The Spiritual Conquest

This book is
No. 11 in Series I: Jesuit Primary Sources
in English Translations
from
The Institute of Jesuit Sources

THE SPIRITUAL CONQUEST

ACCOMPLISHED BY THE
RELIGIOUS OF THE SOCIETY OF JESUS
in the Provinces of Paraguay,
Paraná, Uruguay, and Tape
written by
FATHER ANTONIO RUIZ DE MONTOYA
of the same Society
(1639)

*A Personal Account of the Founding
and Early Years of the
Jesuit Paraguay Reductions*

Introduced by C. J. McNaspy, S.J.
Translated by C. J. McNaspy, S.J.,
John P. Leonard, S.J., and Martin E. Palmer, S.J.

St. Louis
THE INSTITUTE OF JESUIT SOURCES

©1993 The Institute of Jesuit Sources
3700 West Pine Blvd.
St. Louis, Missouri 63108-3386
TEL   314 652 5737
FAX   314 652 0810

First edition

Library of Congress Catalog Card Number: 92-75537
ISBN 1-880810-02-6 hardcover
ISBN 1-880810-03-4 paperbound

CONTENTS

FOREWORD

THIS ENGLISH edition of Antonio Ruiz de Montoya's *Conquista Espiritual*, an outstanding document of Jesuit and colonial South American history and a moving personal record, is the work of several hands. The project owes its initiation to C. J. McNaspy, S.J. In addition to writing the introduction, McNaspy furnished a preliminary draft of the translation, based upon the only text available to him at the time, the somewhat bowdlerized Bilbao edition of 1892. Later, upon Ernesto J. A. Maeder's republishing in 1989 of Montoya's original Madrid edition of 1639, the initial draft was reworked and annotated by John P. Leonard, S.J., and subsequently revised by Martin E. Palmer, S.J., who is solely responsible for its final form, as well as for the translation of the two appendices. These are an early account by Montoya of his spiritual experiences and a set of spiritual counsels compiled by his earliest biographer from Montoya's now lost spiritual diary. In the later stages of the work, much help was derived from the useful annotated Portuguese translation of 1985 by Arnaldo Bruxel, S.J., and Arthur Rabuske, S.J.

In this edition notes have been kept to a minimum; many are merely brief identifications of persons mentioned in the text. The biographical data are mainly from Hugo Storni's *Catálogo de la Provincia del Paraguay* (Cuenca del Plata, 1585–1768; Rome, 1980) and, in the case of Belgian or French missionaries, from the study "Jésuites wallons, flamands, français, missionnaires au Paraguay, 1608–1767," by Pierre Delattre and Edmond Lamalle in *Archivum Historicum Societatis Iesu*, 1947, pp. 98–176.

For completeness' sake, Montoya's cryptic marginal references to contemporary authors and documents have been given untranslated in the notes, usually with Maeder's identification of the sources. For fuller documentation and bibliographical references, Maeder's scholarly edition should be consulted.

A full bibliography of writings by and about Montoya may be found in Hugo Storni, S.J., "Antonio Ruiz de Montoya" (*Archivum Historicum Societatis Iesu* 105 [1984] 425–42). Later publications may be found in the annual bibliographical listings in subsequent issues of the same periodical.

No biography of Ruiz de Montoya exists in English, though the reader may consult Storni's concise article in *The New Catholic Encyclopedia* (vol. 12, col. 706) and an interpretation by the Lutheran scholar John E. Groh in the *Catholic Historical Review*, 56 (1971) 501–533. Also in English are treatments of Montoya in the larger context of the reductions in Philip Caraman's *The Lost Paradise* (New York: Seabury, 1975) and in C. J. McNaspy's *Lost Cities of Paraguay* (Chicago: Loyola University Press, 1982) and *Conquistador Without Sword* (Chicago: Loyola University Press, 1984).

C. J. McNaspy wishes to express his gratitude to his friend and colleague Salvador Loring, S.J., for his assistance with the translation. Thanks are also due to Dr. Teresa H. Johnson of St. Louis University, Manuel Ramiro Muñoz, S.J., and Valentín Menéndez, S.J., for their help with difficult passages; and to John L. McCarthy, S.J., for his invaluable assistance with editing and proofreading.

INTRODUCTION
by Clement J. McNaspy, S.J.

OF THE towering missioners who evangelized South America east of the Andes, the great majority were born either in Spain or Portugal. One thinks of José de Anchieta, Luis de Bolaños, Manuel da Nóbrega, Antonio Vieira, to mention only a few. Two, however, stand out especially as being American-born: St. Roque González de Santa Cruz, a native of Asunción, Paraguay, and Antonio Ruiz de Montoya, born in Lima, Peru—both Jesuits of the same generation, both outstanding founders and promoters of the mission system commonly known as the Paraguay reductions.

Thanks to his martyrdom and beatification (and recent canonization), Roque González is perhaps the more widely known to nonhistorians. Further, as I experienced while writing his biography, *Conquistador Without Sword,*[1] Roque's life is somewhat easier to document, since a thousand pages of detailed testimony had already been gathered during the "process" of his beatification, including tough questions brought up by the official Roman "devil's advocate."

On the other hand, while data regarding the life and work of Ruiz de Montoya are even more abundant, they are also more scattered and thus harder to piece together into a trustworthy biography. Even in his *Spiritual Conquest,* Ruiz de Montoya was, as his first biographer, Dr. Francisco Jarque, discreetly put it, "perhaps more concerned with the substance of the truth than with accidents and circumstances of fixing the times and locating the places where they took place."[2] Ruiz de Montoya, in fact, seemed unconcerned about many of the raw materials that biographers need to work with, such as the year of his birth (variously given in earlier biographies as 1583 or 1585).

We now know that Antonio Ruiz de Montoya was born in Lima on June 13, 1585, the son of a native of Seville in Spain, a captain Cristóbal Ruiz de Montoya, and of Ana de Vargas, a native of Lima. Early biographers, in the pious manner of hagiography, refer to Antonio's mother as "a virtuous woman of high society," though Antonio clearly states that he was illegitimate. In an account of his spiritual journey probably written around the time of his ordination, Ruiz de Montoya describes how he had been afraid that the Jesuits would not admit him into their order: "One night I was praying under a tree, weeping and as it were making loving complaints against our Lord that he had allowed me to be born a natural and not a legitimate child, and that because of this they would not receive me into the Society."³ It is hardly surprising that this disedifying tidbit did not find its way into previous lives of Ruiz de Montoya, the authors, if indeed they were aware of it, probably feeling that it would damage the cause of his eventual beatification.

When Antonio was only five years old, his mother died, and his father decided to take him to Spain. On the way, when they reached Panama, Antonio became violently ill. Afraid that his son would not survive the journey to Spain, his father decided to return to Peru. Not long afterwards, Cristóbal died, leaving nine-year-old Antonio with a perilously sizeable fortune.

Meantime he had been enrolled in the Jesuit school of San Martín, where he is said to have been at first a model student. Before finishing studies, however, Antonio plunged into a life that he would later describe as "worse than that of a pagan, dedicated to the worship of Venus." At the same time he was involved in several violent escapades, himself receiving serious wounds in a sword fight.

These experiences, and others described in his own account of his youth in Appendix I, eventually sobered Antonio somewhat and led him to decide to enlist in the army. He was received by the viceroy, the Count of Monterrey, and was destined to leave shortly for the ongoing war against the Araucanian Indians in Chile. In 1598, these Araucanians had ambushed and slaughtered more than fifty Spanish soldiers, among them their commander, Martín García Oñaz de Loyola (coincidentally a nephew of the Jesuit founder, Ignatius of Loyola), and strife between Spaniards and Araucanians was to continue for years.

However, at the last minute Antonio was deflected from this desperate step by a prudent friend, resolving instead to go on a clothes-buying trip up to the Caribbean ports of the Spanish Main. Looking ahead to this dangerous voyage, he made a general confession during Lent at the Jesuit College. Shortly thereafter, a mysterious experience while he was praying before a statue of the Blessed Virgin began an interior transformation in him, and as a result he returned to the Jesuit college to finish his education, with a view to eventually entering the Franciscan order.

Toward the end of his studies, Antonio made the Spiritual Exercises of St. Ignatius to discern his vocation. On the fourth day he had a vision: he saw an unknown land inhabited by pagans who were being defended from cruel aggressors by transparent, white-robed men. These he recognized as members of the Society of Jesus. This vision decided his vocation. He was accepted as a Jesuit by the provincial superior, Rodrigo de Cabredo, on November 11, 1606. He was then twenty-one years old.⁴

Antonio had been a novice for only some four months (of the twenty-four prescribed for Jesuits) when there arrived in Lima Diego de Torres Bollo

(1551–1638), who had just been assigned by the Jesuit superior general Claudio Aquaviva to establish the new Paraguay Province—a vaguely defined, vast region previously included in the Peruvian Province. Of the novices who volunteered for what must have seemed a remote foreign mission, three were selected on March 7, 1607: Pedro Romero (1585–1645, who would die a martyr in Itatín, part of what was then Paraguay), Baltasar Duarte (1589–1668), and Gabriel Melgar. However, the latter proved too infirm for the long journey, and he was replaced by Antonio.

The three novices traveled to Córdoba, in present-day Argentina but then headquarters of the new Jesuit province of Paraguay. No documents are available to indicate when or where the three young men pronounced their first vows as Jesuits, though probably the ceremony took place in Córdoba two years and a day after their entrance into the novitiate. In any case, Antonio completed his seminary studies in Córdoba and was ordained some time in February of 1611, in Santiago del Estero, Argentina. It is an interesting coincidence that the ordaining bishop, Fernando Trejo y Sanabria, had previously ordained Roque González de Santa Cruz as a diocesan priest in Asunción, in 1598; Roque was to become a Jesuit after spending a number of years as an apostle among the Indians.

Anyone acquainted with Jesuit academic traditions will be surprised at Antonio's ordination after so few years of seminary study. Certain biographers attributed this to his "exceptional brilliance" and eagerness to get on with what he felt was his vocation as a missionary among the Indians. Whatever the reasons, this shortening of the usual Jesuit study program seems to have led later to his not being selected to make the "solemn profession of four vows" (the fourth being one of special obedience to the Pope regarding missions). The same happened in the case of the two martyrs Roque González and Pedro Romero.

This curious fact is explained by the idea then current in the Society of Jesus that only those Jesuits judged competent to teach theology at a university level should make the order's "solemn" profession of four vows. Further, since provincial superiors had to be solemnly professed, none of these three missionary giants ever became provincials, though all of them were judged fit to be "mission superiors" of the entire system of the reductions, a position often more influential in the missions than that of the provincial living in far-away Córdoba. Even so, in an evaluation given years later by Antonio's provincial, Nicolás Mastrilli Durán (1568–1653), we read: "It was a shame to deprive him of studies, since he could have been provincial."[5]

No document informs us as to when Ruiz de Montoya began his study of the difficult Guaraní language—unlike Roque González, who as a native-born Paraguayan knew it well from childhood. Antonio may have learned some Quechua and/or Aymara back in Lima; but even so, since these languages are unrelated in vocabulary and structure to the Tupi-Guaraní linguistic family, contact with them could make little difference. In any case, since his ambition was to work among the Guaranís, he probably took advantage of some colleague or teacher in Córdoba who could initiate him into Guaraní. His subsequent mastery of this taxing language became a matter of amazement to his contemporaries, and his books dealing with or written in Guaraní (like his grammar and 800-page dictionary) make him a recognized pioneer in Latin American linguistics. Indeed, modern dictionaries cite his initial "M" to suggest him as the ultimate arbiter of "classic" Guaraní.

Jesuits had been evangelizing the area where Antonio was first sent to work—Guairá, encompassing several thousand square miles roughly between São Paulo and the Tebicuary River southeast of Asunción—for some time even before the Province of Paraguay was established in 1607. This immense territory lies west of the line drawn by the Treaty of Tordesillas (1494) apportioning the newly discovered world between Spain and Portugal. It was thus, at least in the Spanish view, legally Spanish and lay within the Jesuit Province of Peru.

But Jesuits had already arrived on the coast of Brazil as early as 1549, participating in the founding of the first capital, Salvador (Bahia), and a few years later that of São Paulo, today's metropolis. In a letter dated March 3, 1556, almost four months before his death, St. Ignatius mentions a request for Jesuits received from Asunción (which he refers to as "Paraguay," as it is still called today in popular Guaraní). So many other demands and international complications were pressing that it was some time before Jesuits could reach Paraguay. They arrived in the harbor of Buenos Aires, in fact, on March 8, 1587, responding to the request of Francisco de Victoria, bishop of Tucumán, Argentina—an international trio of them including the Portuguese Manuel Ortega (1560–1622), the Catalonian Juan Saloni (1540–1599), and the Irishman Thomas Fields (1549–1625), born in Limerick. This internationalism is already emblematic of what would be singularly characteristic of the entire history of the Jesuit Paraguay reductions.

When Ruiz de Montoya reached his destination in the missions of Guairá (as he describes in chapter 44 of the *Spiritual Conquest*) he found as his predecessors there two Italians, Giuseppe Cataldini (1571–1653) and Simone Mascetta (1577–1658), "impoverished but rich in joy . . . I was delighted to find myself in their company." His zeal at last had a chance to express itself, as he participated in developing the reduction mission system already under way, a "republic" civilly subject to the Spanish king, but enjoying a large measure of autonomy designed to protect the Indians against the *encomienda* system (in the concrete order virtual slavery under the Spanish colonists) as well as against the slave-raiding *bandeirantes* from São Paulo in Brazil.

Ruiz de Montoya must have met something like instant success in the reduction of Our Lady of Loreto, since only three years later we find this official evaluation given by the provincial Torres Bollo: "Good talent, judgment and prudence, moderate experience, good constitution, great skill in handling cases of conscience, talent for the Society's ministries even as a superior, very good worker among Indians, and excellent religious." On February 2, 1622, Antonio pronounced his final vows (becoming a "professed of the three vows") in the reduction of Loreto.

The historian Hugo Storni[6] divides Antonio's Guairá activity into three periods: as missioner, 1612–1622; as superior of the Guairá missions, 1622–1636; as superior of all the Guaraní reductions, 1636–1637. The second period includes his founding, or participation in the founding, of San Javier, in 1622; that of San José, in 1625; of Encarnación (not to be confused with the modern city in Paraguay, founded by Roque González), 1625; of San Pablo, 1627; of the Siete Arcángeles, 1627; of San Pedro, 1628; San Antonio, 1628; Santo Tomás, 1628; Jesús-María, 1629. All of these reductions lay in the modern state of Paraná, Brazil, though most of them were later destroyed or removed to safer lands in what is now northeastern Argentina.

Indeed, the most dramatic moment of this period of Ruiz de Montoya's life was forced upon him by the slave-raiding *bandeirantes* from São Paulo. Many thousands of Christian Guaranís had already been captured or massacred, and the situation of Loreto and other reductions became desperate. Under his leadership, as we read in the vivid account in chapters 38 and 39 of the *Spiritual Conquest*, some twelve thousand reduction Indians, largely from Loreto and San Ignacio Miní (founded in 1612, shortly after the other San Ignacio in present-day Paraguay, and hence nicknamed "miní" or "lesser"), undertook a remarkable escape from the area in late 1631. This episode has often been called an "Exodus" by such British historians as Robert Southey, R. B. Cunninghame Graham, Philip Caraman, and others, with Ruiz de Montoya accordingly thought of as a new Moses. The metaphor, somewhat overworked today, should not be pressed too literally; for, while to the Guaranís their escape was indeed a matter of life, death, or enslavement, and while it was surely a noteworthy rescue operation in South American history, it enjoys none of the rich "salvation history" significance or typology of the Mosaic Exodus. Ruiz de Montoya's own account, while moving, is altogether unpretentious, in no way suggesting that he thought of himself as another Moses.

Hurriedly, Ruiz de Montoya and his associates persuaded the Indians that the *bandeirantes* were on the point of assaulting them. Some twelve thousand Guaranís were placed on seven hundred *balsas* or large double canoes, plus a few individual canoes, with all their provisions, and the gigantic flotilla set out down the Paranapanema River toward the Paraná. From other Indians they learned, in fact, that the timing was barely right, since the *bandeirantes* reached the abandoned mission towns only two days later.

Even so, the escape was not to prove easy. New hazards, both physical and human, lay ahead. The missioners received word that Spanish colonials of the town of Guairá were lying in wait to snare them at a narrow spot in the Paraná just before the mammoth cataracts (today covered by the artificial lake serving the Itaipú hydroelectric plant, largest in the world). The Spaniards' plan was to trap the flotilla and capture the Guaranís for their own benefit. Ruiz de Montoya, accordingly, went ahead in a small canoe, entered the Spanish fortress, and tried to persuade the new enemy to allow passage for his twelve thousand Christian Indians. He met no success but managed somehow to escape and return to his companions. They decided to try persuasion again, but again failed and had recourse to the stratagem of forcing their way through in battle array. The Spanish fell back, obviously fearing for their lives.

Once past the Spaniards, however, Ruiz de Montoya's people had to face the awesome cataracts of the Paraná, until recently called Guairá Falls or the Seven Falls. They tested three hundred canoes to see if they could stand the Niagara-like plunge; they were, of course, shattered. This entailed a forced march of twenty-five leagues (at least seventy-five miles) through the jungle before they could regain the river, rebuild the lost craft, and try to reach safer lands in what is now the Argentine province of Misiones, where a number of the Guairá reductions were reestablished.

While in his account of the exodus Ruiz de Montoya mentions only in passing occasional strategy sessions with his colleagues, it is evident that unanimity would seldom emerge among men of the stamina and initiative of these early missioners. In their article on the Belgian and French missioners in Paraguay, Pierre Delattre and Edmond Lamalle show that Louis Ernot, for instance, was vigorously opposed to the move.[7] Not long after, in fact, in May of 1632, he wrote to the superior general in Rome, Muzio Vitelleschi, criticizing the haste and costly lack of organization shown in the exodus. On November 30, 1634, Father Vitelleschi replied sympathetically but pointed out realistically that many of the difficulties were unforeseeable. Hugo Storni points out in his article on Ruiz de Montoya that the latter had already written to Vitelleschi in February and April, and that the superior general answered him, also on November 30, 1634, doubtless in the same mail packet, gently remonstrating with him regarding the number of people who died in the exodus, but adding: "I am sure that those who disagreed with you will understand that the decision had to be made, and that it was necessary to avoid greater evils, though some wish that the problems had been better foreseen; still, what is past cannot be remedied; for the future, it will be better to proceed more slowly."[8]

Nonetheless, it is not clear to us, nor apparently even to Vitelleschi, what other course of defense could have been taken, since the *bandeirantes'* threat was both real and imminent. In any case, Ruiz de Montoya's high appreciation of Ernot (as evidenced in chapter 62) shows that, following their disagreements, no bad blood existed between the two Jesuits. Moreover, the selection of Ruiz de Montoya as superior of all the Guaraní missions (1636–1637) manifests the high esteem in which he was held by his fellow missioners.

In 1637 Ruiz de Montoya was sent by the provincial of Paraguay as a special procurator to the court of Spain, to petition relief for the problems caused for the reductions by the attacks of the *bandeirantes* from São Paulo. Thanks to Ruiz de Montoya's notebook, his journey can be traced in some detail: "I left Loreto on the vigil of the Annunciation; left Córdoba, August 11; left Buenos Aires, October 15, 1637; entered Rio on November 6; left Rosario May 19, 1638; crossed the line [equator] on the feast of St. Anthony of Padua; reached Madrid September 22." He traveled to Europe together with a fellow missioner, Francisco Díaz Taño (1593–1677), who had been sent on another official visit to Spain and then on to Rome. They parted at Lisbon, since Díaz Taño had to go first to Seville.

We are fortunate, too, in having a letter of Ruiz de Montoya's written to the same Díaz Taño from Madrid some years later: "I received your letter with great pleasure and not a little envy at seeing your Reverence depart for my homeland while I stay on here in this exile. Not for me all this bustle, hand-kissing, courtesies, waste of time, and especially having my mind occupied with business, anxieties, and projects, which rarely come to anything. In sum, Father mine, I remain here an exile. Not a day goes by but for my consolation I imagine they are already taking me to the ship. But it is God's will that for the time being these remain merely thoughts, so that when I do return I will have a higher esteem for lowly work among my Indians, far from perplexities, free from rivalries and useless anxieties. May you and your companions [the new recruits for the reductions who returned with Díaz Taño in 1640] enjoy this great good even if you accomplish only the conversion of a single pagan. For it often seems that not to convert them in heaps means not filling the void of one's desire; but in this we must move at God's pace without attempting to set a foot beyond what His Majesty wills."⁹

Ruiz de Montoya's task in Madrid was, in brief, to secure a remedy for hazards besetting the missions. On the journey, being eminently a man of action, he spent countless hours writing out specific proposals to present to King Philip IV. According to Ruiz de Montoya's own summary, these were that the king should:

1. Enforce the law established in 1611 in Lisbon (Philip IV being then king of both Portugal and Spain) against enslaving Indians
2. Confirm decrees of Paul III and Clement VIII against enslaving Indians
3. Make the capture of Indians a case for the Inquisition
4. Give the governor of Rio de Janeiro responsibility over south Brazil, since the capital in Bahia was too remote to be effective

5. Invest the bishop with the power of a papal nuncio to repress members of religious orders who harm the Indians

6. Give authorities power to stop boats setting out for slave raiding

7. Forbid the transporting of Indians or other criminals to Brazil

8. Free all captive Indians, men and women, and send them to Buenos Aires, where the Jesuits will undertake to return them to their homes, even if they have to sell their chalices and vestments to pay for it

9. Have bishops excommunicate those who fail to disclose what Indians they are holding

10. Punish the guilty and the magistrates who have allowed these abuses also "to dispel the shame brought on the holy gospel, which has been defamed in the eyes of pagans and recent converts"

11. Allow Indians who no longer have homes or relatives to settle in the Indian villages around Rio de Janeiro

12. Send a serious person zealous for God's service, with armed support, to ensure that the royal orders are carried out.

"In this way," he adds, "two things will be assured: firstly, the liberty of so many persons who are being captured, bought, and sold in their own lands; secondly, the security of Your Majesty's realms in Peru, which they are trying so hard to hand over to the rebels, and where the road is already open from São Paulo to the borders of Potosí. And I protest that my intention is not the death of anyone nor the shedding of any blood."[10]

Another essential issue raised by Ruiz de Montoya was the absolute need that the reduction Indians be permitted to use firearms to defend themselves against attacks by the *bandeirantes*. After endless debates in a special junta, the king signed four decrees directed to the viceroy of Peru, and on May 21, 1640, he signed the main decree on firearms, but leaving its execution to the viceroy's decision. This meant, of course, that Ruiz de Montoya would have to go back by way of Lima.

It was at the end of his long stay in Spain that Ruiz de Montoya published his ringing plaidoyer on behalf of the Paraguay Indians, *Conquista Espiritual Hecha por los Religiosos de la Compañía de Jesús en las Provincias del Paraguay, Paraná, Uruguay, y Tape* (1639), and brought to press the philological works on which he had been laboring for decades: *Tesoro de la lengua guaraní* (1639), *Arte y vocabulario de la lengua guaraní* (1640), and *Catecismo de la lengua guaraní* (1640).

Just as Ruiz de Montoya was setting out again for America, however, a nationalist revolt erupted in Portugal which brought to an end that country's sixty-year subjection to the Spanish crown. This, too, complicated Ruiz de Montoya's work, since the documents he bore were signed by a king whose writ no longer ran in either Portugal or Brazil.

Meantime, back in the reductions it was presumed that the king had approved the petition for firearms, and that in any case natural law made it obligatory to defend the Indians, since the enemy had firearms. Accordingly, the Jesuits secured some from the governor of Buenos Aires. Brother Domingo Torres (1607–1688), a former soldier, taught the reduction Indians how to use the weapons. Under the skilled leadership of chief Nicolás Neenguirú, they won a decisive victory over the invading *bandeirantes*, and for a time the slave-raiding attacks ceased.

While waiting and working in Madrid, Antonio became gravely ill. Following medical practice of the age, the doctors bled him several times. Later he wrote: "They tried to kill me, but I was so anxious to return to Paraguay that I told them, 'Heal me any way you wish, but don't bury me here; I must go back to my province.'" He earnestly begged a friend, "Do not allow my bones to lie here among the Spaniards, even if I die here; make sure they return to my Indians, my dear children, so that my bones may rest where they labored and wasted away."

At last he was well enough to leave, but on the way home he stopped briefly in Loyola as a pilgrim to the house of St. Ignatius. Finally he started for home, but with a long detour to Lima to persuade the viceroy to carry out the King's permission regarding defensive firearms. This required much more time than he had imagined, since the Peruvian authorities were disinclined to establish the dangerous precedent of allowing Indians to use firearms. Then, when he was back in Paraguay, further complications arose. His superior wrote asking him to return to Spain. As he was preparing for the terrifying journey, another letter countermanded the order. It seemed that at last he would be able to go "home," as he called the reductions.

When he got as far as Salta, Argentina, he found another letter from the new Paraguayan provincial, Juan Pastor (1580–1658), who had been appointed in 1651. This ordered him back to Lima to defend still other needs of the reductions. Mustering his failing strength and doubtless deeply disappointed, Ruiz de Montoya returned and carried out the new assignment.

What protracted his stay in Lima was an unsavory development back in Asunción, where the controversial and irregularly enthroned bishop Bernardino de Cárdenas was vacillating between lavish praise and slander in his behavior towards the Jesuits. Since few people knew the Paraguay Province as well as Ruiz de Montoya, he was asked to present its case to the viceroy and other authorities. The entire episode—one of the more piquant in Latin American history—has been vividly recounted by Philip Caraman.[11] Paraguay's leading ecclesiastical historian, the late Bishop Angel N. Acha Duarte, recapitulates it pithily: "Consecrated before the papal bull was sent, Bishop Cárdenas left in Paraguay only memories of his extravagant behavior."

While he worked and waited in Lima, Ruiz de Montoya's reputation for holiness became widespread, and he was able to do a considerable amount of spiritual counseling. The bishop of Guamanga, Francisco de Godoy, tried hard to persuade him to stay and open reductions for the multitude of

Indians in his diocese; failing this, the bishop tried unsuccessfully to have the viceroy forbid Ruiz de Montoya to leave Peru.

One especially important spiritual contact, however, did result from Ruiz de Montoya's delay in Lima. The Venerable Francisco del Castillo (1615–1673), whose cause for beatification is now under study in Rome, was able to have Antonio as spiritual director. He wrote in his spiritual notes, later published by J. de Buendía, about the great blessings he had received "when the venerable and apostolic Father Antonio Ruiz de Montoya arrived here in Lima, through the great consolation and good done to me."[12]

It was largely for Francisco's benefit that Montoya compiled, around 1646, his mystical guide, *Firestone of Divine Love and Rapture of the Soul in Knowledge of the First Cause*. This work survived the centuries in a single manuscript and was published for the first time only in 1991 by the Peruvian scholar José Luis Rouillon Arróspide.[13] Written in a lively and engaging style, it reveals that Montoya had acquired considerable knowledge of Christian mystical literature. Drawing heavily upon earlier and contemporary spiritual writers, it is a wide-ranging discussion of the interior life in four treatises. The first treatise deals with "speculative knowledge of God through creatures" and "seeking the First Cause in its essence, presence, and power." The second describes "the purity of memory, understanding, and will required for divine contemplation." The third is entitled "Active firestone of divine love and rapture of the soul once purged in its powers of memory, understanding, and will"; and the fourth "Passive firestone of divine love in the understanding and will." The work concludes with an epilogue: "Nobility and descent of the perfect man; devotion to the saints; introduction to prayer and advice for prayer; brief summary of the foregoing treatises."[14]

After reading in the *Spiritual Conquest* and elsewhere of Ruiz de Montoya's frequent and rather startling visions and other paranormal experiences, it is interesting to see how forcefully he inculcates in his mystical treatise an uncompromisingly nonimaginative and nonconceptual mysticism of the Pseudo-Dionysian type that has become familiar from the *Cloud of Unknowing*. The *Firestone* makes it clear that Ruiz de Montoya was a paradigmatic "contemplative in action," a man whose extraordinary missionary activity was sustained and animated by an equally extraordinary interior life. In this he strikingly parallels his North American contemporary and counterpart, St. Jean de Brébeuf, S.J., the apostle of the Hurons.[15]

In 1652 Antonio's health declined alarmingly, though everything possible was done to remedy it. On April 11 of that year he died in Lima, where sixty-seven years earlier he had been born, where he had spent a tumultuous youth and achieved a noteworthy spiritual conversion, and where he entered the Jesuit novitiate. Assisting him at his deathbed were a number of Jesuits, including Venerable Francisco del Castillo.

Ruiz de Montoya was so widely venerated that the viceroy and other high officials participated in his funeral, even carrying his casket. The archbishop of Cuzco, Pedro de Contreras y Sotomayor, who had known him back in school days as well as in recent years, offered this tribute: "Ruiz de Montoya is no ordinary saint; he is a giant in holiness, a great saint of the highest order."

When news finally reached the reductions that their hero had died, some forty Indians from Loreto made the journey of several thousand miles across the continent to beg for the remains of Ruiz de Montoya. The request was apparently also made in the name of the Paraguayan Jesuit province, and in any case was granted. Historians speculate on the route taken by this unusual triumphal procession: probably by Salta, Tucumán, Santiago del Estero, and Córdoba, places associated with his Jesuit life; then on to Santa Fe and by river to Asunción; from there through the reductions to the southeast, on to Candelaria (where the mission superior had his headquarters), and finally to Loreto, where the remains were laid to final rest in the sacristy of the church, today lost amid rubble.

Rubén Vargas Ugarte, historian of the Jesuit Province of Peru, sums up Antonio Ruiz de Montoya's life as follows: "His name deserves to be on the list of those explorers and discoverers of hitherto unknown lands who stretched the limits of the known world. As a geographer he was one of the first, if not the first, to map that vast region; as a linguist, in his *Arte y Vocabulario de la Lengua Guaraní*, he explored the structure of that difficult tongue, and his work remains unsurpassed to this day; as a mystic, no less than a man of action, he left us in his *Firestone of Divine Love* a finished guide to the paths followed by souls in the search for God—a work as yet unpublished but which won the praises of other mystics."

Even during Ruiz de Montoya's lifetime, when superiors are not given to indiscriminate encomia, his provincial sent this evaluation to the superior general of the Society of Jesus: "A perfect man, one of great prayer. In converting the pagans he performed works at risk to his life. Very good as a superior. It was a shame to deprive him of studies, since he could have been provincial. In work and wisdom, he imitates the footsteps of our St. Francis Xavier." High praise indeed in any official evaluation. But perhaps even more impressive is the tribute given by the forty Guaraní Indians of Loreto who crossed South America twice, risking their lives to secure the remains of the man they deemed their own saint.

The *Spiritual Conquest*

Anyone reading the *Spiritual Conquest* will encounter almost as many problems as delights. A fervent admirer, the Spanish historian Jesuit Antonio Astráin, feels forced to admit: "He shines neither in order nor in method, nor nicety of style; writing from memory, with no books or documents to guide him, he tossed onto paper episodes and adventures of his apostolic life, often not even indicating their time sequence." (Montoya knew his own limitations as a stylist, and attempted unsuccessfully to have his book ghost-written for him by the leading Spanish Jesuit writer of the time, Eusebio Nieremberg.)

Hence, if the *Spiritual Conquest* should be reckoned some sort of classic, other than purely literary claims must be set forth. For all its stylistic faults, it is a work vibrant with mysticism and dramatic in its portrayal of primitive life in South America. There are passages of considerable narrative power and even lyricism. At the same time, the ethnologist Alfred Métraux praises the work as "the principal, almost unique" testimony of the life-style of South American forest Indians, especially the Guaraní tribes, at the time of the Conquest.

Paraguay's leading secular historian, Efraim Cardozo, assesses *Spiritual Conquest* as uniquely important for its eyewitness information, since almost everything Ruiz de Montoya wrote about he had personally observed during some twenty-five years of work among the Guaranís. Further, while serving as superior of all the Jesuit missions among the Guaranís, 1636–1637, he had enjoyed access to other firsthand documentation. Cardozo also admires Ruiz de Montoya's high "intellectual capacity," evidenced in his unchallenged command of the difficult Guaraní language, notably in his definitive 800-page dictionary of that tongue. Bartomeu Melià, the most respected authority on Guaraní ethnolinguistics, has published an important article outlining some basic traits of the ancient Guaraní culture as they emerge from the data in the *Spiritual Conquest* and Ruiz de Montoya's other works. [16]

To classical scholars the *Spiritual Conquest* will naturally bring to mind Julius Caesar's *De bello Gallico*, a work of comparable erudition though superior in style, still useful to historians and ethnologists despite its apologetic focus; or Tacitus' *Germania*, learned and beguiling even if hardly unsubjective, given its hortatory thrust. These and other classical historians traditionally organize their materials in view of making a moral point. So does Ruiz de Montoya, rather less artistically, but with at least as great interest to readers today.

At the same time, the modern reader will not be altogether comfortable on first plunging into *Spiritual Conquest*. Exposed to, if not trained in, recent anthropological method with its neutral or egalitarian presuppositions regarding all forms of religious experience, many readers may be queasy at Ruiz de Montoya's failure to appreciate shamanism—the religion of medicine men, witch doctors, or the like. If Ruiz de Montoya does not seem as enlightened as his contemporary Jesuit confrère Friedrich Spee von Langenfeld, who in 1631 wrote against the plague of witch-hunts then engulfing Europe, neither does he advocate the execution of witches, as was done as late as 1692 in Salem, Massachusetts.

If anything, to one reading the *Spiritual Conquest* with the optic of the times rather than with facile hindsight, Ruiz de Montoya seems, while not tolerant, at least rather ahead of many of his contemporaries. This, in fact, seems extraordinary in view of his day-to-day physical encounters with shamans who actually did put to death his friend Roque González de Santa Cruz.

In chapter 30, for example, we find Ruiz de Montoya himself threatened with death, while in chapter 11 he objectively quotes the words (as far as he could recall them) shouted by the shaman Artiguaye: "You are no priests sent from God to aid our misery; you are devils from hell, sent by their ruler for our destruction. What teaching have you brought us? What peace and happiness? Our ancestors lived in liberty. They enjoyed all the women they wanted without hindrance from anyone. Thus they lived and spent their lives in happiness, and you want to destroy their traditions and impose on us the heavy burden of being bound to a single wife."[17] If Artiguaye's case is not put as eloquently or fully as those of the Indian leaders Nezú and Potiravá in justification of their killing Roque González, Ruiz de Montoya here and elsewhere seems to try to state the Indians' position honestly as well as usefully, as far as modern scholars are concerned.[18]

We are tempted to laugh when reading Ruiz de Montoya's labored attempts to confirm the legend that St. Thomas the Apostle had evangelized South America. Yet this opinion, which strikes us as so bizarre today, was shared by men as intelligent as Bartolomé de las Casas, Garcilaso de la Vega, and even Antonio Vieira, half a century after Ruiz de Montoya, and a full century later by the enormously erudite Martin Dobrizhoffer in his fascinating *Historia de Abiponibus* (Vienna, 1784, and translated into English in 1822 by Samuel Coleridge's wife Sara!).

More troubling, perhaps, to us moderns are Ruiz de Montoya's blood-curdling accounts of what he judged to be direct diabolic possessions and assaults on the missionary enterprise. In this, as in his treatment of witchcraft, he was, as already suggested, a man of his own and not of the nineteenth century (given the current vogue of satanic and other such cults, one should perhaps not say "of our enlightened twentieth century"). In any case, exaggerated as they seem to us, Ruiz de Montoya's accounts are not those of parlor mystics or others so well described by Ronald Knox in his classic study of mystical eccentricities, *Enthusiasm*. As our brief sketch of his life has shown, Ruiz de Montoya was, and was recognized as, an authentic mystic and a mystical writer of consequence, comparable to many studied by Henri Bergson in *The Two Sources of Morality and Religion*; indeed, he was recognized by those who knew him best as one whose extraordinary prayer life was linked with a strong sense of earthy practicality.

Antonio Ruiz de Montoya is one of a legion of explorers, missioners, and close observers of colonial Hispanic America. At least as much a doer as a "seer" (in both senses of the term), he was a spiritual conquistador whose only weapon was a rough wooden cross which he also used as a walking staff, never a bludgeoning instrument, and whose "conquest" was, at least in intent, altogether liberating. Yet he can hardly be called, in today's terminology, a "liberation theologian." He apparently never thought of working for the Indians except "within the system" of rule by the Spanish crown. Rather he seems a practical liberator, devoting his long, hectic, diversified life to freeing "his" dear Guaranís from what he perceived as spiritual and earthly enemies, and to bringing them safe to God.

The Spiritual Conquest Accomplished by the Religious of the Society of Jesus in the Provinces of Paraguay, Paraná, Uruguay, and Tape

Overleaf: Map of the Paraguay reductions at their greatest extent, in the century following the loss of the Guairá missions (adapted from the *Catholic Encyclopedia*).

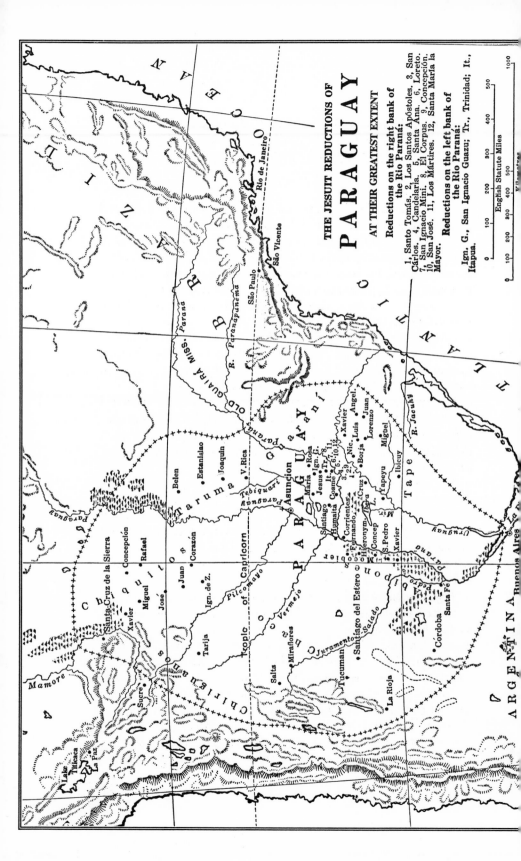

THE JESUIT REDUCTIONS OF

PARAGUAY

AT THEIR GREATEST EXTENT

Reductions on the right bank of
the Rio Paraná:

1, Santo Tomás, 2, Los Santos Apóstoles, 3, San Cárlos, 4, Candelaria, 5, Santa Ana, 6, Loreto, 7, San Ignacio Miní, 8, El Corpus, 9, Concepción, 10, San José, 11, Los Mártires, 12, Santa María la Mayor.

Reductions on the left bank of
the Rio Paraná:

Ign. G., San Ignacio Guazu; Tr., Trinidad; It., Itapua.

English Statute Miles

APPROBATION OF THE VERY ILLUSTRIOUS LORD, DOCTOR DON LORENZO DE MENDOZA, PRELATE OF RIO DE JANEIRO

*H*AVING EARLIER *examined, by command of the Royal and Supreme Council of His Majesty (whom God preserve), the* Treasury, Art, Dictionary, *and* Catechism *of the Guaraní language of Paraguay composed by Reverend Father Antonio Ruiz de Montoya of the Society of Jesus; and having accorded these books the favorable approval they merit, based upon my own knowledge and experience of the provinces of the viceroyalty of Peru, where I have for so long resided, as well as of their languages and of the port of Buenos Aires and the River Plate; I have again been directed by the Royal Council to examine the present work of Father Antonio Ruiz entitled:* Account of the Spiritual Conquest Accomplished by the Religious of the Society of Jesus in the Provinces of Paraguay, Paraná, Uruguay, and Tape.

I affirm not only that it contains nothing against our holy faith and good morals, but that it gives evidence of how much God has accomplished through the zeal, labors, and preaching of these religious men in the domestication, reduction, and conversion of those regions, inhabited by such large numbers of more than barbarian pagans, as can be seen in this work, particularly in chapter 34. All of this is owing to these same religious, who founded in the aforementioned provinces a garden of celestial flowers and a new primitive church, which the wolf out of hell has striven by so many means to ruin and has to a great extent succeeded in ruining, forcing them to flee from the boundaries of their own lands, in fulfillment of the text: "The boar out of the wood has laid it waste, and a singular wild beast has devoured it."[19]

Regarding much of this, particularly the aforementioned fruits of the restoration of so many souls and the glory of God, I am a competent witness because of the close connection of these reductions with my diocese. Only one who knows this as it is, who understands what these religious men have accomplished and what they have suffered by way of poverty and other great hardships in those vast territories filled with wildernesses, rugged terrain, dense forests, and mountains, as they sought out and gathered in these human brutes who fed on one another, and where, as I have said on other occasions, there are none of the riches and comforts found elsewhere in the Indies—only such a person, I say, can appreciate the heroism of the achievements presented in this account.

*Indeed, this province of the Society can claim for itself, without prejudice
to others, the text: "I have toiled more than all of them."*[20]
For all of these reasons it is right that the work be printed.
Madrid, May 16, 1639.

THE PRELATE OF RIO DE JANEIRO

DEDICATION TO OCTAVIO CENTURION, MARQUIS OF MONASTERIO

A GIFT'S SUCCESS *lies in finding a receiver who values it. The
slight gift which I herewith present to Your Lordship may hope for
great success, given Your Lordship's own religious zeal, which I am
confident will increase by reading of the wonderful works of God among
heathen peoples previously so bereft of knowledge of him. Your Lordship's
piety will surely overflow with spiritual joy at these glorious triumphs of
the faith, and your own mercy be increased by so many souls' having
obtained the mercy of God. Your Lordship's devotion will be rejoiced at
seeing how such barbarous peoples have come to know Jesus Christ, their
Creator and Lord.*

*Your Lordship's desires to please God are not confined to your actual
deeds; your achievements, however great, will be surpassed by your
desires. These must always extend beyond one's capacity and thus console
him for the limitations of his own achievements through joy over the
achievements of others. I offer Your Lordship occasion for this in the
glorious labors and services that have been rendered to God in the
remotest reaches of the earth. Your Lordship founds churches and holy
monasteries in order to give spiritual amplitude to the glory of your earthly
title; surely you will rejoice to see how the Church is being established in
regions that lay in the shadow of death and the gates of hell, how the
Faith is being exalted and the devil vanquished, how souls are being
redeemed. The matter is worthy of Your Lorship's piety, and the author's
attachment not unworthy of your kindly favor—of which, over and above
those already received, Your Lorship will grant a new instance by
accepting this slight token of the author's great good will.*

Your Lordship's humble chaplain,

ANTONIO RUIZ DE MONTOYA

CHAPTER 1

Introduction

M Y OWN has been the experience of the great desert father Aphra-ates.[21] When he heard, from his remote solitude, the roar of the waves that were buffeting the bark of the Church and the flames with which the terrible monster, Julian the Apostate,[22] was striving to burn it down, he emerged from his beloved solitude, depriving himself of the animating heavenly breezes that stirred with life and growth the spiritual plantations of the desert; he made his way into the hubbub, disquiet, and traffic of cities and, undeterred by his own uncouth and rustic speech, did not hesitate to thrust himself into the elegance and refinement of royal palaces—all in his attempt to quell the winds, quiet the waters, and quench the flames with which the apostate was scorching the earth. So it was with my own coming to court before the royal feet of his Catholic Majesty (whom heaven prosper with long life). My goal is to make peace between Spaniards and Indians—a task so difficult that for more than a century since the discovery of the western Indies it has been impossible to achieve.[23] I am driven to pursue this goal by Christian charity, by the Indians' utter defenselessness, by the example of my predecessors who conquered them and left outstanding models to imitate, and by my own nearly thirty years of unswerving dedication, before all else, to their instruction and their conversion to our holy faith—my desires being crowned with toil, hardship, and the ever-present danger of death and of being eaten by barbarians.

In this suit of mine, eagerly undertaken because it is grounded in the law of charity by which I love and desire the eternal good of both parties equally, my model has been the high priest Onias,[24] of whom it is said: "When enmities had reached such a pass that some persons were committing murders, Onias perceived how dangerous the quarrel was and betook himself to the king, not to bring an accusation against the citizens but for the common good, in consideration of the entire people; for he saw that without the king's intervention there could be no peace."

I have lived for this whole period of time in the province of Paraguay as a desert-dweller in pursuit of wild beasts—the barbarian Indians. I have tramped through forests and fields to gather them into the sheepfold of holy Church and into His Majesty's service. From among them, I and my companions have erected thirteen reductions[25] or settlements, with unimaginable toil, hunger, lack of clothing, and frequent perils to life—in all this feeling myself a wilderness-dweller indeed.

Social structure For whereas the Indians, who in their old way of life once lived in open or hilly country, or in forests, and in clusters of up to five or six dwellings, have now by our efforts been brought into large settlements and, through the constant preaching of the gospel, transformed from country-dwellers to Christian citizens, all this has for so many years deprived me of contacts with the Spanish and the use of their language (since I am constantly obliged to use the language of the Indians) that I myself have almost become a rustic and a stranger to cultivated language—not the least by having to eat the ordinary food of the Indians: roots, squashes, herbs, beans, and the like. But then came an invasion of hostile forces which obliged me to leave this desert solitude. They burned churches, wounded and maltreated priests, committed sacrileges, robbed church furnishings and the poor treasures of religious men who preached throughout eleven settlements, and, even worse, ejected from four churches the most holy and venerable Sacrament of the altar. I am referring to the citizens and inhabitants of the towns of São Paulo, Santos, São Vicente, and other Brazilian towns settled by persons whose actions had forced them to flee the light of justice. These events have compelled me to travel to the royal court and to His Majesty's feet, journeying some two thousand leagues[26] through the notorious hazards of seas, rivers, and enemies, to register an urgent appeal for measures against these great evils which threaten serious impairment of His Majesty's service—indeed, I would say, grave harm and the threatened loss of the finest jewel in his royal crown.[27]

CHAPTER 2

The province of Paraguay

THE PROVINCE of Paraguay comprised four Spanish cities. Three were settled by people from São Paulo; the principal city, Asunción, is the capital, where the bishop and governor reside. Asunción is situated on the banks of the river called Paraguay, which means the River Paragua, or "Crown of Feathers"; thus in our language it means the same as *Río Coronado*.[28] This is a broad and abundant river, along which quite large ships from the port of Buenos Aires (more than two hundred leagues from Asunción) transport produce of the land both up- and downstream. These products are principally sugar, honey, wine, wax, *garabata* (a sort of hemp), and the so-called Paraguayan herb [the *yerba mate*].

Asunción has fewer than four hundred citizens; and it is commonly said that there are ten women for each man. It has no gold or silver mines, nor does any currency circulate. Commerce is by barter. However, they have devised a system of "hollow weights," as they call the weights used for setting prices. Thus, a coin of eight silver reals will bring three "hollow weights" of fruits of the land.

The land is quite fertile. Wheat grew excellently, but only what was required for Mass breads or delicacies was harvested since the inhabitants highly esteem the flour of what they call manioca, which they make into cakes (in Cartagena, Panama, and Quito it is called cassava[29]). Considerable maize is also harvested; from this they also make cakes, which taste good enough when fresh but are like leather when stale.

There is also a great abundance and variety of beans, which they call *frisoles*, and of squashes of various sorts. There are also local fruits, some of them highly prized; from these they make a variety of preserves in large quantities. There is a considerable yield of excellent wine. All these products are exported from the city in exchange for cloth brought by the merchants.

Wax is harvested from nine or ten different species of wild bees; these have never allowed themselves to be domesticated but live quite well in the forest. Nowadays a good deal of wheat is produced, even though the ordinary bread is made from manioca flour. The principal medium of exchange, which functions like silver, is the herb that we will mention later.

There are handworkers for all the manual crafts and they do practice them. However, nobody looks upon himself as a handworker, since everyone has learned simply by doing the work in his own house. For example, though a shoemaker makes shoes in public, he does not want to be called a shoemaker by trade, claiming that he merely picked up the skill by his own wit. By this subtle distinction they attempt to provide for their needs and at the same time hold on to the noble status bequeathed to them by their ancestors, all of whom belonged to the nobility.[30]

CHAPTER 3

Some animals

ALL THROUGHOUT the country there are numerous species of snakes and serpents. The smaller ones measure about a span, others half a yard; depending upon their species, they grow up to six yards. Once disemboweling a snake that was half a yard in length, I counted fifty baby snakes, all of them already alive. The natives say that the snake conceives through the mouth and that in order to be born the baby snakes tear open the mother and even kill each other. This seems correct, since if they all survived there would be no place to set foot without treading on a snake. Other snakes lay eggs; those I have seen are about a third larger than pigeon eggs. These they hatch by lying on them and thus bringing them to life.

There is one called the rattlesnake. It has a rattle in its tail that resembles the grains inside the shell of a dry bean and makes a similar sound. It produces a new grain each year, and its sound can be heard at fifteen paces. When the strength of its venom builds to the point where it irritates the snake (the way a cold can cause toothache), the snake rattles more loudly. Eventually it bites something and ejects the poisonous fluid which is stored in its gums and which fills a pair of teeth or fangs, rather large at the base but coming to a point like that of a fine needle.

These snakes are all so venomous that anyone bitten on the foot immediately bleeds through eyes, nose, ears, gums, and nails, with so much blood between the fingers and toes that the person is instantly disfigured. The people use numerous remedies and herbs that nature has provided there. St. Paul's stone is a tried and true remedy, garlic is pounded and drunk, bezoar stones and herbs are used. The homeliest remedy, however, is fire; they powder the affected part with sulphur and purge it out with a glowing knife. This remedy is well known and if it is applied in time the person is in no danger of death. The snake's own head, mashed and placed on the wound, lessens the pain and sucks out the poison. The livers are also eaten as a remedy.

There are some snakes four or five yards long that live by hunting. They climb a tree alongside a path and await their prey. They fling themselves down with great speed, encircling the prey with amazing agility and squeezing it so powerfully that in short order it is killed and swallowed. This leaves the snakes so full that they are incapable of movement, and since their own heat is insufficient for digesting a large deer or wild pig, they roll in the sun and thus rot along with the rotting flesh of the prey. The belly breeds maggots, which attract little birds and feed them for many days. Once the putrefaction is over, the snake recovers its skin and is as healthy as before. It has happened that a snake went through all this while clinging to a small tree. As the skin came back, the snake's flesh formed around the tree, and upon recovering its health it found itself caught and unable to get free, and was there discovered alive.

Other snakes live on fish. I saw one snake four yards long with a head like a calf. From the foot of a tree it would lower its head into the Paraná River and expel foam from its mouth. Immediately a shoal of little fish approached to feed on it. The snake would let them feel secure and then with amazing speed open its mouth and make a large catch. After swallowing them it would expel more foam; again the fish would come to feed and again the snake would swallow them.

Others live on rats, rabbits, and the like. They are so poisonous that if a kind of effluvium which they give off reaches the prey, even on the run, it is brought to a stop, not only surrendering but even stretching itself out for easier swallowing. To my astonishment I saw this actually happen: the prey, a span thick, made itself longer and thinner by a third, thus enabling the snake to swallow it quite easily.

There are other snakes large enough to swallow a man. We saw an Indian, six feet tall and quite husky, swallowed by a snake. The man was fishing, wading naked in the water up to his waist. The snake engulfed him, and the next day threw him up whole, his bones crushed as though in a mill. These snakes never leave the water; I have seen them in the largest whirlpools of the Paraná. They have grotesquely large heads—viper-shaped like their bodies—and monstrous mouths.

The Indians say that these animals beget in the same manner as a human male (but it is not the fish-man sometimes spoken of). This was confirmed by the following incident. An Indian woman was washing at the river bank. At the scent of her menstruation, which arouses these creatures, one of them attacked her and carried her off to the opposite side of the river. Then, to prevent her from drowning (another indication of the creature's nature), it dragged her on shore, and there performed its act on her. This left her so utterly undone and overwhelmed that she could not escape. The fish kept her there, returning to see her over the three days she stayed there. She was discovered, and, having told this story and received the sacraments, died.

There are other snakes three or four yards in length that live in swampy thickets. They go out on the banks and await their prey. They spring and encircle it with amazing agility, attempting to stab it in the anus with a sharp pointed bone in their tail. In this way they overpower it and drag it off to their swampy lair. If they meet with resistance, they go back to wet themselves in the water (since dryness weakens them) and then return to the struggle. This was witnessed in the case of an Indian who was attacked by one of these snakes. Even with his arms pinned, he fought back for a time. Feeling itself desiccated, the snake leapt into the water but just as quickly returned to try his luck. This time, however, the Indian was ready; he held his arms high and was caught only around the body. He had a knife at his back hanging from a cord on his neck; he promptly slashed through the snake and killed it—delighted to bring home provisions for several days, for all these animals serve the Indians as food.

An entertaining fencing-match takes place between birds called by the natives *macaguá* and certain small snakes. The bird thrusts its beak through the feathers of its wing, which serves as a shield, delivering the snake a sharp jab; the snake replies in kind. When the bird realizes that it has been struck, it rushes off to a thicket of herbs bearing the same name as itself; it eats twigs from the herb and then returns to the fray, repeating the procedure until it stabs the snake to death and eats it. It immediately repairs to its pharmacy for the antidote, eating fresh sprouts of the same plants, and is thus preserved, cured, and victorious. The natives also use the herb as a remedy for all kinds of poison, and we have seen it effective against headache, fevers, stomach cramps, and other infirmities as well.

The tigers [jaguars] that breed in those lands are past counting because of the vast quantity of wild cattle available to them; this is so great that a cow can be purchased there for what a chicken costs here, its fat alone weighing one and a half or even two *arrobas* [twenty-five pound weights]. Much could be said about the nature of these tigers. A pair of them were going along the shore following the spoor of a water hog; the latter spend a great deal of time in the water, which is their refuge from hunters. The tiger saw by the animal's tracks that it had entered the water. He leaped in after it. Out of curiosity I started saying Hail Marys; when I had got to the sixth, the tiger emerged with his prey already dead. Between the two of them they had a good meal.

The natives have learned that this animal avoids human urine like death. A tiger pursued an Indian in a forest near where I lodged. Though he shouted we could not hear him. He climbed a tree, and the tiger crouched at its foot waiting for him to come down. The Indian flung down heavy branches to drive it off, but it would not budge. He then resorted to the simple means just mentioned and the tiger instantly fled at the smell. It seeks out the poorest meat: if there is a Spaniard, a black, and an Indian, it attacks the black first; if there are only blacks, it chooses the oldest and worst smelling.

There are animals called *antas* [tapirs] that look like donkeys with very small ears. They have trunks, a span in length, which they extend and contract and apparently use for breathing. They have three toes on each foot. From their hide soldiers make helmets that turn aside arrows and sometimes bullets. Their meat is excellent, resembling beef. By day they eat vegetation, by night brackish mud; in some places their traces are as abundant as in a large cattle pen. Hunters come to these muddy spots at night. When they hear the *antas* approach, they suddenly pull out a blazing torch; this dazzles the animals and enables them to kill them. They spend the whole night in this exercise and in the morning track them down, finding them dead a few paces away.

The hoofs of this animal are an antidote against poison, especially that of the left forefoot, which corresponds to the heart. Taught by nature, the animal itself realizes this: when fatally injured, it always falls on the left forefoot and holds it next to the heart; this has been observed many times. In their maw they have bezoar stones, which are effective against poison.

CHAPTER 4

How the members of the Society entered the province of Paraguay

THE FATHERS Provincial of Peru had sent some Fathers[31] on mission to the city of Asunción, five hundred leagues distant from Potosí, the furthest outpost of the province of Peru. There they built a house, preached, and performed the Society's ministries for a number of years. But since superiors were unable to visit this residence because of the distance, they closed it and recalled the Fathers. Only one, an Irishman named Father Tomás Fildi,[32] a man of very mature years and exceptional virtue, was kept there by divine Providence to look after our house and church. Even with the Father living there, there were not wanting religious who wished to take over the house. But he kept it for us, retaining his hope that it would be filled again by men of our own who would come back for the now-ripening harvest of pagan Indians.

In 1603 Father General Claudio Aquaviva,[33] under the inspiration of heaven, as we often heard the venerable Father Diego de Torres[34] declare, put his full efforts into re-erecting the Paraguay mission and setting it up as a viceprovince. Accordingly, he named Father Diego de Torres provincial, sending him six Fathers—three Spaniards and three Italians, the first arrivals in this new province from Europe and the first help that His Majesty bestowed on us.

At the same time when Father Claudio Aquaviva in Rome was founding the province of Paraguay, our Lord was rousing the souls of certain persons in the Indies for this same enterprise and spiritual campaign. Among them was a man[35] who, planning a long journey for the sake of the profits that prompt men to disregard the fear of danger, and given that the danger of the sea is certain, had recourse to a good general confession against any eventuality. After examining his conscience thoroughly, he confessed to a religious of the Society. The latter urged him to make certain Exercises that are given by this holy order. The man, ignorant not only of the marvelous effects of these Exercises but even of their very name, allowed himself to be guided by his spiritual father and accepted. He spent three days in these exercises as if in the galleys, for the earlier objects of his vanities and follies violently rushed in and seized his mind when he tried to fix it on God, death, and eternal punishment or glory. He was thus cruelly tormented by finding himself immersed in dissipation and follies, friends and amusements—things the world deems a happy life whereas they are in reality an unhappy death.

On the fourth day he was as frightened of setting himself to prayer as to an oar, so strongly did the devil vex him there. Animating himself to hope for some spiritual peace, he felt himself desirous of praying, free from thoughts, with clarity in his mind and good affections in his will, and intimations of spiritual consolation. Quite abruptly, he felt as if in a foreign region, so distant and far away from himself as if it were not he. At that moment he was shown a vast plain of pagans, who were being chased by men bearing weapons in their hands. When the latter caught up with them, they bludgeoned them, wounded them, and ravaged them, seizing and kidnapping great numbers and setting them to hard labor.

At the same time he beheld a group of men who shone brighter than the sun, robed in white garments. He could tell that these belonged to the Society of Jesus—not by the color but by a certain understanding that enlightened his mind. The whiteness (as he himself explained to me, his closest friend while he was still a layman) had highly mysterious meanings which I must omit so as not to lose the thread of my narrative. These men were striving with all their might to drive off the others, who had the appearance of devils. The whole scene resembled the Last Judgment as it is customarily depicted, the angels defending souls and the devils assailing them. He perceived that the members of the Society were doing the angels' work. This sight enkindled in him a burning desire to be their fellow in this noble task. Immediately after that he saw and felt experientially that Christ our Lord was coming down from on high, clad in a flowing heavenly vesture like a cloak, thrown back under his arm. Drawing near to the man as he knelt there, he placed his arm on his shoulders. He drew the man's face toward the wound in his side and placed his mouth upon it; there, for a good length of time, the man imbibed a sweet exhalation that came out of the wound, the smell and taste delightful beyond anything that can be imagined.

Here he understood that Christ Jesus, the delight of souls who make themselves one with him by grace, was choosing him for the province of Paraguay, where great numbers of pagans only waited to hear the good news of the wedding of the Lamb; and that he was impressing on his soul a burning desire to dedicate himself to their conversion. The man many times assured me that the sweetness he experienced at this was so intense that it all seemed to happen to him in an instant, although by the clock more than an hour had elapsed. His earlier repulsion and dislike toward the Society changed then into a deep and heartfelt affection; he acquired a high esteem for its institute and a desire to ask for admission as a member. However, for many days the lofty idea he had formed of its apostolic institute made him afraid to reveal his desires. Finally, upon his sharing them with a very holy and learned man, the latter encouraged him to try and achieve his holy desires, telling him not to mention his vocation and call to Paraguay to anybody but to leave everything to Divine Providence alone, without recourse to human means, so that God alone would be credited with the conclusion of this happy beginning.

He followed this advice quite strictly, but the Lord likes to make his mercies known, and when the person who receives them says, "It is good to hide the secret of the king,"[36] the Lord knows how to make it manifest for his own glory and our good. And so the Lord made this known to a holy woman of very proven spirit. Once, while conferring in the church with her confessor, she said to him: "Father, do you see that brother just coming out of the sacristy to serve Mass at the high altar? Well, know that he is destined to go to the province of Paraguay which they are now talking about starting, and he must suffer many travails there; but the Lord will go with him and be his help." Asked by the confessor if she had known him before, she replied that this was the first time she had ever seen him—that it had been revealed to her by the Lord. The religious in question lives in that province today, and his apostolic work there is highly esteemed and appreciated; he related this to me as his intimate friend. The matter of our Lord's revealing that he would go to the province of Paraguay was also related to me by the holy woman's confessor. Moreover, I heard from her own mouth other things unconnected with my story but having to do with the same person.

CHAPTER 5

The province of Paraguay is founded

THE APOSTOLIC man Father Diego de Torres (whose life it is hoped will soon appear in print), first provincial of the Paraguay province, finding himself with a certain number of his own men—few enough compared to the vast harvest offered by almost countless pagans—along with the six workers earlier whom Father General had sent at no other behest than that of heaven's divine inspiration moving him to start the province so as to enrich itself from the treasury of souls there, inaugurated his province auspiciously. Passing over the schools that were founded, the enthusiasm with which the Spaniards welcomed them, and the abundant fruits gathered, all of which will in time adorn a long history, I shall discuss only a number of matters pertaining to the Indians. This is my sole intention here, and it is this that the apostolic provincial made his chief concern, as he sent the Indians apostles and angels of peace to announce eternal salvation to them.

The first mission he undertook was toward the south. There he sent the venerable Father Marciel de Lorenzana,[37] a man noble by blood but far nobler by his holiness; his life was written after his death by the present Father Provincial, Diego de Boroa.[38] Father Lorenzana eagerly offered himself to obedience and to the vicissitudes which can commonly be expected in enterprises among unbelievers. He founded the first reduction which the Society erected in that province. "Reductions" are what we call towns of Indians who, formerly living in their old fashion in forests, hill

country, and valleys, and along hidden streams in clumps of three, four, or
six dwellings situated one to three or more leagues apart, have been through
the Fathers' efforts assembled into large settlements, to a civilized, human
way of life, and to the raising of cotton with which to clothe themselves—
having previously been accustomed to live naked and leaving exposed even
what nature has concealed. This reduction is called San Ignacio, located
about twenty-five leagues from Asunción. Here we will have to leave off for
the time being while we ascend eastward into the province of Guairá. From
there we shall come back down—fleeing perhaps the townsmen of São Paulo
—to discuss this and the other reductions of the Paraná River.

CHAPTER 6

Entry of the Society of Jesus into the province of Guairá

AT THE same time, then, Father Diego de Torres dispatched to the town
of Guairá (composed of only thirty men) Fathers José Cataldino[39] and
Simón Masseta,[40] both Italians, valiant missionaries and faithful sons of the
Society, as apostles to the pagans there. Guairá was a hundred and sixty
leagues east of Asunción. Farther in the same direction was Villa Rica,[41]
sixty leagues beyond Guairá, a town of a hundred men. This whole territory
is rugged and mountainous, so that travel between settlements was by river;
there are quite large ones here, the Paraná (frequently called the River Plate)
reaching at certain points a breadth of two leagues in this region.

The Fathers performed their ministries in the town of Guairá, and then
moved on to Villa Rica. This entailed considerable hardship since the long
journey required two boat trips. The first was from the town of Asunción to
the port of Maracayú, a journey of thirty to forty days through uninhabited
country on a difficult river, with provisions having to be carried for the whole
period. From Maracayú there is a stretch overland to the great falls of the
Paraná, one of the wonders of the world. This takes six to eight days of
tramping on foot through swamps and over rough paths and dangerous
streams. When the latter are in flood, passage is afforded to the traveler by
the tips of trees, poles being tied from one to the other with reeds which
easily break, so that it is extremely dangerous.

From this waterfall one embarks again. After a journey of two leagues
further upstream was the town of Guairá. Traveling eight days upstream from
there by another river called the Huibay, one reached the settlement of
Espíritu Santo, now totally devastated by the townsmen of São Paulo, as we
shall mention later. Here the Fathers fell quite ill; indeed the lack of doctors
and medicines brought them to the verge of death. On recovering, they
performed their ministries with great fruit for souls. There was a priest in the

town, a professed religious of a certain order, who decided to change his habit. Claiming that his own had been stolen during the night, he took that of St. Peter, thus living and dying as a secular priest. He baptized numerous adults with no instruction beyond pouring the water on their heads.

After completing their mission among the Spaniards, the Fathers turned their attention to the conversion of the Indians for whom they had been sent. Although in those parts there were numerous areas of pagans apparently ready to receive the gospel, heaven guided them along a river called the Paranapane, which means "unfortunate" or "luckless." It turned out to be unfortunate for the devil but fortunate for heaven, for in this province a great treasury of souls was enrolled for heaven by baptism. In this enterprise the Fathers were accompanied by a townsman of Guairá in the guise of interpreter, a man desirous of doing good. They traveled up this river for ten or eleven days through entirely uninhabited country, finally reaching a town right on the river bank and bordered on one side by a stream called the Pirapó. It was inhabited by about two hundred Indians, and they received the Fathers with great love. Here they raised the standard of the Cross and put up a little hut for a church; they called it Nuestra Señora de Loreto and halted there for some days. Learning about the people who lived along these rivers, the two Fathers set out together with their companions to bring the people (who, as we said earlier, lived scattered in tiny clusters) together into large settlements. They found twenty-five small hamlets and some villages of reasonable size. The Fathers preached to the pagans, explaining why they had come: to make them children of God and free them from slavery to the devil.

On the other side the Spanish layman was going about his own business in a way that nearly got the gospel and its preachers driven out or cast into discredit. The Fathers noticed that one time he came to the house without his hat, later without his cloak, then without coat or doublet, and then without trousers and with nothing on but white pants and a cloth tied on his head. Bemused by this oddity, the Fathers asked an explanation. His reply was: "Your Reverences preach in your way and I preach in mine. I have no words, so I preach with deeds. I have given all my clothes away to gain the good will of the principal Indians. If I can win them over the rest will do what I want." Who would not be edified by so zealous a deed? The Fathers were embarrassed that they had nothing to give, such was their poverty.

Having finished his business, the Spaniard asked leave to depart. Hardly had he gone when the Indians revealed that he had been auctioning his clothes off, purchasing with each garment an Indian woman or child. The Indians thought he was acting under the Fathers' orders and for a time lost some of their earlier confidence in them; however, being given a satisfactory explanation by the Fathers, they recovered their confidence in them. This is a plague that dogs the gospel: on the heels of the liberty acquired through baptism follow slavery and captivity—not by diabolical but by human device

—to block the spread of the gospel; for this traffic leads to internecine wars so that they can sell one another, to robbery, killing, and an increase in the number of concubines.

CHAPTER 7

Father Antonio Ruiz goes to the mission; the so-called Paraguayan herb

THE FATHERS had been at the Pirapó for about six months—a year and a half having gone by since their departure from Asunción—when I was dispatched to the region by Father Diego de Torres. My departure, however, had hung in the balance. After he brought me to Asunción from the city of Córdoba (about two hundred leagues), and I already had my foot on the road to my mission, he told me: "I did bring you for the apostolic mission of Guairá, but now my need for you requires changing my plans and sending you to Chile." My heart froze at this unexpected decision. Without answering a word, I fled to the Blessed Sacrament. The upshot was that he soon changed his mind and assigned me to Guairá.

Father Antonio de Moranta[42] and I left together. Halfway on our forty-day journey through uninhabited country, our supply of jerky and manioca flour ran out. We still had a little maize-corn; we each ate a handful at midday and another at night. This scarcity made Father Moranta painfully ill; and, when reports warned us of other difficulties awaiting us further on, necessity forced him to turn back from the port of Maracayú.

The Indians of this town welcomed me with great love. Counting them, I tallied a hundred and seventy families. Passing through this place several times on later journeys, I counted within a few years no more than fifty. The cause of this widespread decline in the number of the Indians subjected or given to Spaniards in *encomienda*[43] has ceased to be a matter of inquiry: it is too well known, and so commonplace that it is not wondered at or even noticed. I remained a number of days in the town administering the sacraments, and by continuously hearing and speaking their language eventually acquired facility in it.

The town is situated in a small clearing surrounded by immense groves of wild forest, containing stands, two, three, or more leagues in length and breadth, of the trees from which the so-called Paraguayan herb[44] is harvested. These trees are quite tall, leafy, and thick, with thickish tongue-shaped leaves. The trees are felled; thick new shoots sprout from the stump and in three years they are as large and fine as when cut down. The branches are placed on grids and roasted over a low fire. The leaves are then laboriously ground by the Indians. The latter, with nothing to eat all day but the mushrooms, fruits, or wild roots they happen to find in the forest, are at constant labor and toil under an overseer, whose wrath the poor Indian, the moment he rests for a moment to catch his breath, feels in the form of words or sometimes nicely delivered blows. The work on this herb has consumed the lives of many thousands of Indians. I can testify to having seen in those woods huge piles of their bones. It pains one's eyes to see them and breaks one's heart to know how they died, still pagans, roaming these forests in search of vermin, toads, or snakes, and, unable to find even these, drinking quantities of this herb, which swells their feet, legs and bellies, while their faces display nothing but bone and death's-head pallor.

Once one or two hundred hundredweights have been accumulated in any of these encampments, eight or nine Indians are loaded up. Each carries five or six *arrobas* a distance of ten to twenty leagues, the Indian himself weighing far less than his load and being given nothing for his nourishment. Curious persons have made the experiment of weighing an Indian against his load on a scale: even with many additional pounds on the Indian's side he did not outweigh his heavy load. How many have been left dead beside their loads, the Spaniard less concerned over the poor Indian's death than at having no one to carry the load! How many have plunged with their burden down steep ravines, where we have found them at the bottom throwing up bile through their mouths! How many have been devoured by tigers in these forests—more than sixty in a single year!

These things cried out to heaven. To remedy these evils, his Catholic Majesty dispatched Doctor Don Francisco de Alfaro,[45] a judge presently on the Council of Finance and a man born for the task. The first-hand inspection he carried out of nearly all of Peru, visiting the provinces and administrations and enacting just ordinances, brought him to that territory, a place where no judge's robe was seen before or since. The West accordingly holds him in high regard and is eager to see him on the Council of the Indies so that, having laid down such Christian ordinances while there in person, he might here [in Spain] by his memorials and sagacious counsel ensure their execution.[46] Under severe penalties he prohibited forcing the Indians to harvest the herb; indeed he prohibited the Indians themselves from doing so even voluntarily during the four months of December to March, an extremely unhealthy period throughout the region.

Such were the injunctions of this most righteous judge. But they are not obeyed, although His Majesty confirmed each of his ordinances to the letter, altering nothing. But certain procurators (not of the Indians, who have none, but of the Spaniards) have come to this court with reports, the falseness of which was not realized, and obtained from the Council a restriction—or rather, extension—of some of the orders. Passing over the rest so as not to transgress the brevity I aim at in this account, I shall give an idea of them all by a single instance. Dr. Don Francisco had assessed the Indians five of the "hollow weights" mentioned earlier. Although his wish was to banish from the world the abominable practice of personal service (which today His Majesty, whom God protect, has sternly ordered to be banished from the Indies, though there are not wanting those who repeal this banishment),[47] he was unable to do so at the time and hence ordered that for the five weights each Indian should render a month's service.

The said procurators came to the court here, and, with no one to speak on behalf of the defenseless Indians (even though it was the Indians' sweat and blood that the procurators spent at court—I can testify that they seized the Indians' oxen, horses, mares, and other property, telling them that it was to finance the procurator who was going to represent the interests of the country, and that it was common property whereas it was actually the Indians' individual property), the procurators obtained a ruling which rather than improving the Indians' lot condemned them to pay double tribute—ten pesos paid with two months of personal service. If this were all, the poor people might have borne it. However, one must reckon that to do this enforced labor many travel thirty, forty, or fifty leagues, or even the hundred and sixty leagues between Maracayú and the Paraguay. The result is that after losing eight, fifteen, or twenty days in getting there, and two months in paying their tribute, they are forced by fear of harsh compulsion to stay at least a month more, sometimes two or three more.

I am witness to the fact that in Guairá Province, the most honest *encomendero* employed all the Indians granted given to him in *encomienda* for six months of the year without any pay, while the less honest hold them for ten or twelve months. And if this be so, as in fact it is, what time does the wretched man have left to support his wife and raise his own children, who are sometimes strangers to him, having been born during such long absences? This topic requires more space than I have here.

Besides this swindle of doubled tribute, there is another through which the Indian pays more than the ten pesos' tribute by being cheated out of the regular wage of a day laborer in that land. The law provides that a day worker be paid a real and a half a day, and thus receive forty-five reals a month—with the additional factor of being free to hire himself out. The poor Indian, however, obliged to pay with his very person, is forced to serve at forty reals a month. He thus ends up paying ten reals over and above the double tribute imposed on him, for a total tribute of eleven pesos and two reals[48]—an intolerable burden in such a poor country.

I got off my subject by going into the injustice done to the Indians, but with good reason since this herb plays an important part in it. I shall now go back and finish my discussion of the herb. I carefully inquired about its origin from Indians who were eighty to a hundred years old. I learned as a certain fact that in their youth the herb was not drunk or even known except by a great sorcerer[49] or magician who trafficked with the devil. The devil showed him the herb and told him to drink it whenever he wanted to consult him. He did so, and, under his tutelage, so did others whom we have known in our own days. The witchcraft they perform commonly derives from this herb. The older Indians took up its use, but with moderation. They claim it has the following effects: it lightens work; it sustains them (we have daily experience that an Indian can row for a whole day with no sustenance beyond drinking the herb every three hours); it purges their stomach of phlegm; it makes the senses alert; it dispels drowsiness when one wants to stay up at night without sleepiness (in this it seems to resemble somewhat the Chinese herb called *cha*, which takes away sleep—even the name of the herb is not much different, being in the native language *caa*[50]).

The native Indians take it with moderation once a day. The Spaniards have found it a remedy against all ills and claim that it is a well-proven remedy against urinary illness, and for this reason they use it in those regions without any moderation or restraint. I have observed that excessive drinking of the herb has caused some persons for extended periods to lose their judgment—which is so lacking in large numbers of persons that they spend more than 300,000 pounds annually on mere vomitives.[51] I do not doubt its effectiveness, although I have never tried it. However, it deserves condemnation because of the abuse made of it, the hardship involved in its cultivation, the high esteem it enjoys, its sustaining and stimulating effect on workers, the high prices it commands (in Paraguay a quintal or hundredweight goes for twenty-five pesos, at Santa Fe for sixteen to twenty silver reals, and at Tucumán for thirty-five to forty pesos, the price continuing to rise proportionately as one approaches Potosí), its superstitious employment in sorcery, and even for its odor and taste (that of sumac), in which it closely resembles the Peruvian herb called *coca*.

CHAPTER 8

Effects of the prevailing poor treatment of the Indians

I DO NOT propose to list the injustices regularly done to the Indians. This would involve recapitulating numerous other authors, and, with the addition of what I myself have seen, would produce a quite substantial volume. The injustices that brought me here to court will of course have to be reported in their proper place; I shall speak at present of their consequences. The first is that the pagans are unwilling to receive the gospel. A second is scandal given to those already Christians: with their ears they hear the justice of God's law set forth, but with their eyes they see man's contradiction of it in practice. In many regions we have heard this argument from the pagans and have seen them shun our preaching, which is rendered abhorrent by bad Christians. I will give just two instances of this.

Opposite the city of Asunción, on the other side of the River Paraguay, live two nations, one called the Guaycurús and the other the Guaicurut, each numbering about five hundred or fewer Indians. Their dwellings are of cowhide and thus portable. They are huge in stature; the men go naked, while the women are decently clad. They wield spears and clubs, which they hurl with speed and accuracy, as well as bows and arrows. They do not farm; instead they steal whatever they can from the crops of the Spanish. They regularly enter the cattle ranches, killing whatever they want and taking the fat and meat to the owner for sale to him. They stroll through the town in perfect safety, but any Spaniard going onto their lands has none, for they will slit a Spaniard's throat as readily as a cow's. They are so fierce that Spanish power does not suffice to curb them.

The governors asked the men of the Society to tame this barbarous people by means of the gospel. The difficult task was undertaken by Father Pedro Romero,[52] a truly apostolic man, whose labors among them merit a lengthy history. He tried everything that his ardent zeal could devise to wrest them from their bestial customs and root them in Christianity. But after many years he had no success, for they mocked our faith. What use was this apostolic man's preaching to them the beauty of chastity when they saw Venus being worshiped in the town? They used this argument to support their bestial practices, in which they are determined to live until death. As a result, the apostolic man had to abandon these barren plantations, managing to cull only a few flowers, infants who before being withered by death received the water of life. He was forced to leave by a bishop, who promised to put another priest there; but within two days the barbarians forced the latter to leave, never to return. The governor and people urged the Society to take them in hand out of concern for the general good of their community, since the priest got them to return stolen horses and other property.

The Spaniards were also on guard against the Indians' schemes; even today they do not feel their lives safe in the town, living in unbearable anxiety with sentinels posted day and night. Their wish, however, was not successful, for once rivalry takes over it sweeps duty before it, even when it costs the loss of souls.

There is another region of baptized Christians called Calchaquí, where His Majesty possessed a people of his own which paid him no small tribute. There were secular priests in the village missions and religious orders in the town. The Indians were so oppressed by the ceaseless toil of raising cotton and weaving canvas, and their wives so harried with the ceaseless spinning that was harshly exacted from them, even from those busiest caring for their own children, that necessity forced them to seek relief. They arose and killed a good number of Spaniards; the survivors had to abandon the city and all their possessions—which were not small—and take refuge in the city of Corrientes. Despite efforts to retake the country, it has proved impossible, even when undertaken by that great and noble soldier, Commander Manuel Cabral,[53] who has rendered His Majesty most loyal service with his person and his fortune. On the contrary, with the seven hundred horses left them by a certain retreating general as booty, plus the weapons they captured, the Indians are so well armed and defiant that all hope of conquering them has been given up. This took place but a short while ago in the provinces of Paraguay and Buenos Aires. The like happened almost contemporaneously with another nation, also called Calchaquí, in the district of Tucumán. They had been conquered through the gospel preached by the members of the Society, who had five settlements there. They were distressed by the infamous personal service, as were the preachers of the gospel, being eventually obliged to bid farewell to the Indians, who were left deeply sorrowful and grieving, the Fathers no less so at abandoning them.[54]

Their departure delighted the Spaniards, but when the natives saw how much they had lost and what labors were laid upon them, they took up arms, threw off the yoke, and overran the Spaniards' land and ranches, killing many and destroying their property, cattle, and crops. They emptied a town of Spaniards and were ready to put an end to them all. In this desperate situation it was necessary for the Royal Audiencia of Charcas[55] to send the attorney-general as commander. Neither his authority nor the forces he brought (at great expense to the Royal Exchequer) were enough to undo the harm. In the end, with the whole province devastated of both men and property, their final recourse was a peace settlement that left the Indians upon the lands which they enjoy today. They still wish to have the gospel, however, for they all request priests and insist that their revolt was not against the gospel but against tyranny and injustice. Moreover, if in the province of Uruguay, where the gospel penetrated unarmed, five priests of the Society shed their blood in noble martyrdom, this is not a weakness of the gospel but its strength and a powerful watering for growth; nor is it dishonor for Spain but honor and increase for the Royal Crown, for this blessed watering has produced a rich harvest of twenty-five settlements or reductions maintained by the Society today strong in faith and obedience to His Majesty —to whom, as I in their name have set forth in my memorials, they promise whatever tribute His Majesty may be pleased to lay on them.

This digression has been essential for my purpose. I shall now resume the thread of my journey.

CHAPTER 9

Father Antonio Ruiz de Montoya arrives at the reduction of Loreto,
where Fathers José Cataldino and Simón Masseta were stationed

I ARRIVED AT the reduction of Our Lady of Loreto anxious to see those outstanding two men, Fathers José and Simón. I found them in great poverty but rich in happiness. The patches on their clothes could no longer be distinguished from the original cloth. The shoes they had brought from Paraguay [Asunción] had been repaired with bits of cloth cut from the hems of their cassocks. I counted myself blessed to be in their company. The hut, furnishings, and food closely matched those of the anchorites: bread, wine, and salt were not tasted for many years. We occasionally saw meat in the form of game, which was brought to us every once in a while as alms. Food mainly consisted of potatoes, bananas, and manioca roots. There are two species of the latter, a sweet one which can be eaten without harm, either roasted or boiled; and a harsh, bitter one which is fatal when eaten in this form; it becomes edible when grated and pressed out, and the juice is widely used to flavor things boiled in it. There is the tradition that they were given this food by St. Thomas the Apostle:[56] he took a stick, made a cutting, and ordered them to plant it; and so they do. Although the cutting has no roots, it produces quite thick ones within eight to twelve months. If the sweet manioca is planted together with the bitter, it will lose its sweetness and turn bitter and poisonous. We were forced by necessity to plant with our own hands the wheat required for hosts; half an *arroba* of wine stood us for nearly five years, as we used only the minimum needed to consecrate. Moreover, so as not to burden the Indians, we had our own little garden of the ordinary roots and vegetables which we lived on.

Father José and I traveled up the rivers to invite the Indians to gather into large settlements in locations that had already been designated for them. We arrived at a village ruled by a great cacique who was a great magician, sorcerer, and familiar of the devil. His name was Taubici, meaning "devils in a row" or "row of devils." He was extremely cruel: upon the slightest annoyance he would have Indians killed at whim, and so was held in awe and served at the merest hint of his thought. Shortly before our arrival he had had an Indian killed because he had put him in charge of a sick little son of his and the boy died. When he wanted to talk with the devil, he ordered everyone to get out of his house and to give it a wide berth all around. Four of his favorite girls would stay in his company. He would order part of the roof of his house taken off for the evil spirit to come in. Then the wretched fellow would have fits; his women would support him, holding his arms and head as he made wild faces and gestures. With these tricks and shams of his, he would afterwards publish numerous lies about future events —some of which occasionally came true, having been gotten by hints from the devil. This man received us well and, evil though he was, saved us from death. Some of the Indians decided to kill us the very night of our arrival but, having determined this, thought it better not to act without consulting him. His reply was: "If you want to kill the Fathers, do it yourselves. I will not get involved in it."

This expression of disapproval sufficed to keep them from taking our lives. They were discussing this at midnight; at the same hour I awoke with a start from a dream that they were going to kill us, so that we spent the rest of the night preparing for death.

This cacique went down to the reduction we had named San Ignacio,[57] where Father Simón Masseta was in charge, and began to establish himself among the Indians through his evil tricks. Though many refused to give him credit because they were pledged to the faith preached by the Fathers, nevertheless something happened to him which gave him considerable credibility. There was an Indian who had two plantings of sugarcane in his plot. This being a novelty, his neighbors stole some from him. The man took what remained and brought it to Taubici, telling him that the reason he was bringing him this puny gift was that the rest had been stolen. Taubici asked about the culprits; the Indian replied that he did not know who they were. Taubici said: "Do not worry, the robbers will be found out and will pay for it. I will punish this insolence with the sickness of the bowels." So it was; a short time thereafter the illness broke out in that and the surrounding towns, and a number of persons died. This so enhanced Taubici's reputation that when Corpus Christi came Father Simón warned the people that no one should leave the town until after the celebration. On the same occasion Taubici took a mind to leave the town and go to his own. Gathering a party to go with him, he settled on his departure. The Father urged him and the others, especially those already Christian, to attend the procession and Mass first and then leave. Having no success with them, he declared to them in his zeal: "Since you refuse to honor our Creator and Lord, and despise my warnings, fear with a certainty that he will soundly punish you where you are going."

It happened as he said. They started out cheerfully, mocking and joking about the Father and his warnings. Just as they reached their village, about twenty leagues from San Ignacio, they recognized some Indians in canoes on the river. Taubici went to them, thinking they were his friends. As soon as they recognized him, they killed him in revenge for a man that he had killed. His companions took to flight in their boats, with the others in pursuit. Many were wounded; some jumped to land to escape with their lives into the thick forest; some rowed hard and got out of danger. They returned without their leader, taught a good lesson by this chastisement to mistrust the ministers of the devil and to believe those of God. This won great credit for the gospel.

We arrived at another town governed by an honorable cacique who was eager to hear things concerning his salvation. The devil aimed at obstructing his good desires and so stirred up one of his chief ministers, a great preacher of lies who went on mission from place to place deceiving these poor people and preaching that he was God, the creator of heaven and earth and men, that he sent the rains and took them away, bestowed fertile years so long as they did not anger him but, if they did, stopped the waters so that the land became barren again, and other nonsense by which he attracted many silly people to himself. This man came to visit the above mentioned cacique Maracaná. The latter arranged for three of his relatives to throw him in bonds. The magician leapt from his boat and started preaching a great harangue in a loud shout, as is the old custom of these brutes. His theme was their stubborn foolishness in making up gods for themselves. He arrived at the cacique's house and proffered his usual courtesies. The cacique asked him who he was and why he came. He answered: "I am the creator of things. I make fertile the fields and punish those who do not believe in me with many grave diseases." The cacique signaled to the three young men; they tied him up, though it took a while because he resisted for some time, telling them that he would kill them with his saliva and spitting in their faces. The good cacique said: "I am going to test the truth of what you say about giving life to others. I will be able to tell by whether you escape the death I shall now inflict on you." He had him taken to the river and thrown, with a large stone fastened to his neck, out into the current; there the wretched man ended his miserable life.

CHAPTER 10

Customs of the Guaraní Indians

THE PAGANS lived, and still live today, in quite small villages (as already mentioned), but not without government. They had their caciques, who were universally recognized as possessing noble status inherited from their ancestors, based upon their having had vassals and ruled over people. Many acquire noble status through eloquence of speech, so great is their esteem for their language—rightly so, for it is worthy of praise and of being celebrated among the tongues of renown. By their eloquence they gather followers and vassals, thus ennobling both themselves and their descendants. The common folk serve them; they clear their ground and sow and reap their crops; they build their houses and give them their daughters when they crave them. In this matter they behave with pagan freedom: we met some with fifteen, twenty, or thirty wives. A surviving brother sometimes takes his dead brother's wives, but this is not common. In this regard they show the greatest reserve towards their mothers and sisters, and would not even think of having relations with them, considering it a crime against nature. Even after becoming Christians, if they are related to a woman in any degree, even one that is dispensable or licit without dispensation, they will not without dispensation admit her as wife, asserting that it is their own blood; they avoid unnatural crime like death; nature is thereby assisted for evacuation through the passage; they will die rather than admit such.[58] To this day Christian caciques do not today marry common women, but those from the prominent families; they are very particular about this, even though common women be naturally endowed. Many arguments confirm that they never had permanent wives. Being people without contracts of any sort, they never had any thought of the burdensome contract of permanent marriage. Moreover, as lovers of freedom and ease, they considered it disgraceful for a man to be bound to one wife by a tie he could not dissolve at will. Others have found grounds for the opposite opinion; my purpose is not to decide debates. They knew of God's existence, and even in a certain way of his unity. This is gathered from the name they give him, *Tupá*.[59] The first syllable, *tu*, expresses wonder, while the second, *pá*, is an interrogative; thus it corresponds to the Hebrew word *Man-hu*, "What is this?," in the singular. They never had idols, though the devil was already imposing upon them to venerate the bones of certain Indians who had been famous magicians during their lifetimes, as we shall see later.

They never offered sacrifice to the true God, nor did they have any more than a simple knowledge of him. In my own view, this was all that remained among them from the preaching of the apostle St. Thomas, who, as we shall see, proclaimed the divine mysteries to them.

They count years by winters, which they call *roy*. Their counting reaches only the number four, and from there, somewhat confusedly, up to ten. Hence we are progressively teaching them our number system, which is essential for confession. They know the time of sowing from the movement of the Pleiades. They held as a quite certain doctrine that there is an enormous tiger or dog in the sky, and that, in certain fits of wrath, it devours the sun and the moon—what we call eclipses. When this happened they would demonstrate grief and astonishment.

While one of a man's wives was giving birth, he would go on a strict fast for fifteen days, eating no meat; even when game appeared before him he would not kill it. For the entire period he would maintain the greatest seclusion and isolation; the good health and rearing of the child depended on this.[60] They practice a sort of baptism or name-giving. When they capture someone in war, they fatten him up, giving him freedom to choose food and women at his pleasure. Once fattened, he is killed with great solemnity. Then, all touching the corpse or striking it with a stick, each

or enemies

person takes his name. They distribute pieces of his body throughout the region. The piece is boiled in a large amount of water and made into a pottage. Each person receives a mouthful and takes his name. Women give a bit of this gruel to their nursing children, giving each one its name. This is a solemn festival among them, performed with great ceremony.

They welcome guests or those coming back from a journey with a ritual lament, in this manner. The guest enters the house and seats himself, with his host beside him. The women then come out, surround the guest, and without exchanging a word raise their voices in a ritual wail. In this lament they recall the guest's family members, their deaths, their heroic feats and deeds while alive, and the good or ill fortune that has befallen the person. The men cover their faces with their hands in a display of sadness and of weeping; they endorse in low voices the elegies being sung by the weeping women. The more important the person, the greater the weeping and wailing, giving the impression throughout the whole neighborhood that someone deeply beloved by the household has died. Then they wipe away their tears, cease their lamentation, and bid the person welcome. Unfortunate is the person who is not received in this fashion.

Upon their husbands' death, wives fling themselves shrieking from a height of three yards, sometimes suffering death or crippling from the impact. The devil keeps them deluded, persuading them that death is not something natural and common to all but that every death is an accident.

They thought that the soul accompanied the dead body in its burial, though separated. Accordingly, many buried their dead in large jars, setting a plate over the mouth so that in this hollow space the soul would have more room, although they buried the jars up to the neck. When we would inter Christians in the earth, an old woman would come up on the sly with a strange little sieve; this she would surreptitiously pass over the grave as if taking something out of it. They claimed she was removing the dead person's soul so that it would not suffer by burial with the body.

At the beginning of a girl's first menstruation, they place her in her hammock or net, sewing her up in it like a corpse in a shroud and leaving only a breathing space. They give her very little to eat. This ordeal goes on for two or three days. When they are done, they hand her over to a very tough, hardworking woman who exercises her in heavy, toilsome, and fatiguing housework, in which she is exercised very hard. The aim of all this is to make her a good worker, not dainty. She spends this time—normally eight days—dirty and harassed. Here they find out if she is valiant and hard-working. After this, they cut her hair after our fashion, clothe her, and adorn her with the best they have, which are blue beads and other trinkets. From then on she can have relations with a man; before this menstruation it would have been a sacrilege.

They hold it a fact proven by experience that if a deer enters a settlement and is not killed, someone in the neighborhood through which it escapes has to die. The devil has at times concurred with these superstitions. We witnessed this in a town of Spaniards. A man had married; as the groom was engaged in wedding revelries on horseback with some other men, a deer being pursued from the countryside ran down the street. Their revelries were heightened by the attempt to catch it, but it got away. With great sadness an Indian asked: "Who from this house will have to die today?" That very night the groom took sick and did not reach the morning alive. They have the same notion about toads: if one gets into a boat, some person in the boat has to die. One time, when traveling on a boat with more than twenty people, for two days we all heard the continuous noise of these vermin. Aware of this superstition, I carefully observed the actions of the Indians. They were upset and anxiously watched for the little creatures, but failed to discover if there actually were any. In fact it was a device of the devil which for two days produced the music of toads without there being any at all. The Indians were in anguish, but as recent Christians they cloaked their uneasiness out of respect for me. Just a few days later, on the same trip and in the same boat, several people fell ill with a pestilential fever; even though I bled them, four died.

They know by tradition about the general deluge, which they call *yporú*, which means "very large flood." The same tradition is found in Peru, as an author of our own time writes.[61] The superstitions of the magicians are based on divination by bird songs, about which they have invented numerous fables, as well as on fraudulent treatments of the sick: the magician sucks the affected part and then, extracting from his mouth items he had concealed there, shows that by his power he has removed the cause of the person's illness—a fish bone, a coal, or the like. The worst and most pernicious are the buriers. Their trade is killing. In the house of a person they want to kill they bury leavings from his meal—fruit skins, pieces of charcoal, etc. They sometimes bury toads with fish bones stuck through them; this slowly debilitates the person they want to kill and he dies without any other accident. We have many times seen this happen unmistakably. Regarding some I learned that the devil would appear to them as a little black man with a basket in his hand, urging them to go bury. In a room where people were present day and night we found more than three hundred holes and burials of items that the devil had given them. When one of these men wanted to kill one of the Fathers by such means, the devil replied that he was powerless against these religious.

CHAPTER 11

Our method for ending these abuses and preaching the faith

AT THIS time a companion joined us. He was Father Martín Urtasun,[62] a native of Pamplona, where he abandoned his inheritance as eldest son, an income of three thousand ducats, for the rumor of rich mines of souls in the poor province of Paraguay. We divided ourselves between two settlements, Loreto and San Ignacio, a pair of us working in each. We set up a school to teach the youth reading and writing, and indicated a period of one hour every morning and evening for the adults to come to catechism classes. Although in these classes and in the sermons we gave each Sunday we treated the mysteries of our holy faith and the commandments of God with all clarity, we kept silence in public on the sixth commandment so as not to wither these tender plants and arouse hatred for the gospel. Those in danger of death, however, we instructed with all clarity. This silence lasted two years, and was quite necessary, as the outcome proved, as we shall see. The devil tried to tempt our purity through the caciques' offering to us some of their women on the complaint that they considered it unnatural for men to engage in domestic work such as cooking, sweeping, and the like.

We gave them a full account of priestly chastity, explaining that this was why our first concern had been to enclose a small area around our house with a stake fence to keep women from entering our house. They marveled at our doing so; however, being barbarians, they did not find it admirable since among them it was a matter of honor and prestige to have numerous wives and serving women, a widespread failing among pagans. Besides the town of San Ignacio, Fathers José and Martín had two others as colonies to which they went as needed. Father Simón and I had one at Loreto, three quarters of a league distant. Its cacique was a valiant and respected Indian named Roque Maracaná, who was venerated by the whole territory. We took turns every Sunday going there to catechize these people, all recently settled. As they were very numerous, this gave us a great deal of labor, although it was welcome because of the large numbers being won for baptism. We had adults and sick people with whom we were obliged to handle the topics of marriage and monogamy, and this demanded much effort. This was our regular practice: at daybreak we would visit the sick; then we would celebrate Mass, with a sermon after the Gospel, after which the pagans were dismissed, much to their chagrin at seeing themselves ejected from the church like dogs. They envied the Christians who stayed behind, and this spurred them to learn the catechism for baptism as soon as possible and to set aside every obstacle. Taking time out at noon to pray the hours of the divine office, we would return (still fasting so as not to annoy the Indians by asking for anything) to the church where we gave instruction, baptizing up to two, three, or four hundred each day. Night had already fallen when we would return to Loreto exhausted and with our heads bursting, still fasting and with no desire to eat. Our Father Martín Urtasun soon died from this toil, as I shall recount.

We Fathers in San Ignacio had a prominent cacique who, after varied fortunes in different places, where he was baptized and married, finally by his eloquence became as it were lord of the people there. He was a servant of the devil. Attracted to a woman, not for her beauty but her noble status, he repudiated his legitimate wife, banishing her to a farm and putting the girl in her place with the title of legitimate wife. With shameless effrontery he asserted that she was his legal wife, and she had herself waited on as mistress of numerous serving women. The poor wretch went even further with his fraudulence; to gain greater prestige with his followers, he pretended to be a priest. In his private chamber he would put on an alb; robed in a mozetta of brilliant feathers and other adornments, he pretended to say Mass. He would spread a table with cloths and place upon them a manioca cake and a painted cup of maize wine; muttering a number of ritual formulas, he would show the cake and wine as priests do, finally eating and drinking everything. His vassals consequently venerated him as a priest. His life was exceptionally scandalous as he had a large number of concubines, with the full consent and encouragement of his pretended wife. We baptized eight of his infant children—the year's crop—all of them blessed indeed for they died shortly after being baptized. Our own purity and modesty was an offense to him; he disliked our obliging the sick and those who wanted to be truly cleansed through baptism to give up their concubines. His resentment reached such a pitch that he began to incite his vassals' minds against us. In various gatherings he told them: "The devils have brought us these men, for with new teachings they want to take away from us the good old way of life of our ancestors, who had many wives and servant women and were free to choose them at will. Now they want us to tie ourselves to a single woman. It is not right for this to go any further; we should drive them out of our lands, or take their lives."

There were many among them who had love for us and esteemed our virtue, good example, and teaching. These put him off with the suggestion that it would not be good to carry out his design without consulting Roque Maracaná for his opinion, and that, if he agreed, it could be put into effect. Then this cacique, whose name was Miguel Artiguaye, came to visit the Fathers, seemingly friendly and with smiling countenance. After a few words of courtesy, he turned into a wild beast and burst out shouting: "You are no priests sent from God to aid our misery; you are devils from hell, sent by their ruler for our destruction. What teaching have you brought us? What peace and happiness? Our ancestors lived in liberty. They enjoyed all the women they wanted, without hindrance from anyone. Thus they lived and spent their lives in happiness, and you want to destroy their traditions and impose on us this heavy burden of being bound to a single wife." And as he left the room he said: "This shall not be; I am going to do something about it." The Fathers, who had listened like lambs to this wolf's howlings, tried detaining him to reason with his irrationality, but without success. On the contrary, he went on shouting with uncontrollable diabolical fury: "We can no longer tolerate the freedom of these men who want to compel us in our own lands to live in their evil fashion."

CHAPTER 12

Departure of this cacique from his town to discuss his evil intention with Roque Maracaná, and what happened to him

THE FOLLOWING night Miguel conferred on this matter with his people, as did the Fathers with God. The upshot was that at daybreak a great racket and din was heard throughout the settlement—preparations for war, drums, flutes, and other instruments. Three hundred warriors assembled in the town square, armed with shields, swords, bows, and great quantities of arrows, all splendid with rich painting and variegated feathering. On their heads they wore gorgeous feathered crowns. The most elaborately decked out was the cacique Miguel. He wore a rich robe all of varicolored feathers very skillfully woven; on his head was a feathered crown. He was armed with a sword and shield; at his sides walked two burly young fellows each bearing a bow and a large quiver of arrows for the cacique. At the head of all these people he set off to embark on the river. They left the landing with a great show of bravery, to the sound of flute and drum.

Let us leave them for the moment on their way downstream and return to Father José and his companions. Apprehensive about this journey, they could only conclude that it was to consult with Roque Maracaná about their deaths and then, with his approval, to kill Father Simón and me at Loreto and then return to kill themselves. This was confirmed by the opinion of some who remained in the settlement. Further, the cacique Miguel had been heard to say: "These Fathers will wake up one morning with their heads gone." The probability of the cacique Roque's going along with him was increased by his own vested interest in the many young women he possessed and by his being a very unrestrained and impetuous young man.

Amid these discussions the Fathers withdrew to hold a spiritual conference on how they should go about preparing to meet death. They decided to make a general confession of their entire lives (although in the general confession of his whole life which Father Martín made a few months later as he died in my arms, I found nothing that was or that I could conjecture to be serious). They made their confession for death, placing themselves in the hands of God, whose protection was their only defense. In this predicament our Lord came to his servants' rescue in the following manner.

Beyond San Ignacio there was another quite large town made up of people whom we had settled there. Their cacique was an excellent Indian named Araraá. Immediately upon hearing of the cacique Miguel's defiance, he dispatched a good boat with a message to the Fathers: "I have learned of that cacique's shamelessness and of his plan to kill you. I would be greatly pleased if you would come to this town of yours for protection against your enemy. You will not lack for anything you need or for people to defend you, for I have vassals who will be able to do it. So that your coming will not be delayed for want of a boat, I am sending you this one and look forward to seeing you here in this town of yours."

Unwilling to show cowardice and trusting in God, the Fathers preferred to await whatever happened. So, replying to his offer with gratitude, they remained in continuous prayer, which is mightier than any weapons, as was proved that very day.

The cacique Roque—along with Father Simón and myself—was quite unaware of all this agitation, when he heard a great hubbub and the beating of drums. He asked his servants what this unexpected occurrence was all about. Once fully informed, he called for sword and seized a shield, showing himself valiant (as indeed he was) and very well disposed. The cacique Miguel leapt ashore. His soldiers lined up in two rows, with himself as commander in the middle, grasping his shield and girded with his sword. In the style of the ancient nobles, he began striding and shouting aloud: "My brothers and sons, the time is over for bearing the evils and disasters these men we call Fathers have brought on us. They shut us up in a house (he meant church) where they harangue us and tell us the opposite of what our ancestors did and taught us: our ancestors had many wives, and these men take them away from us and demand that we be content with one. We do not agree to this; let us take measures against these evils."

The cacique Roque advanced a few paces from his house, escorted by only twelve or fourteen of his vassals armed with bows and arrows. Miguel paid his compliments. Before letting him go forward, Roque asked: "Are you bringing letters from the Fathers of your town for the Fathers down here?" Miguel replied: "This is no time for letters but for honoring our ancestors' way of life and for doing away with these Fathers and enjoying our women and our freedom." At this, Roque lunged at him; seizing him by the front of his clothes and giving him a couple of hard jerks, he flung him to the ground. Miguel, his shield, and his sword went rolling off in different directions. Turning to his men, Roque said: "No one shoot an arrow. Let them start; I will finish them off if they do, for I am going to punish this fellow's impudence." Poor Miguel, seeing how ill he was received, shouted to his men: "Let's retreat, let's retreat!" They all did so. He had himself taken across the river, about a musket-shot wide. There he leapt ashore, stripped off his fancy clothes along with his crown and feathers, dressed in a shirt or coat he got from an Indian, left behind his sword and shield, and, with a staff in hand like a penitent, set off for his own town alone with a servant.

The Fathers there were anxious to learn if they had already killed us, expecting their own end as well, when they caught sight of Miguel, unrecognized in his garb. He came in the Fathers' doors, fell to his knees, folded his hands, and said: "For the love of Jesus Christ and St. Ignatius, I implore you to forgive my stupid insolence towards you. I was crazy and had lost my judgment; but now I have got it back, because God has punished my pride, and so I beg your forgiveness. You have preached to us how readily God forgives those who offend him; imitate him and forgive me. Furthermore, I beg you to shield and defend me, for I have good reason to fear that these people will kill me. I certainly deserve death for my folly, but as true Fathers and servants of God you have to pardon and protect me."

Father José took him in his arms. As a father, after all, even to such an evil son, and as true and loving shepherd, he raised him from the ground and consoled him, warning him to look out in the future and to choose the true path after experiencing how badly his mad schemes had turned out. Thus was the tempest calmed. Miguel pretended to give up his concubine, the cause of all this trouble, and brought his true wife home. Outwardly pretending to live a good life, he continued to live a bad one, and thus died an evil death, as we shall recount.

CHAPTER 13

The Fathers send Antonio Ruiz to Asunción, and what befell him

BECAUSE OF the great distance between the reductions and the city of Asunción, we had no correspondence with our superiors. They were accordingly concerned about us, their concern growing daily because of reports they got from some Spaniards of Villa Rica who claimed that we were idle and merely wasting time, and should be withdrawn. (Their motive for this was inexcusable: they were eager to get us to abandon our flock so that they could get in and shear them.) Because of this report, our superiors had already decided to summon us. The Fathers accordingly decided to send me.

I departed, much grieved at leaving my companions and forsaking such apostolic work. I traveled by river as far as the falls of the Paraná, and thirty-five leagues overland from there. Shortly before I arrived at Maracayú (already mentioned), a fierce downpour accompanied me nearly the entire

[handwritten margin note: Suffering priest's]

day. I walked, barefoot, through a continuous stream from the falling rain that coursed along the path itself. I took shelter under a tree for the night with five companion Indians, for the sixth had stayed a league behind with the blanket, hammock, and bit of manioca flour which constituted all my equipment and supplies. I sat down, with my head leaning against the tree, and spent the night, neither I nor my companions eating a mouthful, since there was nothing. The water gushing along the ground was my bed, that which fell from the skies my roof. I yearned for day, so long was the night.

At break of dawn I tried to stand, but found myself crippled: my leg was as stiff as a board and acutely painful. I worked up the courage to walk, leaning on a cross that I carried and dragging my leg along the path of running water. I got over each of the many logs that lay across our path by sitting on it and lifting my bad leg over with both hands, with excruciating pain; I would then get up and continue my way. Heaven knows how unbearably I suffered.

I reached the port of Maracayú. There I found a reputable Spaniard who dealt in the herb. I explained my difficulty, hoping he would help me out with a boat he had there. He refused it to me, the Lord allowing this so he could reward obedience. I decided to continue my journey overland, for a distance of a hundred and fifty leagues rife with hostile Indians and sorcerers, drawing confidence from the fact that my journey was out of pure obedience. During the whole of that day I covered only half a league, resisting the Indians who kept trying to get me to let them carry me on their shoulders in a hammock, which I refused to allow. *[handwritten margin note: Refused help]*

At sundown we halted under a tree. My knee was swollen, my muscles like iron. At every movement I felt as if I were being stabbed with spears. I lacked even a bandage to wrap my leg with. Deciding that my best medicine would be prayer, I commended myself to my glorious father St. Ignatius, and reminded him of the benefits he promises in his letter on obedience to those who let themselves be blindly guided by that virtue, and of the victories sung by the obedient. I spent a good deal of time on this, since the pain kept me from sleeping well into the night. Hardly had I dozed off for a few moments through exhaustion, when I felt St. Ignatius at my feet. He touched my foot and said: "Go on with your journey; your foot is healed." I immediately woke up (I am not sure if I was asleep) and tested my leg: it was healed. Bending it, I felt no pain. I stood up, walked about, kicked with my lame foot, and found myself completely well—healed, full of energy, without fatigue. I fell to my knees and thanked God for working such wonders through his saints.

In the morning my companions were intending to carry me on their shoulders and made the necessary preparations. I challenged them to a race, starting the contest myself and getting a substantial lead on them. They were dumbfounded, unaware of what a good physician had cured me. The following day I came across some Indians who told me about a boat that was on a stream and advised me not to go by land or I would surely be killed by the barbarian Indians who lived in those woods. In this boat we reached the city of Paraguay [Asunción].

CHAPTER 14

My arrival at Paraguay [Asunción] and return to the missions;
death of Father Martín Urtasun

ARRIVING AT Asunción, I reported the glorious work being done by my companions back there and requested some men. However, the scarcity of manpower left my wishes unfulfilled. Retracing my steps on the long narrow path back to my beloved reductions, I arrived at the landing at Maracayú. Here I once more met the man who had refused me the boat. He complained strongly about me, falsely claiming that after being refused his boat I had stolen it. I showed him the boat that I had used—it was the same one in which I returned. What had happened was that as soon as the man refused me his boat the devils sank it in the river and filled it with sand. When he went to look for it and could not find it, he decided that I had taken it and angrily accused me. However, as some Indians were swimming in the area, their feet struck the sides of the boat, which was quite large. They told the owner. He hired a score of Indians for a goodly sum to bring it up on the following day, though some thought this could hardly be done because it was so large and filled with sand. On the appointed day they arrived to find it floating on the water, quite clean. There are many such evil spirits in the forests there.

I reached my longed-for missions very eager to assist my companions. We spent six months working as described above, with numerous conversions, many baptisms, and much growth of the faith. Then superiors summoned Father José to the congregation,[63] leaving just three of us. A few days later we were only two, for Father Martín Urtasun died of sheer toil. His death was hastened, not by want of luxuries, doctors, or medicine—none of which we had—but by want of a rational person's diet. His greatest luxury was an occasional small bird brought him from the hunt in the woods and a bit of manioca flour, which even someone in good health needs a strong appetite to eat. For more than eight to ten years we never laid eyes on bread.

Several times he asked for a lump of sugar to alleviate the heat of the fever. When I inquired why he asked for it, since he knew that we did not have any, his reply was: "I know; I only ask in order to fob off nature, which keeps asking me for it and is not going to get it." To think that this man, born noble, heir to an estate, raised in luxury, should die of starvation! He made a general confession of his whole life, although it contained no serious sin, as I mentioned. He was distressed to be dying in bed—a little mattress and blanket—which he thought too luxurious, for his desire had been to die a martyr, dragged off and cut to pieces for Jesus Christ.

"How soft I am," he told me many times, "dying like a seeker of ease in bed." He made frequent heartfelt acts of desire for martyrdom. The day he died I found him despondent in appearance and asked him why. His answer was: "Father, what a journey this is, how fearful! One must practice dying for a lifetime in order to die well just once. Since my soul will have to go for many months without the suffrages that are supposed to be said for me, given the long journey before the province learns of my death, I beg you to make up for this by offering twenty Masses for me, the first one at the moment of my death."[64] I promised him fifty. He asked for extreme unction, saying he wanted it now so that he could receive it while fully conscious. He received it with great emotion and consolation. As the holy man was promising to assist me with his prayers in heaven, he suddenly lost his power of speech: they were his last words. I then asked if it was the Mass he wanted at the moment he died; he answered yes by moving his head. At midnight he gave his soul to the Lord, as peacefully and calmly as if he were falling into a quiet sleep, displaying in the beauty and serenity of his face the beauty of his blessed soul.

Some months later, at a time when a religious who was a close and devoted friend of his was afflicted and overwhelmed by his labors among the pagans, he comforted him one night by appearing to him in brilliant light, encouraging him to perseverance and patient suffering in his labors, and saying to him, "This is the glory enjoyed by those who labor for God."

CHAPTER 15

Conversions made; individual cases

THE NUMBER of workers declined, but not the amount of toil and labor. Some of the sites where the Indians had gathered together were very *cold.* unhealthy, and while we attended to one place people would die without confession in another. With this ceaseless toil I was eventually laid low by a severe illness of fevers that were hastening me to my death. I endured this crisis alone, abandoned by a number of Indians I had had with me.

One night I thought was my last. Grasping a small image of the Crucified that hung from my neck, and placing myself in his hands, I committed my spirit to him, with deep consolation and joyful jubilation at seeing myself dying bereft of all human help, not even having a person to make a light in the darkness of my hut. I was glad that I was already clad for burial, since I had not even had the strength to disrobe. Then came our universal physician

in his infinite mercy, which he never denies to those who throw themselves
into these eventualities for love of him; he came to this man with tokens
that he would quickly recover his health; and so he did.

My companion and I made plans to gather all these people into two
locations which experience had assured us to be healthy, so that, assembled
there, they would no longer be in danger of dying without baptism or
confession. All the caciques agreed, with the exception of the above-
mentioned Roque Maracaná, who shamelessly declared that he would not do
it. I told him that willy-nilly he would do what God pleased.

His town was the one most in need of moving, being the most unhealthy.
The move to Loreto involved three quarters of a league and there was as yet
no construction: only the materials had been piled up. We resorted to prayer,
which our regular experience had shown to be powerful and effective.
Hearing of my illness (from which I had already recovered), Father Simón
came down to see me on the eve of Epiphany. The two of us recommended
the matter to God that day in prayer. At midnight we heard a great hubbub
among the people of the Loreto reduction where we were staying. I awoke
my companion. Unsure what the cause might be, we guessed that another
uprising like the previous one might be afoot to kill us. We spent the rest of
the night in prayer.

Scarcely had morning come when the cacique Roque entered our house,
with an escort of servants and his sword in his belt. Our suspicion that they
were planning to kill us grew. I asked why he had come so early in the
morning (I have mentioned that his village was three quarters of a league
from Loreto). "You must know," he answered, "that though you wanted me
to move to this place, I was unwilling; I considered it debasing for me to join
another town, since my ancestors and I always had a separate one of our
own. But last night, I had hardly closed my eyes to sleep when I was
wakened by a voice saying: 'Move, do as the Father tells you.' I awoke and
saw no one—I had a light in my room—and the same thing happened a
second and third time. I began to be afraid that unless I did this God would
take away my life. So right then, in the middle of the night, I called my
people, told them what had happened, and gave orders that we should
straightway set out with axes to clear the spot here that you had assigned
me. At the same time I had my part of the roof of my house taken off and
brought here by river so that they could set up a shelter or lodging for me
this very night, where I was able to rest. During the night my vassals cut
down a large tract of woods to construct their houses and mine. I am
resolved never to go back to the place I abandoned and never to go away
from this one. I came to tell you this so you will not worry, and I would like
for us to go and see last night's work."

So he spoke. We were left amazed at how easily divine providence can
employ awe to turn a heart of stone into wax. We proceeded to the site. But

for the testimony of our own eyes we would have thought it beyond belief that so much work could be accomplished during the night, its darkness vanquished by huge bonfires in the light of which the whole task had been carried out. Only God's right hand could have achieved this, and we gave fitting thanks.

Through these events the word of God continued working and the gospel gathered strength. Accordingly, we began to preach more vigorously against sexual disorder, and the caciques quickly began giving back their concubines. One cacique heard a sermon, and was pierced by the word of God. Hardly had the preacher come down from the pulpit when this man followed the Father, bringing along six concubines—it ought to have been seven, so that the seven sins would leave his house. The people gathered at this spectacle, so unusual among these barbarians that it startled and astonished them all, and generated no little edification inasmuch as it was being done by the leading cacique of the settlement. He said: "Father, I am this people's cacique and ruler, and so it is good for me to start giving good example by getting rid of these impediments. I here bring you six women who have been my concubines. Marry them off or dispose of them wherever you wish. They will never set foot in my house again."

This deed resembled that of Ananias, who cheated on the price he presented to the Apostles.[65] This man cheated on the number of his concubines: he had left behind thirty, well hidden away, some having belonged to a brother of his. Divine justice seized him with a serious illness. Seeing himself caught out in his chicanery, he composed his soul and died—albeit not suddenly—a short time later, deeply repenting his wrongdoing and leaving us tokens of his eternal salvation. There were other incidents of the same sort.

A Father was once praying after midnight when he heard a voice in Spanish (there being no one but himself in the settlement who spoke or understood it) saying, "Marry the man." Three times at short intervals he heard the same words: "Marry him right now." He decided it was a hoax of the devil. Morning arrived, and right off a quite prominent cacique came to him and said, "Father, marry me." The Father had for a long time been urging this man to get married, for he was now a Christian and kept a beautiful Indian woman as a concubine; but the man had no intention of marrying her and kept postponing it day after day. The Father asked him, "Son, why this sudden change?" "Father, marry me," he replied. The Father kept asking the reason, as he saw him now boldly demanding what he had earlier obstinately refused. "Marry me right now," said the Indian; "I do not want tonight to be another troubled and heavy one like last night. I lay down to sleep last night, and at my first slumber some unknown person struck me in the side and said: 'Marry! Why do you not do as the Father tells you?' I awoke but spied no one; I could see that all my people were asleep. I lay down again, and no sooner had I shut my eyes when the same thing happened a second and then a third time; I saw no one. I shouted out: 'Leave me alone; I promise I will go in the morning and ask the Father to marry me.' I was so afraid that I was unable to sleep, waiting anxiously for the day so I could come and ask you to rectify my condition." Seeing how well the two admonitions tallied, and being assured there were no impediments, the Father married them. The two led quite upright lives, dying some years later with numerous tokens of their salvation and bequeathing their virtues to three sons who are alive today.

CHAPTER 16

A tumult raised in Loreto by a secular priest, and his attempts to expel the Fathers

THE COMMON enemy of humanity, spiteful at seeing two poor priests rob him of the prey over which he had exercised such undisturbed possession for almost countless years, undertook to do battle with us and thwart our efforts. As his instrument he employed a priest who decided that, with the people there now pacified as a result of our labors, the secular clergy would be able to instruct them better than we could. He accordingly attempted to get the Indians to expel us from their lands, using as his agent the cacique Roque, the same who on another occasion had saved our lives. The latter, along with two other caciques, heatedly agitated for our banishment. The people split into factions, with the majority being on our side. Father Simón preached to them a sermon to this effect: "Sons, do not be upset by these difficulties threatening us. Their author is the devil, who through his servants is trying to cut the cord of your salvation. They will soon pay for their rashness with their deaths, and everything will be quiet again." God fulfilled his servant's prophecy. When their agitation for our exile blazed most fiercely, Roque and his two companions, then at the height of their health and vigor, the oldest being thirty-five years of age, fell sick on a Monday and were under the earth by Friday, along with the whole commotion. To make this example clear to everyone, the Father buried the men side by side in the middle of the church in three separate holes, with a marker over their graves. The adherents to their faction were thereupon reconciled with the Fathers. The priest who was the chief cause of all this did not escape unpunished, dying shortly afterwards from a poisonous snakebite.

Around this time Father José Cataldino returned, so that we were even more triumphant over our past adversity. It happened about this time that a good Indian fell ill. He had always been thought a Christian, and as such went to frequent confession and annual Communion. I went to see him. He made his confession, but had no serious sins since he had lived quite uprightly. He remained ill for more than two months and kept sending for me every day. Since he barely brought up matter for confession, I guessed he must be concealing something, but after close questioning failed to come up with anything. There were days when he would send for me three times. The day he died he urgently called me three different times, one after another. I asked if the devil was deceiving him into holding back some sin but he said no. At this point an elderly woman came forward. "Father," she said, "this man is not able to die because, as I understand it, he is not a Christian." I inquired about his baptism and he himself confessed that in a Spanish town where he had gone as a young man he had been baptized by a priest who threw holy water on everyone in the church; some drops had fallen on him and he had given himself the name of Juan. This was the *Asperges* ceremony performed on Sundays in the churches. I explained to him that he was not a Christian. Earnestly begging for baptism, he sat up in bed to receive it; and as soon as I poured the water on him he leaned back and handed over his soul in my presence.

CHAPTER 17

Further incidents in the reduction of Loreto

IN THIS reduction we had an excellent Indian who was gifted with sincerity and a fine soul. He fell ill, confessed his sins, and died—receiving the other sacraments as well since by this time we were giving Viaticum. (In this matter many priests will be called to account for their negligence: to escape the labor of preparing the Indians for Communion, they condemn them as uncouth and unteachable.) I designated the spot for his burial. Some hours later I noticed one of the Fathers burying a dead person there, and assumed that it was the man. Around midday they called me on behalf of this dead man. The messengers claimed that he had risen from the dead and that the whole town was coming to see him. Going, I found they had undone his shroud. His face was pleasant and cheerful, and the people gathered around astonished. He told me that he had died and that there near his bed (he pointed to the spot) his soul had met a fierce devil who said: "You are mine." "No I am not," he replied; "I made a good confession and received the sacraments." "Not so," countered the devil; "you did not make a good confession. Years ago you twice got drunk, and you never accused yourself of the fault." "True," I said, "I failed to confess those sins, not through wickedness but because I forgot, and so God has already forgiven me." "No, he has not," said the devil, "and so I am going to take you because you are mine." At this the apostle St. Peter appeared to him accompanied by two angels—one of whom he recognized as St. Michael and the other as his guardian angel—and their presence put the devil to flight.

This good Indian had never seen a picture of St. Peter, but he described him to me exactly as painters portray him and writers depict him. He covered the man with his cloak, and escorted by the two angels they crossed the forests. Passing lovely fields they came within sight of a vast walled city, gleaming with great light and splendor. They came to a halt and St. Peter said to him: "That is God's own city that you see; there we dwell and live with him. But you must return to your body, and on the third day (it was a Friday) you will go into church." Thereupon the man found himself once more in his body. I asked him what he thought his having to go into church on the third day meant (though I was privately certain that it meant he was going to die on the third day). He replied: "It means I will be buried on Sunday. I have come only to warn my relatives to believe what you Fathers preach and teach about the other life and to learn how to make their confession." I gave him the best possible treatment to see if he would get through Sunday alive. On Friday and Saturday he ate heartily, conversing on these days with all the people who flocked in to see and hear him, enjoining them to live good lives and to profit by the Fathers' teaching. The whole time that he remained alive, he displayed a great longing to die so that he could once more behold the marvels that he had seen and that he said no words of his could express.

On Sunday, after confessing only the matters the devil had reminded him of, since he had nothing else troubling him, and after also publicly confessing them in the presence of all the people, he fell asleep in the Lord. We buried him that evening, his prophecy thus being fulfilled. This incident had an excellent effect on everyone and was a great warning to make a good examination of conscience before confession. It resulted in a great number of general confessions.

Failing to have his way with this dead man, the devil decided to try his wiles on the living. Seeing his unbelieving followers now turned into devout Christians, he aimed his shafts at deceiving them with specious devotions. In the reduction of San Ignacio, five devils appeared. Four were dressed like ourselves in black cassocks, trimmed with tinselly bands, their faces very handsome. The fifth appeared in the form in which the Blessed Virgin is portrayed. However, as the devil is always a liar, even when counterfeiting the truth, his very deceptions betray the mark of his lie: the woman was carrying two children in her arms. The figures came up to a group of Indians. The latter halted at the sweet sound of their antiphonal singing as they walked along and imitated the tune of the litanies of our Lady as sung in figured choral music in the churches there. The Indians noticed, however, that they uttered no praises or comprehensible words. They thought this must be something from heaven, to judge by their voices, ornamentation, and beautiful faces. In all simplicity they asked them who they were. "We are angels from heaven," they replied; "we bring here the Mother of God, who is very fond of your Fathers." "Well, if that is so," said the Indians, "let us go to the Fathers' house and the church." The simple folk thought they were sure to come and bring us something we would like very much. The devils replied: "It is not good for us to go to the Fathers' house; we will stay out here and assist them. We will speak to you slowly and teach you what you need to know and the Fathers do not tell you." At this they disappeared.

They appeared with great frequency in various guises. Sometimes when a group of Indians were together, some saw and heard them while others could not hear them. There was a prominent cacique, a fine Christian, who, when others heard and saw them, was alone unable to see them. Somebody suggested that he go into the woods and take a discipline—perhaps then he would see them. He took the advice, and both heard and saw the devil in the form of a tall, well-set man with a musket on his shoulder, like the *maloqueros*[66] who today go out to subjugate the Indians. Now and then this figure acted as if he were firing, and they saw flames emerge soundlessly from the barrel. This was a presage of what was done in subsequent years by the townsmen of São Paulo. The Fathers attempted to drive this riffraff away by exorcisms. They would disappear for a time, and later return. Sometimes they spoke well of the Fathers, at other times ill, now calling them their friends and at other times saying they could not bear to see them. Finally they were bold enough to declare that we ought to be killed, whereupon the Indians ceased acquiescing in the devil's pretensions. In our sermons we tried to get them to avoid listening to or looking at the devils, although curiosity drove them to do so. The devil ended up none the gainer by all this; rather he lost considerably, for the Indians were reinforced in their faith and in love for the Fathers.

At that time I was in Loreto roofing a belfry which housed a very fine bell given us by His Majesty. I was suddenly upset by the thought that one of the Indians working there was going to fall off the belfry and die unconfessed, or that a bolt of lightning would strike him or the church, killing him and breaking the bell. I fled to the Blessed Sacrament, which we had already placed there, and begged that if any of this did happen it would all fall upon the bell, for I would be deeply grieved to see an Indian die without confession. It was a Saturday afternoon. The bell rang several times that day. At nightfall it rang for the Ave Maria and then for the souls of the dead. At the first stroke of the bell on the following day, we could hear that it was broken. I was very consoled at its loss—although it was much treasured in those parts—because the Indian had been saved. Hardly three hours later Father José wrote me from San Ignacio, three leagues from Loreto, asking me if it was true that the bell was broken, since at dawn a devil had appeared to some Indians and said, "See my power; I have just come from breaking the bell at Loreto." I wrote back, telling my story and saying that the father of lies had spoken the truth. At this same time, we were quite disquieted and concerned over a noise that from the beginning to the end of our Sunday sermons would disturb the peace and profit of the listeners, since they were unable to hear anything. We thought it was because of the nursing children, and tried to solve the problem by getting the mothers to leave so that the sermons could be heard with profit. But the noise continued as before. It was so bad one day that in the middle of my sermon I paused for a considerable time trying to tell where the wretched noise was coming from. I saw all the people (probably more than two thousand of them) strangely quiet, without talking or moving. But I noticed that from among them there came a buzzing sound which was producing this evil effect. Deciding that it had to be the devil, I alerted my listeners to the fact and told them we should pray the Lord to deliver us from this disruption of his divine word. It then ceased, and on another day the devil stated that he came every Sunday to church and lodged in the first beam there, from which he caused the humming sound. We prayed hard to the Lord to rid us of this. His Majesty did so, for from that time on, even with a huge crowd in church, everybody could hear quite well, in as much silence as if not a soul was there.

CHAPTER 18

Other occurrences

OUR LORD used these visible events to bolster both our preaching and the new Christian commonwealth there so that they would believe in invisible truths—those regarding death as the common lot of all mankind (for they had lived under the illusion that it was not such but always the result of some accident); regarding souls remaining in their graves (a widespread error among them produced by the wiles of the devils who had deluded the sorcerers whom the people considered as gods); regarding the suffering undergone for a term by souls in purgatory and for ever by those condemned to hell; and regarding the glory enjoyed by the just in heaven. "Prophecies are given to believers, not unbelievers; but signs are given to unbelievers, not believers."[67] So the Apostle teaches, and we certainly saw it in practice, as I shall now confirm by other occurrences.

At Loreto we were dedicating a new church to the sovereign Virgin on one of her feast days. The night before, as more than sixty persons were celebrating the festival by moonlight, they all beheld three figures emerge from the old church opposite the new one. They were clad in snow-white garments that gleamed like burnished silver. Their faces seemed three suns, their hair like threads of gold falling on their shoulders. Out between the two churches stood a beautiful cross with three steps at its base. These the figures gracefully mounted, and then stood against the cross and looked toward the altar of the new church, which as yet had no doors. The people stood and gazed spellbound, contemplating their beauty and the graceful form of their bodies. They were not all the same size; each of the three was different. Some of the children who were there were so inflamed with love for them that, quite without fear and in all simplicity, they went to them in brotherly affection to be with them and enjoy the lovely spectacle from closer up. Very gradually, the figures withdrew and returned to the church from which they had emerged, leaving everyone annoyed and blaming the children for causing them to lose this delightful vision. I do not propose to comment on these things, but simply to tell the story. I will only remark that the sovereign Virgin of Loreto has always shown herself pleased by the smallest services given her. I could give instances of this were I permitted to stray from my purpose, which is merely to report the means used by God for the conversion of the Indians of this province and their growth in the Catholic faith.

Father Juan Vaseo,[68] a Fleming, who did apostolic work in the reductions there and brought music to a marvelous level among the Indians (more about him will be said later), was quite ill in Loreto. Through the window of his room he heard a noise outside, and finally someone rapped at the window. The Father asked who it was. The knocker replied, "Come, Father Juan, let us go to heaven." He knew the voice very well; it was one of the singers he was teaching. The Father was amazed to hear his voice there, knowing him to be quite sick in his own house and unable to get up. The Father asked us about him and about the state of his illness. We told him he had just died. The good Father then said, "My own hour has come, for he just called me and invited me to go to heaven with him. It is a great consolation for me to die struggling blessedly to the last for the conversion of the Indians." Shortly thereafter he died.

During an outbreak of smallpox a young man, highly skilled and adept in music, fell ill. I asked the Lord to preserve his life. On the eve of his death, I went to visit him. Seeing him close to the end, I told him that I wished he would recover but that we should be conformed to the will of God. He replied: "Father, I have just come from visiting the Blessed Sacrament. Our Lord let me know that I must die very soon, and so I am very consoled and anxious for his will to be fulfilled." "How were you in the church?" I rejoined; "You did not go there; you cannot even move." "Father," he answered, "I was in church; my guardian angel carried me there because I so longed to visit the Blessed Sacrament. If you do not believe me, I can give you signs. The first is that they were burying such-and-such a person; I did not know he was dead until I saw him being buried; he was buried by Father so-and-so. The second sign is that you were by the grave, kneeling on the

Gospel side. The third is that you were very fervently commending me to God. I could not have known any of this unless my angel had shown it to me. To see you assist me so earnestly in God's presence gave me great joy and increased my love for you. I will pay you back in heaven, where I hope to go very soon." All the signs were correct, and it was quite true that I was commending him to God with deep feeling and conformity of will, asking God to give him either life or death, whichever was better for him. The lad died the following day, excellently disposed and with indubitable tokens of his salvation.

There were various occurrences having to do with souls in the pains of purgatory. They would appear visibly and furnish us material for sermons. I will mention only one case. As one of the Fathers at Loreto was sleeping, he dreamt around midnight that he saw a soul, most despondent and clad in rough, mournful garments. It was walking down a certain street of the town, sighing and appearing to be in great torment. It entered the church by the main door and knelt down in the middle, making vehement acts of repentance and sorrow by heavily beating its breast. A good while later it left by the other door of the church—both doors being shut. It moved off towards the middle of the town square and was disappearing from view. At this point the Father awoke. Unable to tell if it had been a dream or if he had actually seen it, he said a few prayers for the soul. Feeling an impulse to say a Mass for it, he decided he would not unless somebody in the town told him he had seen the soul. Immediately upon arising in the morning he saw a cluster of people standing there talking about this soul. One person left the group and came over to the Father; he told him how he had seen the soul at midnight while standing at the door of his house. Asking for details, the Father discovered that the Indian had seen it on the street exactly as he had seen it in his cell. The signs tallied perfectly, and so he said the Mass for the soul.

Although I said I would only narrate one incident, I will add another which I had decided to pass over as not involving Indians but which I believe will be found edifying. One night two priests were praying before the Blessed Sacrament. After a good while the two of them went out to attend to an obligation of obedience. The one walking in front noticed that opposite where they were going there was a figure like a white cloud against the wall. He noticed that it was walking and coming towards him, and that, passing in front of the gleam of a candle that shone into the passageway, it was transparent and moved like a cloud. It was of human stature but without distinction of limbs. It moved toward the Father and penetrated him, going right through his body. He felt a contact such as glass might feel when penetrated by the sun. This made him take a step backwards. He turned around to see if he could still see it, but neither he nor the Father behind him saw it, the other Father seeing only the movement of the man in front of him. This penetration left him deeply consoled and with glimpses of heavenly glory. He had no doubt it was a soul from purgatory, but could not tell who. That midnight a Spanish friend of his, who had died sixty leagues away, appeared to him in his room. The man's face was very sad and sallow, his visage that of a corpse. He begged for help in his suffering. The Father requested Masses as alms from his companions and himself said several for the man, whereupon he understood that his imprisonment in purgatory had ended.

CHAPTER 19

Events which show how much the devil takes account of our actions, however small

MANY THINGS pass right by us in this life which the devil stores up and engraves in his memory. They appear small to us, but at our final agony he will paint them to us as important and weighty. In this regard I shall recount two incidents that had good effects on the Indians. Among the devotions progressively introduced by us and today practiced to such good effect in this new Christian commonwealth was the following. When the Ave Maria was rung in the morning, our own door was opened so that the men who wished might come in to visit the Blessed Sacrament and spend some time in prayer. To ease the way for them by example, a Father would be present in the church performing the same exercise. I took as my job the opening of the door at the reduction of our Lady of Loreto (truly she has been the lady and teacher of those souls). One morning when I opened the door a young man was already waiting to come in. I had hardly turned my back to enter the church when I heard a bustling of people at the same door. I thought it was caused by people coming to perform their devotions, but it was three devils, one in the form of Father Juan Vaseo (whose death, already mentioned, had taken place five years earlier). They wore black cassocks. The principal one had a face strongly resembling the Father's; he spoke to the young man as follows: "Francisco (that was his name), do you know me?" "Yes," the boy replied. "How are the Fathers?" "Fine," he answered. "I have come to see you and console myself by seeing you and how well you are living and making progress. What did you do with the five beads left over from the string I gave you for the purchase I commissioned you to make?" The boy answered, "I spent them right away, because you gave them to me for myself." The devil answered: "It must have been so; I do not remember whether I let you have them or whether you kept them without showing me. Kneel down in front of me and worship me." The simple, guileless lad knelt down; he was hardly on his knees when the riffraff disappeared.

The young man, who up to this point had been without apprehension, now began to be afraid. He came into the church, weeping and calling aloud to me, repentant for having knelt down before the devil even though he had not thought that it was he. (I myself, annoyed by the sound of this long conversation, had felt like going outside and telling the people either to come into the church or to leave, supposing that they were Indians.) The devil does not lose track of our smallest affairs. I gathered from this incident that the lad had failed to give the Father the five beads, and that the devil was accordingly calling him to account. This incident became widely known and numerous people came to confess such trifling things as taking a gourd, a pepper, or the like. This scrupulosity has endured to the present day, even over things equally trivial, to the point of causing real disturbance.

This incident was shortly afterwards duplicated by another quite similar case of which, although I was a witness, I will for reasons of my own omit certain details. I had thrown into my cell a little string of some twenty little glass beads. A young man who served us in the house took them. He fell sick, so seriously that I realized that he was going to die on me. He was in a room attached to my own, where I had him staying because he was in such danger. At about eleven o'clock at night, he saw (he had a light) five ferocious devils coming in through an angle or corner of the wall. One had the head of a pig, another that of a cow, and so forth, with the feet of cows, goats, and huge birds with large claws and spindly legs, the eyes shooting rays as of fire. Knowing I was so close by, the boy was not afraid. He saw them prowl around the room as though looking for something on the floor and in the corners. "What are you looking for?" the young man asked. They replied, "Some beads that you took the other day from the Father's room." "I have them on my breast," said the youth, "in this bag with an Agnus Dei."[69] "That's what we are looking for," they said; "let us have them so we can return them to the Father." The boy saw them getting closer. Calling on the name of Jesus, he got up and came to my room asking to go to confession. I found this odd, especially since I saw the tears rolling from his eyes. I told him to go to sleep, that it was too late. I thought he had some insignificant scruple, for I knew of his good life from the confessions he made each week without fail. Then he recounted to me the mummeries the devils had practiced on him, and there was no getting him away from me until he had confessed this trifling matter. The next day he told everyone what had happened and it did a lot of good. This is God's purpose in ordering such things. We ourselves have experienced the good such incidents do by way of growth in virtue, lasting devotion, and the rejection of every sort of vice.

The people there have everything in common in their houses and no one steals anything. To illustrate this I shall recount an amusing story. One midnight I was in a corner of the church praying to our Lord when I heard footsteps in the courtyard. Surprised to hear such a sound at that hour—the more audible because of the nighttime silence—I saw a quite tall Indian coming into the church by the door that leads to our house. I could see that he was carrying a small basket. Wondering if it might be the devil, I let him keep coming in. He directed his steps toward the high altar where the Blessed Sacrament was reserved. Thinking he was going to commit some disrespect at the altar, I arose, went towards him, and asked who he was. As soon as he heard me he turned and ran toward the door. I rushed after him, but with great agility he leapt over the enclosure of the house. I was left annoyed at his escape and absorbed in suspicions that it might have been an Indian sorcerer trying to commit some impiety in the church. However, I reassured myself at the thought that there was no longer any trace of such persons. Anxious to discover who it was, I decided to try measuring the footprint, and possibly track him down that way. I got a candle and found a very clear footprint in the sand. I measured it with a stick. As I thought about it, it occurred to me that the form I had seen resembled a big fellow who was known in the town. I sent for him in the morning, measured his foot, and found it exactly the size. "You are the one that came into the church last night," I said to him; "tell me, what were you after?" Trembling and disconcerted, he confessed that it was he, and that his reason for entering the church was the following. While going through the forest he had found a wedge (one of the iron hatchets they use). He had looked for the owner; failing to find him, he had employed the wedge for himself. But hearing how the devil was keeping track of people who held things that belonged to others, he had wanted to give it back. Seized with shame, he had been afraid to bring the wedge to me, and so had awaited the silence of the night to bring it to the Blessed Sacrament and place it there on the altar. I was much edified by this action. He brought me the wedge in his basket and I gave it back for him to use as long as he did not know the owner, for there is a considerable scarcity of metal tools there.

And if the upright life they generally lead stimulates them to rivalry in acquiring virtue, the death of the cacique Miguel—the one I already mentioned as wanting to kill the Fathers—served them as an anchor for perseverance. He had given much scandal to the towns there. While the rest had renounced vice and embraced virtue, he alone persisted in his evil life with his old concubine. He kept her well hidden, but no matter what one does the evil odor of that vice cannot be kept from being known and spread abroad. Attempts were made to cure the blight; the girl was taken away from him and exiled to a Spanish town so that the distance would make him forget her. It would have been miraculous if such an inveterate fault had admitted of sorrow and amendment. But, swept away by his disgraceful attachment, he did not shrink from abdicating his honor. Even though ruler of a splendid town in his possession, he forsook his goods, forgot his friends, and, without a care for his true wife whom he abandoned, made himself an exile, going off alone in quest of the woman who had caused him these losses and ultimately the loss of his soul. He found his treasure, and to avoid the risk of her being taken from him again, he took his concubine and the little son she had borne him to a remote forest, where he toiled with his own hands to support himself, a thing he had never done before. There he lived, his hardships, great as they were, lightened by his disgraceful love. After all the delays granted him by God, the day came when the poor man fell ill from toil and age. In a short time he rendered up his unhappy soul in his concubine's arms. She herself was wise enough to return to our reductions, where she repented of her past life, did penance, and by this means obtained a happy death.

CHAPTER 20

Entry of the Fathers into a new province of pagans; the martyrdom of an Indian

THROUGH THE munificence of our lord the King (heaven grant him new kingdoms and a long life), the number of priests and other workers laboring in the vineyard there increased. Consequently we made plans to win further territory and souls for heaven. Leaving behind four fervent workers in these two reductions, three of us prepared for this new and perilous entry. The Indians advised us to send people ahead of us to scout the land and, given the opportunity, to explain our intentions to the pagans there. Two men offered to serve as our precursors, with a mind to sharing in our enterprise. One was a man of mature age and a newcomer. The other, a young man, had been raised in our school. Both were married.

They entered the pagan territory and explained our wishes and determination to come in and announce the gospel. They were immediately taken captive, with a view to killing them in one of the baptism ceremonies described earlier. They were offered women and unrestricted freedom to do whatever they desired. The older one accepted the offer and soon took a woman; the young man, remembering what he had learned in our school (so important it is even among Indians to instruct youth well), refused to accept any of their offers. The better to persuade him, they offered him a very select girl who, attracted by the young man's fine presence, wanted him to desire her. The chaste youth refused even to look at her. The pagans pressed him to look at her, but he replied that the Fathers taught that one should not look at women, since sin entered the soul through the eyes; that God's law forbade impurity and adultery; and that he was married according to God's command and could not take another woman. They threatened that unless he took the woman they would kill him. "Kill me," he answered; "you will only kill my body, not my soul, for it is immortal; I trust that when I die my soul will go to enjoy God for ever." Faced with this courage, the pagans planned to kill him; the girl's father himself, intoxicated with rage at seeing his daughter spurned, rushed at him and with bestial ferocity stabbed him to death. They cut up his body and ate it. His wretched companion lived for a number of days with the woman they had given him and finally, with great solemnity, was also killed and eaten.

The blessed death of this Indian martyr hastened our steps to convert these beasts and bring them to change their brutish way of life, or else to offer up our own lives to their ferocity. The three of us—Fathers José Cataldino, Diego de Salazar,[70] and myself—arrived at a small town where we were most hospitably received. Hardly did those who had martyred the Indian hear of our presence in their territory when, ravening like dogs to eat us, they quickly gathered in great numbers and rushed down the mountains like raging tigers. The women in the village where we were staying raised the lament for our funerals; the men, by now fond of us, confessed they were too few and weak to resist this throng. The confusion in the town grew, and a happy death for us drew on. I went to Father José and repeated the words of St. Ignatius Martyr: "I am Christ's wheat; may I be ground by the teeth of beasts so that I may be found to be pure bread." I added, "Father mine, I think that this will be our pilgrimage's final day." The noble man replied just as calmly and peacefully, "May God's will be done."

Turning to some Indians who were putting up a hut to serve as our church, he instructed them on what needed to be done and, unmoved, gave a hand with the work himself—certainly the act of an apostolic man who beheld God's providence present in all that he did. Even the pagans who were doing the work could see it. A prominent cacique—no doubt led there by God for our defense—had come to visit us, a man much respected for his noble status and eloquence. When he saw that they were quite close, he went out to meet them. He gave them an elegant speech, telling them that we had entered their lands not to fight, since we bore no arms, much less to take away gold or silver, for they had none, but only to make them children of God and teach them the good way to live. They did not easily yield to reason, persisting in their desire to kill us. In the end, however, they gave in to the good cacique's arguments. They all went back to their lands, and we started a reduction there which we called San Francisco Javier. Within a few months it grew to fifteen hundred townsmen. Even those fierce beasts entered it and were tamed, turning into gentle lambs. This change was brought about by the word of God and the baptism which they all received, growing daily in faith, in virtue, and in love for us.

CHAPTER 21

Our entry into those lands; traces of St. Thomas the Apostle that we found

A S OUR manpower increased we made fresh sallies into pagan territory and won new children for the Church. The venerable Father Cristóbal de Mendoza[71] moved to the province to help us with the harvest, the fruit of which he secured for himself, winning the palm from us by gaining the palm of martyrdom—not in the province or sequence of events I am now discussing but in the province of Tape, a jurisdiction of Buenos Aires of which I will speak later. Father Francisco Díaz,[72] a man of many parts, remained at the reduction of San Javier. He was an outstanding missionary. The academy had offered him a chair because of his solid teaching, but he descended from it and became a great teacher of pagans. With San Javier so well covered, Father Cristóbal de Mendoza and I left for the province of Tayatí, a rugged, forested land populated by pagan Indians of the same tribe and language as the previous one. This conquest by the Society was carried out always on foot, over more than eighteen years, because the region was entirely without mounts. We always bore in our hands a cross two yards tall and a finger thick, so to make our preaching visible by this sign. The people there received us with extraordinary shows of affection, with dances and rejoicing, something we had never experienced before. The women came out to greet us with their little children in their arms—a sure token of peace and friendship—and lavished upon us their customary food of roots and fruits of the land. At our surprise over this unexpected welcome, they explained that through an age-old tradition handed down from their ancestors they believed that when St. Thomas (usually called *Pay Zumé* in the province of Paraguay and *Pay Tumé* in Peru) passed through their lands he told them: "In time you will lose the doctrine that I am now preaching to you. But after a long period, when some priests who will succeed me come carrying a cross as I do, this teaching will be heard by your descendants."

This tradition made them give us such an extraordinary welcome. We built a fine settlement there. It was a first stage for others that we erected in that province.

The grounds for believing that St. Thomas illuminated the western as well as the eastern world with his presence and teaching are numerous. First, the name they give to priests affords considerable light for resolving any doubt. They call a priest *Abaré*, meaning "a man removed from sex"—a chaste person. This name was not applicable to any of the Indians from their earliest ancestors down to St. Thomas, but only the saint himself. The Indians commonly say that he was *Pay Abaré*, Father-priest, Father in the strict sense, a man different from others in being chaste. All this is implied in this short word. Even after St. Thomas it remained applicable only to priests: whereas the term *Pay*, "Father," was appropriated by old men, magicians, and sorcerers as a term of honor for themselves, they never took the title *Abaré*. The reason for this, in my view, is clear. The virtue of virginity, chastity, or celibacy was so unknown that formerly they identified it with unhappiness. Happiness meant having many wives, many children, and a household; any deficiency in this regard was attributed to misfortune. Indeed, this feeling persisted for a long time even among the Christians we baptized, as will be evident from the following incident.

A cacique who had become a Christian was widowed, and we undertook to get him married. He gave his yes to a woman, but she refused him. This became public knowledge. Insulted and humiliated, he abandoned his vassals, his houses, and his land and went into perpetual exile rather than live with this affront. There was another man, born a eunuch; when his defect became known, he wandered through the forests like a deer or a wild animal to escape being seen. We made great efforts to bring him into the town, but were unable either to tame him or to keep the boys from scaring him off, until our insistence and eagerness to baptize him prevailed. So far are they from ascribing to themselves the title *Abaré* or a reputation for chastity. Even the magicians and sorcerers who oppose the gospel that we preach call us *Abaré* in opprobrium. However, the Christians have now learned the sublimity of the virtue of chastity through our preaching, so that married men accuse themselves of having gone to their wives one or two days before receiving Communion, and numerous unmarried men undertake to consecrate themselves to celibacy. There have even been those who attempted to castrate themselves, so enamored were they with the virtue of chastity.

CHAPTER 22

Other traces left by St. Thomas in the western Indies

THERE IS a firm tradition in Brazil, among both Portuguese settlers and indigenous inhabitants of the Main,[73] that the holy apostle began his overland journey from the island of Santos, situated in the south, where to this day one can see traces which reveal the beginning of his journey or track: the footprints the holy apostle left on a great rock at the end of the beach where he landed across from the bar of São Vicente. It is officially attested that these traces can be seen to this day, less than a quarter of a league from the town. I have not seen them myself; however, two hundred leagues inland from the coast my companions and I did see a path, about eight spans wide, on which the grass grows very short although on either side of the path it grows nearly half a yard high. Even though these lands are burned over when the grass dries out, the grass always grows back the same way. This track runs through the entire country, and I have been assured by some Portuguese[74] that it runs quite unbroken from Brazil and is commonly known as the St. Thomas Road. We have heard the same story from the Indians of our own spiritual conquest.[75]

In Asunción del Paraguay there is a boulder next to the city. On its surface are a pair of human footprints, resembling those of sandals, impressed right into the rock. The left footprint is ahead of the right, as if the person were straining or leaning hard. The tradition among the Indians is that the holy apostle preached to the pagans from this rock, and that the fields there would fill with people who came to hear him. As we have already mentioned, they also have a tradition that the holy apostle gave them the manioca plant, which is the natives' principal bread. Moreover, Doctor Lorenzo de Mendoza,[76] bishop of the diocese there, in an official testimony regarding the above-mentioned footprints, as he learned it from the natives, certifies that, because of their ancestors' ill treatment of him, the saint told them that by rights the manioca roots should ripen in only a few months, but that as a punishment it would take them a year; and so it does today.

CHAPTER 23

Further traces of the saint in Peru

BEING NOW committed by my wish to pursue the holy apostle's traces, I am obliged to leave my own province for that of Peru. However, I do not consider this a digression, my goal being to trace the saint's presence in Paraguay and the truth of the natives' tradition that he carried a cross with him as the companion of his pilgrimage.

The fact that Peru was reached by one of Christ our Lord's disciples is attested by the tradition of the whole country. Father Alonso Ramos of the holy order of St. Augustine states in chapter seven of his book:[77]

The natives of Peru, especially the highland folk, hold as a nearly immemorial tradition that a man walked through here preaching the true God, and then was never seen again.

And in chapter eight he writes:

They tried to stone him on the site of Cacha, five or six days' journey from Cuzco in the direction of Collao. There, even to this day, rocks can be seen that are charred with fire, they say by a flame sent from heaven to avenge their rash insolence and free the saint from their sacrilegious hands. The holy man passed on. Leaving for the Collao territory, he intended to see and if possible cast down the famous altar and shrine that the Collas had on the island of Titicaca.

Further on the author writes:

> At that time he preached to them belief in and divine worship for a single God. Seeing how little progress he was making with this truth and how stubborn and obdurate the people remained, he began to reprove them harshly, so that they came to have a great detestation for him.

And later in the book:

> They held him in such great veneration that in time they called him *Taapac*, which means "son of the Creator"; and they tempted him with riches and comforts.

In chapter 9 the author writes of a cross that was raised by the holy disciple in the town of Carabuco. At sight of it the idols fell dumb and gave no replies. Learning the reason, the pagans removed the cross and tried to burn it. Failing at this, they buried it next to a lake. With water flooding this site or sepulcher, the cross was discovered more than fifteen hundred years later, whole and entire, as can be seen today.

Continuing, the author declares:

> Around 1600 inquiry was made of a very old Indian, Don Fernando, about a hundred and twenty years of age. He stated that they had received from their ancestors a tradition that they had seen in their lands a man of great stature, white and blue-eyed, dressed nearly like themselves. He preached, crying out that they should adore only one God; he condemned vices. They said he carried a cross with him, and was escorted by five or six Indians. Devils fled from the cross, and frequently urged the Indians to kill the man, saying that unless they did so much harm would befall them and their oracles would give no replies. The Indians bound the saint and scourged him. The witness further testified that every time they inflicted any suffering on the saint certain gorgeous birds would come down to keep him company— now that he himself was a Christian he thought that these were probably angels. He stated that he had heard it said that after the saint's scourging the lovely birds came down and unbound him, and that the saint spread his cloak over the lake and sailed off across it (the lake is eighty leagues in circumference). As he passed through a reed marsh, he left a path which has survived to this day as a sort of alleyway. It is venerated by all; sick people eat these reeds or cattails and are cured. He also stated that it was known by tradition that the saint left a tiny coffer on a mountain.

When the Arequipa volcano erupted on a mountain near the sea, a man who was looking after a farm in the valleys there beheld so much ash coming down from above him that it resembled a mighty river. He waited for the flood to subside. As he explored the area he made, close to the said mountain, the discovery of a tunic. It was impossible to tell if it was of wool or cotton. It was long, apparently seamless, and approximately the color of a sunflower. With it were a pair of shoes shaped like triple-soled sandals. The inner sole was imprinted with the sweat of the foot. They were of a very large man. This was a cause of amazement to everyone. The relics are widely deemed to belong to the holy disciple of the Lord. One of these sandals is preserved in a silver casket by a prominent lady, and works many miracles.

The venerable Father Diego Álvarez de Paz[78] of the Society of Jesus, author of the marvelous volumes on *The Spiritual Life*, affirmed that he had often seen this sandal, declaring that it emitted an odor and fragrance so sublime that it surpassed all other odors.

Two leagues outside a town called San Antonio in the province of the Chachapoyas, a place where I have been, there is a stone slab higher than a man and six yards across. Side by side on its surface are a pair of footprints, each about fourteen inches long. In front of the footprints are two depressions, into both of which a knee would fit. This indicates that the saint knelt there, as is universally believed. Alongside these marks on the rock is that of a staff about two yards long. Its joints are visible, indicating that it was a reed or noded stick. It may be surmised that the saint laid the staff down in order to fold his hands in prayer. It is well known that the holy archbishop of Ciudad de los Reyes [Lima], Don Toribio Alonso Mongrovejo,[79] went in person to see this, and on bended knee thanked our Lord for letting him behold these traces of the Lord's holy disciple. He attempted to move the stone, but this proved impossible. Even before the Spanish conquest of Peru, Guarcar Inga's[80] governor, Colla Tupa, who invaded the province to conquer it, had attempted to convey the stone to his own province but failed. He consequently left a decree that all the Indians should worship it. The archbishop ordered a chapel erected over the slab so that the relic could be fittingly preserved. This is well known in Peru. The whole story has been extensively treated by Father Alonso Ramos. In one chapter of his history he states:

> With regard to this glorious saint, I have heard inquisitive persons state that he came to this part of Peru by way of Brazil, Paraguay, and Tucumán. Moreover, when the most reverend Lorenzo de Grado, former bishop of Paraguay, passed through the sanctuary of Copacabana[81] in 1619, he declared that there are strong indications throughout the diocese of Paraguay that one of the Redeemer's disciples came through there. From there he is said to have proceeded to Chachapoyas, and thence to the valleys of Trujillo, and subsequently to those of Cañete. There is considerable evidence for this. In Calango, a mission of the Fathers Preacher, there can be seen today a large slab with the footprints of a tall man and some characters written in a lan-

guage that must be Greek or Hebrew, since persons who have seen them have been unable to determine their meaning. The older Indians say regarding the characters and footprints in the stone that a tall blue-eyed white man with a long beard had made these markings in the stone with his finger as a demonstration and proof to them that the God he preached was mighty and his law true.

Thus far our author.

Furthermore, there is persistent report of a very ancient tradition that the saint ordered the Indians in Peru to build a temple to the true God that he preached. They did so. They had brought a great quantity of straw for thatching it, and, as the saint slept upon it one night, the devil appeared, fierce and terrifying. He commanded the Indians to burn him together with the straw, reproaching them for their credulity towards an outsider and a stranger. They set the straw on fire. As it blazed up, out walked the saint through the middle of the flames, quite peacefully and calmly, leaving the pagans dumbfounded.

CHAPTER 24

That this disciple of Christ our Lord was St. Thomas; the evidence for this

SINCE I would swerve from the brevity I aim at in this plain account were I to launch upon a detailed proof that this disciple of the Lord was St. Thomas, I will touch upon only a few basic points. My starting point will be the scripture text: "Go into the whole world, and preach the Gospel to every creature."[82] This commission was given to the apostles alone. St. Ambrose comments on this text: "Christ urged his apostles, whom he sent to the various parts of the world, to preach the Gospel to the entire globe." The apostles undertook this task: they had been charged to carry it out and to circulate through the entire world with their preaching. If this is so, as it most certainly is, how is it thinkable that they should have left all America in darkness and deprived of the light of the gospel? Mathematically, America constitutes nearly a third of the earth.

A strong argument for St. Thomas having been the one who enlightened the Indians of the western world with his preaching is the fact that it was he whom Christ our Lord chose to be the apostle of the most abject people in the world, blacks and Indians. According to Origen, Eusebius, and others, he preached to the brahmins.[83] He brought the teaching to the East Indians. According to St. John Chrysostom, the Ethiopians were washed white with the preaching of this holy apostle.[84] The Abyssinians who inhabit Ethiopia hearkened to his voice and today venerate him as their first apostle. This evidence, together with the traditions mentioned earlier, make it highly likely that St. Thomas preached throughout the West. He began in Brazil—either reaching it by natural means on Roman ships, which some maintain were in communication with America from the coast of Africa, or else, as may be thought closer to the truth, being transported there by God miraculously. He passed to Paraguay, and from there to the Peruvians. He is known by name in Paraguay even today, being called *Pay Zumé*; and by the same name in Peru, as *Pay Tumé*. This is clear from an account that I have in my possession by Doctor Francisco de Alfaro,[85] presently a member of the Council of Finance, who is the greatest expert known today on affairs of the Indies, having traveled near and far throughout Peru and Paraguay. In his account he states:

> While visiting the jurisdiction of Santa Cruz de la Sierra, I learned that throughout the country there was knowledge of a holy man they called *Pay Tumé*, who had arrived from the direction of Paraguay and had come from very far away, so that I concluded that he had reached the Santa Cruz country by way of Paraguay from Brazil.

Thus far Doctor Francisco.

Accordingly, he is still known as *Tomé* in Brazil, Paraguay, and Peru. That the holy apostle passed through Brazil to Paraguay and Peru is affirmed by Father Pedro de Ribadeneira,[86] of our Society. He writes:

> Not only did the holy apostle preach throughout all these provinces and nations, but the Brazilian natives (as Father Manuel Nóbrega,[87] former provincial of the Society of Jesus there, writes) have knowledge of St. Thomas and of his passage through their own country, which displays a number of traces and signs of this which were seen by the Father with his own eyes.

Thus far this author. Thus, the tradition in Paraguay that the saint passed through there reaches near-certainty. He had prophesied in the eastern Indies that his preaching of the gospel would be revived, saying: "When the sea reaches this rock, by divine ordinance white men will come from far-off lands to preach the doctrine that I am now teaching you and to revive the memory of it." Similarly, the saint prophesied in nearly identical words the coming of the Society's members into the regions of Paraguay about which I speak: "You will forget what I preach to you, but when priests who are my successors come carrying crosses as I do, then you will hear once more the same doctrine that I am teaching you."

From his teaching and instruction, there has survived to our own time a knowledge of the hidden mystery of the Holy Trinity—even though, through the loss of recollection, they used to celebrate in Peru a major festival of this mystery in a superstitious fashion. They had three statues of the sun, named Apointi, Churinti, and Intiqua or Qui, meaning Father and Lord Sun, Son of the Sun, and Brother of the Sun. That the saint explained to them the unity of these three divine persons is witnessed to by an idol that they called Tangatanga, in which they worshiped this three-one and one-in-three. I hold it quite probable that they had gotten this from the apostle, applying it to their own idols. Thus I surmise that the name given to God in Paraguay, *Tupá* (the equivalent of *Man-hu*), was devised by the Indians themselves when, upon hearing the marvels that the saint proclaimed to them about God, they said in amazement, *Tupá* ("What is this?")—something great!

CHAPTER 25

That it is quite probable that the holy apostle carried a cross with him in the West

THE APOSTLE St. Thomas must certainly have had a deep devotion to the wounds of his divine Master, given the special favor which the Lord showed him by allowing him to touch them with his hands.[88] He bore them engraved upon his heart; but, being unable to bear them externally to show the pagans, he doubtless employed the instrument of the cross upon which the wounds had been made. Thus there is every reason to believe that the saint carried the cross with him. The sign which he gave in the East of the preaching to come was a cross of stone:[89] the pagans of the East came upon him in a cave in front of a cross which he had carved in a rock and before which he constantly prayed. In Meliapur, the place of his martyrdom, they display a cross carved in stone with several bloodstains. Other marks of his appear on this stone. Even in such tokens of stone he would not let the West fall short of the East, as we have already seen regarding the marks which can be seen to this day graven on stones. Unknown letters were found on stone in the East; the same are visible today in the West. He was slain by a brahmin upon a stone. The cross brought by the saint to the West is so heavy that it seems of stone—on the basis of both its weight and its incorruption—for, as we mentioned earlier, it remained underground and covered with water for more than fifteen hundred years, and can be seen today as entire, solid, and firm as a cross of stone might be. It has, moreover, a unique odor and gives no indication that it was ever subject to rotting.

Now we must determine whether the saint fashioned this cross in Carabuco, where he set it up, or in Brazil or Paraguay.[90] The reason for asking this is that it was quite high, nearly two and a half yards, thick and unworked—after being carved in our own day it is still a span square and so heavy that half of it, while being transported to Chuquisaca, broke down a pair of mules which carried it on pack frames. Here at court there are reliable witnesses who saw it being transported. I myself have experimented several times with tiny fragments of it: when dropped in water they fall straight to the bottom. It would thus seem that the saint would not have burdened himself for so many leagues' distance with so heavy a load.

Despite this, it appears nearly certain that it was brought there by the saint from some place far away. He certainly did not make it in Carabuco. The entire region is bare not only of timber usable for construction but even of ordinary firewood. This is noted by Doctor Francisco de Alfaro in his report: "I observe that all the lands surrounding the lake (and I have traveled them all) are quite without timber or even firewood." He likewise remarks that the cross must have come from a considerable distance, for he affirms that he had never seen wood of that species anywhere in Peru, so that it was clearly not made there. Indeed, nowhere in Peru is there to be found any incorruptible wood of its type, weight, fragrance, consistency, and color. Moreover, it is certainly not to be found anywhere in Paraguay. During the nearly thirty years that we members of the Society have traveled those forests in quest of pagan Indians, we have never seen such a species of wood. I have a fully authenticated piece of this miraculous wood in my possession. Comparing it with a species of precious wood in Brazil, called *yacaranda* by the natives and *palo santo*[91] by the Spaniards, out of which they fashion artifacts in imitation of ebony, I find that it is of the same species. This is also confirmed by witnesses familiar with this wood whom I had test its color and smell, and especially its weight. When dropped in water, quite small particles of *palo santo* sink straight to the bottom, just as the holy relic does. The conclusion is that the holy apostle fashioned the venerable cross in Brazil, where he initiated his preaching. He thereby imparted to this entire species of wood the efficacy for human health which experience has shown us that it possesses. Drinking water in which it has been boiled is highly beneficial, especially for treating dysentery—hence the common name given to the wood is *palo santo*. The distance the saint carried the cross to Carabuco, where he raised it, is more than twelve hundred leagues.

Thus, all this confers a high degree of probability upon the traditional belief in Paraguay that the holy apostle declared that when successors of his came bearing crosses like his own the people would once again hear the doctrine that he had taught them.

Objections may be countered by saying that a man who, in order to construct a material temple in the city of Meliapur in the East, carried an enormous timber which a great number of men and elephants could not move, would easily have been able to carry this precious wood for the spiritual edifice of his preaching, and that the One who transported him from one to the other Indies without the aid of a galleon would have rendered his cross as light as a straw.[92]

CHAPTER 26

How the holy apostle erected this sacred cross in Carabuco; its discovery and its effects against the devils

MY COMMITMENT to discuss St. Thomas's cross requires me to discuss its erection by the saint's own hands, its discovery in our own days, and its effects in past and present. I do not consider this a digression from my purpose; my topic is the conversion of pagans and the preaching of the gospel, and this cannot be achieved without the cross—a cross that is indeed quite heavy at times but which, being Christ's yoke, he himself renders light.

It is established from tradition that the saint erected this divine standard in Carabuco, a town of the most idolatrous and superstitious pagans that were known in Peru. At the sight of it, the idols, hitherto quite talkative, fell dumb. They warned the Indians that unless the cross was gotten rid of they would grant them no favors or responses.[93] This was the reason why the Indians threw the precious relic into the lake. Though it sank by its own weight to the bottom in the pagans' presence, it appeared in the morning on top of the water. To remove once and for all this threat to their idols, they pulled the cross from the water and consigned it to the flames, attempting to reduce it to ashes. Despite their best efforts, the flames made not a mark upon it, except what was needed to confirm to our own eyes in these our days the universal tradition of the Indians: on one side it has a slight scorch mark.

Seeing both the elements of fire and water powerless against the wood, the pagans decided to consign it to the earth. They dug down some five yards, so close to the water that for most of the year the spot is covered with it. There they deposited this treasure. The better to conceal it, they turned the place into a sewer. The time came that had been set by the Lord for the emergence of this proof of the truth of his gospel, which would make clear that the holy apostles had preached throughout the entire world. The following is an account of its discovery, based on the history of Father Alonso Ramos of the Order of St. Augustine:

It was the great feast of Corpus Christi. The Indians of Carabuco were all eating together in the square, a widespread custom in those lands when celebrating festivals. Under the heat of the wine, a fierce contention erupted between two factions in the town. Coming to blows, they also broke out in shouts, trading insults with each other. The Anansayas, who were recent arrivals, said to the Urinsayas, who were natives of the town: "You are vicious sorcerers; your ancestors stoned a saint who preached to them the faith and belief in a single God. They tried to burn a cross that he bore, and you keep it hidden. You know very well where it is but will not let it be seen." This came to the notice of the pastor, Father Sarmiento, an excellent servant of God. By dint of blandishments and threats, he found out the place. There he dug down five yards and brought the cross up.

Our Lord accomplishes numerous miracles through this cross, especially against lightning and fires. Many are recounted, and many are recorded by Father Alonso Ramos. I will mention only one. An Indian woman wore a tiny bit of the cross over her heart. A lascivious youth attempted to rape her. She told him about the relic she wore in an attempt to scare him off, but he persisted in trying to force her. Thereupon, on a bright and perfectly clear day, a lightning bolt fell and killed him, leaving the Indian woman free and unharmed.

With this I conclude my account of the cross and of the traces and signs of the glorious apostle in the West. I now return to my reductions, hoping that someone will make use of this sketch to give the matter a thorough treatment.

CHAPTER 27

Manifestations of the devil through an Indian who ceased attending Mass on feast days

WITH THE constant preaching of the gospel, the new Christians continued to make much progress, and excellent customs became established. One, a highly praiseworthy practice, was that they would all hear Mass very early in the morning before setting off for their fields. From this holy practice they have experienced an increase of blessings, material as well as spiritual. Those who did not follow this practice have experienced poverty and misery. I could cite numerous cases of persons who, hearing Mass every day, acquired an abundance of goods with middling toil; whereas those who failed to do so, sometimes toiling and laboring straight through on a feast day, barely managed to support themselves.

An Indian in one of the towns would not go to Mass either on workdays or on feast days. He persisted in this for a full year. As we saw earlier in this account, the Lord would teach the Indians through outward things and signs and thereby move them to faith in invisible things and those of the soul. This was the procedure he employed to teach this Indian and prompt him to join the town. One Sunday, while everyone else was attending the Mass and sermon, this Indian alone stayed behind on his farm. There the devils began mooing like cows, bellowing like bulls, lowing like oxen, and making the sounds of goats. Terrified, the poor Indian fled into his hut, so panicked that he would not venture out. People came to him late in the day and the Indian told them of his woes. Going through his fields they saw the tracks of various animals, and a human footprint no bigger than a newborn baby's. Worst of all, the whole field was left yellow, as if singed by a fire. The same thing happened the following Sunday. They reported this to me, but did not mention the Indian's evil habit of never hearing Mass. I advised them to put up crosses and to sprinkle the entire place with holy water. They did so, but the same din by the devil recurred on the following Sunday. They brought me word that crosses and holy water had been of no use. Everyone in the district went to confession, no one certain whether it was his own fault that the devils were molesting them. The only one who did not confess was the ill-behaved Indian. To demonstrate that he was the one responsible, the devils came from a good distance as if charging (only the noise and voices were heard) towards the Indian's hut. The Indian used the name of Jesus as his defense. They asked me to do something about it. After Mass I went to the place, about half a league from town. The whole settlement had already assembled to hear the devil. Reaching a stream that is crossed by boat, I beheld a crowd of people dashing into the water and wading fearfully across the stream in flight from the devil, who was violently attacking the house. We crossed the river, and saw the footprints, and how they had deliberately trampled and ruined the whole field, its yellow color strongly suggesting burning and the crop, still in its early growth, scorched and withered. I asked who lived in the hut, and at that point they told me of his wrongdoing. I took surplice and holy water and, in the name of Jesus Christ and through the merits of his servant Ignatius, charged the devil to leave the area and to harm no one in any town. I placed there in a closed jar a piece of St. Ignatius' cassock. The devil never returned. I brought the Indian into the town. He made a good confession and was thereafter an exemplary Christian.

CHAPTER 28

The corpses of four dead Indians which they reverenced in their churches

THE DEVIL universally attempts to mimic the worship of God with fictions and frauds. The Guaraní nation has been unsullied by idols or idol worship; by heaven's grace they are unencumbered by lies and ready to receive the truth, as long experience has taught us. Despite this, the devil has found fraudulent means for enthroning his ministers, the magicians and sorcerers, to be the pestilence and ruin of souls. In one reduction we suffered a great trial. All week long it would teem with people; only on Sundays, when with much ringing of bells we tried to assemble the people for the Mass and sermon, everyone would vanish. We carefully sought out the cause in order to take countermeasures, but proved unable to discover it. Then, in

great secrecy, a young man revealed to one of the Fathers that there were
three dead bodies, on three hills, that talked; they were warning the Indians
against listening to the Fathers' preaching. The young man claimed that he
had heard them talk, speaking evil of us and our teaching, strongly endorsing
their own ministers and wholly discrediting us. There was a widespread rumor
that they had risen from the dead and were living in the flesh just as before
they died. It was because of these stratagems of the devil that the people
were not coming to the sermon or to catechism. Five of us priests met to
discuss the problem. We decided that at one o'clock in the night four of us
would go out very silently in search of these bodies. Father Francisco Díaz
and Father José Doménech[94] went to a hill adjoining the town where one
of them was. The holy martyr Father Cristóbal de Mendoza and myself went
in search of the others. Father José Cataldino stayed behind in our house to
keep the Indians occupied and distract them. Though we set out after
midnight through the rear courtyard, without a sound, our departure was not
stealthy enough to prevent an Indian gatekeeper of ours from hearing us. He
informed the people in the town that, tired of seeing them not come to
church, we were leaving.

The people flocked to our house and asked Father José about us. He
succeeded in quieting them. Father Francisco Díaz and his companion
managed to make their way in the dark over a rugged, almost trackless ridge.
Mounting the top of a rise, they found a temple where the dry bones in
question were venerated. All around it they saw numerous hermitages in
which those who made the pilgrimage there lodged, just as is done in
novenas—for the devil tries to imitate everything. They found the temple
alone and unguarded. This surprised the guide the Fathers had brought, since
it was said that there were always people there, day and night. The temple
was spacious and well fitted out. In the interior was a dark, two-doored
compartment, in which the corpse was suspended on a net or hammock
between two poles. The ropes were decorated with a variety of brilliant
feathers. The hammock was covered with two precious cloths of colored
feathers, striking to the eye. There were devices for perfuming the place. No
one dared enter it but the priest who posed questions in the people's name
to this oracle. In the front part of the temple were numerous benches where
the people sat and listened to the replies given by the devil. Hanging from
the walls and beams all over the temple were numerous offerings of fruits of
the earth in curiously worked baskets. The priest would eat from these
offerings and give what was left over to the farmers as something sacred, from
which they anticipated great blessings upon their crops. The Fathers gathered
up the bones, feathers, and ornaments, and in complete silence brought them
to the town, unbeknownst to anyone.

Father Cristóbal de Mendoza and myself had a somewhat lengthier
adventure. We walked that night along ridges, valleys, and lakes, speeded by

our desire to discover this devil. At about eight in the morning the guide we brought led us into the temple. We were thrilled at the sight, confident that the devil could now not escape from our hands. However, all we found in the temple were offerings hanging there. Our hopes seemed dashed, since the guide had known this spot but did not know the place where the body had been transported, as the tracks indicated. Both frustrated and anxious to achieve our quest, we decided to follow the most worn path among many that we found. We ran across a pagan boy who, though he stoutly denied it at the time, we later learned was the sacristan or assistant in the temple. We tied him up and alternately threatened and promised him gifts to get him to guide us. He refused, but while continuing to refuse led us over dangerous cliffs, very high indeed. We got past them on all fours, clinging to the rocks. Once past this obstacle, we came upon a half-finished tent or hut. Its curious and recent construction suggested to us that they had begun it for the body and then sent the body further on for greater safety. As luck would have it, we ran into an Indian who resolved our doubt. He gave us the following account. "At midnight," he said, "the body that was worshiped in the temple you saw cried out and begged them to show it kindness by removing it from there. 'Take me away from here,' it said, 'for those evil men are coming after me to seize me so they can burn me. Get me away quickly! If they harm me I will make fire fall from heaven and consume them, I will make the waters rise and flood the land, I will summon my friends in São Paulo to take revenge for the wrong they have done me.' At this warning, those guarding the body undertook to rescue not only that body but another a good distance away. They thought a pair of devils would put up a better defense against a pair of priests (a providential disposition of heaven to enable us to seize the two of them). They reached the spot which you saw there half-built. But the devil, insecure there, cried out 'Get me away from here fast! the Fathers are getting very close.' They immediately took them away. I left them a fair distance from here, still escaping."

Thus far the Indian's account. As we later learned, he had himself gone with the bodies but, upon seeing how the devil feared us and fled, had decided that he was weak indeed and that our friendship would serve him better than that of those poltroons. Unwilling to see them in our hands, and knowing that they would at the very least be burned, he bade them farewell.

By now it was two o'clock in the afternoon. We had not had a moment's rest. With encouragement from this report, our anxiety to catch the prey beguiled away our terrible exhaustion. By the Lord's will, we caught up with them at five that afternoon. Those who had been carrying the bodies for so many hours on this hasty flight had succumbed to fatigue. They had stowed the bodies away as best they could, never believing that our exertions would suffice to overtake their own speedy advance. When we burst upon them, they all ran off. Among them was a priestess who had been moved by the bodies' misfortune and had followed to comfort them, carrying for this purpose a pair of large vessels in which she put burning coals to counter the cold and damp of the forest. They all fled. Only two had the courage to await us—and even try to kill us, aiming their arrows at us. God overturned their courage, and we were able to capture and bind them. Thanking God for this outcome, we opened up the nets and discovered some evil-smelling bones. Even adorned with beautiful feathers they still retained their filthy ugliness. One body had been that of a great sorcerer of ancient times. The other was a man we had found living when we first entered the province. By his looks we had judged him about a hundred and twenty years old. We had often invited him to be baptized, but he never accepted. Only in his last agony, at certain signs which he gave, did Father Simón Masseta baptize him. He was interred in a small church which we soon after abandoned. Many people claimed that cries were heard from his grave saying, "Get me out! I am smothering here! Get me out!" They did so, placing him in the temple, and there the devil spoke through him as has been described.

CHAPTER 29

What was done with the bones

IT WAS essential to make a good demonstration to confound the priests of these idols and to undeceive the towns; for not only this town but also the others had been led astray. First, we forbade all Christians to eat any of the offerings, since they had been made to the devil. We brought the bodies to the town. The inhabitants split into factions. Some deemed our action very harmful, since in those bodies and the worship they rendered them they had possessed a guarantee of good crops, fertile years, and favorable health. These persons were quite convinced that, though dead, they had come back to life, their former flesh restored and improved with youthful vigor. In confirmation of this they claimed they had seen them move inside their hammocks and heard them speak for the common good of the whole people. Others were unsure whether all this was true and wanted to see this deception with their own eyes. Others decided that, since they had failed to escape our hands even by speedy flight and had been captured and brought back by us, it could only mean that their power was very slight.

All the people assembled in the church and were given a sermon. It dealt with the true God, with the worship owed him from his creatures, with the devil's artifices and impotence, and with the lies and deceits of the magicians. Upon completion of the sermon, one of the Fathers went out in surplice and stole, accompanied by servers with holy water and a large finely bound book, from which he read a part of a chapter in Latin. He urged the people to make an act of contrition for believing in this nonsense. They were all kneeling with hands joined and eyes cast to the ground. They made their fervent act of detestation for every vain belief and idolatry, embracing only the true teaching of the Roman Catholic Church. They cried aloud to God for pardon so feelingly and devoutly that we were moved to tears. After this one of the Fathers mounted a platform that had been erected on the square so that everyone, including women and children, could be undeceived by the sight of the cold bones. The Father displayed them, naming the persons whose bones they had been. It was amazing to see the people's rejoicing as they beheld this public discrediting of the great fraud regarding the corpses which everyone had claimed were alive. They competed with one another to bring firewood for burning them. This was carried out in my presence, so that not a single bone could be carried off and the lie thereby perpetuated.

At this they took courage and showed us another recently dead body. Though we had tried to baptize the person in his illness, they had concealed him, intending to build him a temple. He too underwent the penalty of fire. Once this disturbance was removed, the people came to church regularly, the pagans fervently requesting baptism and the Christians confession. Thus a great deal of good was reaped in the town, the people heartily blaming themselves for taking as truth the deceptions of our common enemy.

CHAPTER 30

Our entry into the province of Tayaoba

W E HAD already founded five settlements. Leaving Fathers there to develop them, we set our sights on moving into the province of Tayaoba. This was the name of a prominent cacique who ruled numerous towns and gave his name to the entire province. It fell to me to get the door of this tightly closed province opened so the gospel might enter. The province had an almost innumerable population which was vigorously given to their pagan customs, highly warlike, and very accustomed to eating human flesh. This land of ridges, valleys, and streams harbored large numbers of sorcerers sunk in great errors and superstitions. These stubbornly spurned other teachings, preaching their own as wholly true. Many pretended to be gods (a common delusion among these poor people), fabricating a thousand ruses in proof of their divinity, in which the people foolishly believed. Since these persons possess extraordinary eloquence, they are venerated by the common folk, who are vanquished by their contrived and disjointed lies.

Pursuing my journey, I arrived at a quite small hamlet or village of barely sixty inhabitants. They received me in a friendly manner, which I reciprocated by preaching the gospel. All of them were baptized. I stayed in this village for two months, inquiring about the customs of those who lived in the province and trying to disseminate from there word of my coming and my intentions. The key and guard post of the province was a town situated a day's journey from where I stayed. I sent some small gifts to its inhabitants— fishhooks, knives, beads, and other little items valueless here but prized over there. In this way I succeeded in attracting some of them to visit me. I explained what I wanted, telling them that I wished to enter their lands to proclaim eternal salvation to them. Trusting in their assurances, I set out a few days later on the river by canoe. I reached their town in daylight after traveling the whole day at top speed. They made a show of receiving me well, but this was a pretense. As they spread word of my arrival, people poured down from the hills throughout the night, intending to eat me and my whole party, about fifteen persons. As I learned later, they were eager to try the flesh of a priest, which they thought would be different and more savory than others'. I took all this furtive noise as a bad sign, and spent the night preparing for any eventuality.

Day had hardly broken when a great sorcerer entered my hut and asked for me. Seeing me on my knees in prayer, he sat down not far from me in deep silence. I continued praying for some time, begging God to bestow the light that this blinded people lacked, so that they would cast aside the errors of paganism and be converted to his divine faith. I arose and, with loving and soft words, addressed him and the other eight important sorcerer caciques who had assembled. I told them that I had been drawn to their lands not by a quest for gold or silver, of which they had none, but for their souls. These, though still black with paganism and sin, could be washed white with what I brought, namely, the water of baptism and true belief in one God, the creator of all things. I went on to tell them of Jesus Christ, the Son of God. I was starting to speak of the eternal punishment of the wicked, when one of them cut me short and shouted, "He lies!"—repeating it over and over—"He lies, let us kill him!" The others answered the same. They ran out to get their weapons which, to avoid arousing suspicion, they had left carefully hidden, along with a large number of people in reserve, concealed in the forest.

I was deeply satisfied at having thus proclaimed the gospel to these barbarians. Without budging from the spot, I stood waiting for them. One of the Indians in my escort entered my hut and begged me to leave. He returned a second and third time, saying, "Father, for the love of God, let us go; they are going to tear you to pieces!" Flinging his arms around my neck, he persuaded me by his pleas to leave. In him I seemed to see not an Indian but an angel from heaven. Hardly had we left when we began to feel the arrows they were shooting at us. Seven of my Indian escort fell at my side, shot to death. For me this was to die seven deaths of my own. But my own good fortune did not direct a single arrow towards me so that I could accompany in death those who had accompanied me in life—not just physically but also in the resolve to help me proclaim the gospel. Indeed, with this resolve they had prepared themselves the day before by confession and Communion as if for death. With Christian fervor they had said to me: "Come, Father, let us go preach the faith to the pagans. We shall give our lives for Jesus Christ in your aid and in the defense of the faith that you preach."

Beside me stood the good Indian who had pulled me out of the hut. He saw me surrounded by volleys of arrows and in evident peril. To save me from the hands of death, he exposed himself with manifest risk to his own life. Without saying a word to me, and with all the speed that the crisis demanded, he pulled the cloak off my back, and my hat as well, and said to another Indian: "Get the Father into the woods!" Donning my cloak and hat, and running by himself through the field in sight of the enemy, he gave me time and opportunity to take refuge in the woods, which were quite thick. As they saw my good Indian in my cape and hat, I heard the pagans say, "There goes the priest! Shoot him, let us kill him!" Amazingly, not one of the huge shower of arrows touched him, although all the people there are quite skilled archers.

I got into the forest with three Indians. To avoid leaving a trail, we separated into four, keeping each other in sight—a tactic employed in such situations—and made our way through the extremely dense forest. The loyal Indian who had risked death for my sake kept running for a considerable distance. When he decided I was well into the forest, he took thought to his own safety and gave his pursuers the slip. He caught up with me and gave back my cloak and hat. Then, supposing that the people were still in pursuit of me, he fearlessly returned to face them, with the intention of protecting my life at the risk of his own. We pursued our course, ignorant of where it led. Luckily we found a hidden trail where we could hide our tracks. It was a gully which served as a run and wallow for wild pigs; it was sunk in the ground, muddy all through, and so well covered over and concealed by thorny reeds that we considered ourselves fortunate indeed to find such a hiding place. We scrambled along it. It was barely wide enough for us to go single file. The height was even less. Crawling through the stinking mud on arms and knees, we had to push our faces through mud or risk hitting our heads, if we raised them even slightly, against the sharp thorns on the reeds. I suffered sorely on this narrow, filthy, thorny path. We emerged from it like wild pigs out of the muck. I came out with my head slashed from the thorns and blood running down my face. One of my companions wiped it off with the tears of his eyes. I wanted to hurry on since I was sure the enemy were still behind us; but I was so exhausted, and my heart was so pierced through by my seven companions' death and so agitated by a desire to imitate them, that I pled with those accompanying me to go ahead and save their own lives, so that their children would have fathers and their wives husbands, and not be widowed and orphaned by their deaths. With a manly spirit they affirmed that they thought nothing of wives or children—that they would rather die at my side in this glorious enterprise than live with the shame of having abandoned me among the pagans.

At this point we unexpectedly found ourselves at the river we had come up the previous day. We heard the sound of rowing. We took it to be that of enemies patrolling the river in search of us. Fearing this, we entered the woods. But it occurred to me that we did not know what we were running away from, and I asked my companions to wait for me there. I said I wanted to find out who these people were, and that if they were enemies they should make their escape. They refused, and so we returned to the river together. There we found two Indians in a canoe. They were friends, both caciques from the town we had left the previous day. Quite surprised, I asked them what they had come for. They replied that they had heard what happened and were coming in search of me. This left me dumbfounded. I could see a palpable providence of God. The distance there had required eight hours of continuous rowing by young men, eight or ten in a boat. Yet these two old men, each past eighty years of age, had made the long trip in an hour and a half. We got in the boat and reached the town. There my grief started over again, for all the women and children ran out to meet us, weeping aloud at our suffering. My furnishings were gone, taken away by the barbarians to give to a great sorcerer whom they acknowledged as their lord. The paten they broke into pieces to make a necklace. They took the hammock and blanket which constituted my entire gear. I was left with nothing but the clothes on my back, a fire my only blanket against the intense cold of the harsh winter nights.

CHAPTER 31

My second entry into the province

THE DEVIL aimed through this severe reverse at frightening us off this important enterprise. However, our avidity to win such a host of souls for heaven made us disregard these sufferings. I recommended preparations for a second assault on the citadel, so fortified with the devil's trickery and so heavily garrisoned by his servants. I found the Indians undismayed: though the death of their seven brothers and my seven companions might have discouraged them, I let them know how glorious was the deed they had done and how they already possessed their hoped-for reward in heaven, since they had sealed with their blood the faith they had just received; and this put new heart into them.

During this period it occurred that, at nine o'clock, in the deepest dark of the night, we heard, coming from a deep forest ravine between whose walls there ran a strong and sometimes torrential river, a cry of woe so full of pain and feeling, so piercing and repeated, that we were all puzzled by it. Neither the loud din of the river nor the great distance from which the sound originated in the slightest diminished the ringing, piteous cry. My first thought was that it was some soul terribly tormented in purgatory. I went out to the little town square. Many people were already waiting there, for from the way it sounded it was nearing the settlement by the minute. It passed through our midst like a ray of light, in the visible form of a shape like a white cloud the height of a human being. Entering the church, it disappeared a few feet past the entrance. I said a few responsories for it, and Mass the next day. The Indians were all astonished at seeing something from the other life so clearly. They all said that it must be the soul of one of my companions.

I was wholly intent on meeting the great cacique Tayaoba. I thought that once I won him over I would have the rest on my side. The Lord decreed that my wish be fulfilled. Drawn by curiosity to see me, another great cacique visited the settlement. He brought his wife and two of his children, a sure token of friendship. He never took his eyes off me. I found this quite odd, but he soon relieved my perplexity. He said to me: "Father, do not be upset that I am watching you so closely. This was my purpose in coming here. I came to see with my own eyes whether what the sorcerers maintain about you is true. They say that you are not like human beings, that you are monsters, that you have horns on your head, that you are so savage that your everyday food is human flesh, and that your behavior is churlish. This falsehood is what has brought me here, and it is what has for so long kept Tayaoba from coming to see you. But I will soon go and bring him to you without fail." This he did a few days later, bringing the good old man to see me together with his wife and four children, twenty more having been left behind in his lands. I received them with great honor and caressed his little children a great deal, something these people think highly of. Out of my poverty I gave him and his escort whatever trifles I had. Word of Tayaoba's coming sped throughout our towns. People raced thirty or forty leagues to see him, amazed at the sight of such a renowned man. I then brought up entering his land; he was quite pleased to hear this. We decided to forgo the river route and so went up-country by land. We walked for three days. Then we came upon a rather broad open area, the journey up to that point having been though quite dense forests. I, and the Indians as well, decided that it was a suitable spot for founding a fine town. We immediately raised a beautiful cross, which all of us venerated. My own dwelling was the shade of a tree. In it I had a painting, half a yard high, of the Immaculate Conception. My arms were a cross which I always bore in my hands. A host of people came to see me, including many of those whom I mentioned above as wanting to kill me. They could see that I was defenseless, since I had only thirty Indians with me—although Tayaoba had sent for his own people, foreseeing what in fact happened. The sorcerers plotted to kill me. As quickly as possible, before Tayaoba could gather his people, a host of enemies converged on the clearing throughout the night, roughly three thousand Indians. We essayed erecting a palisade to defend ourselves, but the darkness of the night did not permit this, and we were too few to do it anyway. It was already past midnight. According to their custom, they would attack at daybreak. The Indians advised me to leave the clearing under the dark of night and take shelter in the thick forest. They would wait to try their hand, and at the first skirmish escape. The good Tayaoba said to me: "Father, at dawn we must fight, and I may be killed. Make me a son of God by baptism." The other pagans there said the same. I had already taught them something of the divine mysteries and they were catechumens. I baptized them, Tayaoba receiving the name of Nicolás.

I had hardly moved away from the tree, in the company of three Indians and a little boy who served my Mass, when in total silence a troop of pagans assaulted my lodging from one side. Hearing their noise, we quickened our steps and plunged into the forest. With the darkness of the night and our hasty departure, the holy painting was left behind. My sacristan realized that he had forgotten it. Without saying a word to me, he went back to recover his picture. He was recognized by the enemies, who had already torn the picture to pieces. They bound him and took him to their town. At dawn there was an engagement. It was of short duration because our men were so few. They killed a number of the enemy, who were so numerous that they were an easy target, and escaped unscathed.

A cacique on the other side had promised his concubines that as booty he would bring them a goodly portion of my body for the victory feast. This man had an enemy in his own town, who came with him to seize this opportunity to kill him. This he did: standing at his side in the first onslaught, he treacherously shot him through with an arrow.

I and my companions traveled that whole day through the thickets of the dense forest. I was burdened with anxieties, torments, and distress at seeing Satan thus victorious in his opposition to the gospel. Many thoughts ran through my mind. What tormented me most was that the door to this whole vast province still seemed tightly closed against the holy gospel. Exhausted, we reached a stream at four in the afternoon. Here we halted to rest for the night. We carried nothing with us to sustain nature: none of us had eaten since the previous day. Nor was there anything with which to strike a fire. Need and skill did so, however: one of my companions made fire with two small sticks. The others scoured the woods and quickly returned with food. They brought a bundle of mushrooms wrapped in large leaves, as well as some large tree roots the color and shape of turnips; the other had an armful of tree branches. The mushrooms, wrapped in leaves, they placed upon the embers and cooked. The tree leaves, right on the branch, they parched over the flames. When the meal was cooked, they laid a table for me with leaves called *bihao* on the Main[95]—they are quite large—and upon them placed the leaves and mushrooms. I remained for a time gazing at my meal, deeply moved at the sight, until my companions bade me eat. Whoever has not tasted the food of hardships for the conversion of pagans cannot appreciate the taste of these plants. I tried the mushrooms, but they were tough and resistant. I ate some of the leaves: without exaggeration, they tasted like salted sardines. For dessert they brought me the raw roots; they had the taste of manioca roots, but were quite tender. There was no drinking cup, but ingenuity supplied. An Indian took one of the large leaves. Shaping it into a cone and fastening it with a thorn, he filled it with water and placed it in my hands. I ended giving thanks to the Lord for this savory meal—for so it truly was, especially to the soul. This was a trial event to allay my fear of hunger and hardship. Never again on similar occasions have these given me any concern. My only concern has been not to abate the trust that is owed to God's omnipotence.

CHAPTER 32

How some Spaniards entered a small settlement of unbelievers, and what happened to them

NEWS REACHED the Spanish town of Villa Rica that the Indians of Tayaoba had twice repulsed me. Deciding their arms were strong enough to avenge this insult and in the process bring back a supply of Indian women and children to serve them—the usual aim of these incursions—they organized their campaign. Pitying their scanty forces, I went down to the town and tried to dissuade them. I told them the great numbers of men there, the peril of numerous dangerous passes. Seeing them persist in their intention, I formally petitioned the authorities not to let them enter, being sure none of them would come out alive. Seventy Spaniards, with five hundred friendly Indians, set off up-country. I decided I had to go with them as far as a certain territory in order to defend from their hands a group of people who had entrusted themselves to me and through whom I hoped to win over the remainder. They were now peaceful, and would doubtless treat the Spaniards peacefully. The latter would seize them and carry them off as prisoners—even hang some of them to justify their business. My misgivings were not idle, as the outcome demonstrated.

Father Diego de Salazar was with me on this journey. The soldiers reached a hamlet of perhaps eight small houses of pagans where there were many of those who had tried the second time to kill me and had seized the little boy who served my Mass. As soon as they heard us, the enemy dashed out like lions and felled four friendly Indians with their arrows. At the sound of musket shot they withdrew into the forest. What with the cries of the wounded and the volleys of arrows being shot at us by the enemy, fear grew so great that some of the Spaniards attempted to turn back—a poor tactic since the Indians would attack them in the difficult passes and easily destroy them. They changed their mind and put up a palisade, no longer to conquer the Indians but to avoid being conquered themselves. Our Indian friends came across some large pots of meat boiled with corn. They brought me a dishful and invited me to eat. I ate some of it, thinking it was game. But they shortly brought up the head, feet, and hands of the boy they had seized from me. That it was he was confirmed by some enemy young men that we caught: they told us they had killed him the previous day with the customary ritual which I described earlier.

The enemies kept consulting and holding great councils. They attacked our palisade and wreaked considerable damage on us with their arrows. They inflicted casualties on both Indians and Spaniards, if not mortally yet badly enough to keep them from wielding arms. Many of the barbarians were killed by musket fire. The battle went on. From the fort our Indians shot quantities of arrows at them; they shot them back, inflicting great damage on us. My companion and I attempted to end the battle by ordering our friendly Indians not to shoot any more arrows but to collect those of the enemy instead— once out of weapons, the latter would leave the way free for our retreat, since the Spaniards had no further thought of plunder. We explained our plan, but they recklessly rejected it, claiming it was our shooting the arrows which deterred the enemy from approaching the fort. This was a baseless argument since they themselves were doing it to greater effect with their muskets.

By the fifth day from our arrival, some four thousand picked Indians had assembled. The Spaniards held a council of war. Seeing themselves arrived at the last day of their lives, they agreed that, once the palisade was penetrated by the enemy, they would form a circle and in this way defend themselves until their ammunition (which was very little) was exhausted. Then they would use their swords—when they reached that point it would mean that their end had come. The friendly Indians, seeing how perilous the situation had become, said to me: "You warned these men about all this danger, but they followed their own leaning and incurred it anyway. So it is only right for us to look to our own lives and get away secretly through the forest. Let them stay here since they were so bent on coming to their destruction." I replied that it would not be an honorable deed to abandon the Spaniards in such clear danger and that we ought to fight: at the last moment we would find a way out, being capable of making our escape through the forest, and I had confidence in God we would all get out alive. I told them to stop shooting arrows at the enemy. Even though the Spaniards disagreed, we considered this the only way to bring the battle to a halt.

A closely fought battle then broke out. Behind their embrasures the Spaniards were now fighting for their lives. We brought our Indians back into the square. In an instant the enemy covered it with arrows stuck in the ground, which our men then picked up. The enemy did the same a second and third time, but our men did not loose a single shaft. Suddenly the flutes, drums, cries of the enemy halted in their bewilderment at finding themselves weaponless. The Spaniards were also bewildered, not realizing what had produced the change. Finally they understood and, as we watched the enemy departing in droves home to their own lands, we raised thanks to the Author of all.

Chanting not victory but good fortune, the Spaniards directly began planning their return home. We had been joined by a good number of the Indians for whose sake we had made this journey with the aim of saving them from the Spaniards' hands. Fearful of being killed by the hostile Indians, these Indians refused to return to their own lands. We all set off in flight from the danger. The Spaniards deemed it an indignity to return home covered with wounds, in flight, and with no captives. They consequently chose as their prey the poor sheep who had trusted and followed us. They decided to hold a trial, claiming that these Indians had twice tried to kill me and should be brought to punishment. This they did, sentencing two of the caciques to be hanged. I learned of this and warned the caciques. I advised them to get on the other side of the mountains by the ridges there, with all their people, and to return to the same spot eight days later. There they would find me and we would discuss the proper settlement of their houses.

At midnight, in complete silence, the poor people departed, fleeing from the justice that should have protected and favored them. Morning came, and the captain sent his sergeants to seize all the people. Discovering that the Indians had eluded them, they made great efforts to determine by whom or how they had been gotten out. They could find out nothing, until the captain himself came to me and asked if I had seen them. I said yes, that the previous evening I had suggested they go into the forest and seek out sites for their clearings and plantings. Taken aback and quite unhappy, he replied, "They had recourse to a good saint." Realizing they were not safe from the enemy, the Spanish left the region. My companion and I stayed behind, and were rejoined by the Indians who had fled. Sites were designated and they established their houses and clearings. They were all baptized and some are alive today, excellent Christians.

CHAPTER 33

The Society makes a third attempt at the conquest

IN THIS citadel of theirs the devils doubtless exulted, absolute lords of a host of souls, having twice triumphantly expelled the holy gospel from their lands. I did not despair of victory. The advice given me—that I should give up this utterly hopeless enterprise—only further inflamed my eagerness for the conquest. Letters from friends, urging me to abandon these repeated perils and withdraw to rest and take care of my own life, spurred me to set it at hazard. I invoked the aid of the seven archangel princes of the heavenly army, dedicating to their valor the first settlement that I made. I had a painting of these princes, a yard and a half high. This I placed in its frame and carried in procession for three days as I walked towards the open region where they had driven me away and seized the young boy; I had an escort of only thirty Indians, so that the victory over these hellish brutes would be ascribed to God alone. Our procession arrived within sight of the open area.

I could not espy the cross which I had set up and whose loftiness had shed beauty over the fields. I found it reduced to ashes by the barbarians. I therefore raised another in its place. We quickly built a palisade and a little church, where I said Mass daily. There we awaited the fury of those tigers. They thought from the way things looked that I had large numbers of Indians inside the fort, and came to examine our defenses. However, our people met them at the gate and would not let them inside. We lacked food, and I lived for many days on shoots of wild shrubs, parched tree leaves, and wild thistle roots. Each day brought news of councils being held against me. The one who burned with the most frenzy and eagerness to eat me was a magician named Guiraberá. He had himself called God and had obtained sway over the people with his lies. His regular food was human flesh. When building a house or carrying out some work, he would regale his laborers by having the fattest Indian under his jurisdiction brought so they could feast on the poor man. To those who came to see me, after I had told them the purpose of my coming, I gave small fishhooks, needles, and pins, things not much valued over here but greatly there. They grew more fond of my words. My companions assisted with their own, speaking well to the pagans. The latter, once well informed of my intentions, began coming in droves every day, bringing their women, their children, their sick, and their scant possessions, leaving behind their farms and gardens and the lands on which they had been born in order to settle on this site and hear the word of God. In this place were settled all those who had tried to kill me the first time and who killed the seven Indians, as I mentioned earlier. The spot was also settled by those who had expelled me the second time and killed the boy who served my Mass. Here they displayed their grief for the wrongs they had done me; here they confessed their guilt and were washed in the sacrament of baptism which I gave them. About fifteen hundred families united on the open land there. The number of infants baptized was quite large, and heaven took for itself the firstfruits of many who, just washed, took their flight heavenward.

CHAPTER 34

How the great magician Guiraberá was progressively abandoned and himself succumbed to the truth

THE GREAT magician Guiraberá, seeing that the lies and fables he told to win credence were unavailing to keep the people from racing to hear God's word, decided to visit us himself. We indicated one of our towns to him. Three of us priests gathered there and let him know he could visit us there in complete safety. He came escorted by three hundred Indians armed with bows and arrows. Before him walked a very prominent cacique holding high a naked sword in his hand. There followed a troop of his concubines finely decked out and holding pots and other articles for his use. He himself strode in the midst of this retinue, finely dressed and constantly bestowing blessings like a bishop—even this the devil put him up to. Meanwhile his people cast pieces of cloth on the ground so that his feet would not touch the earth, many even stripping off the clothes they wore and placing them with unflagging concern and care under his feet. He declined to enter our house, presumably fearing that we would kill and eat him. We went out to the doorway. There they set up a seat for him, decking it with a variety of cloths; similarly for his feet. Seated on three chairs, we listened to his oration, that of a man who owed his high enthronement to his eloquence. He voiced his pleasure at seeing us, since he hoped we would consider him a friend, and other matters very finely worded. We responded succinctly, saying we would speak with him at greater leisure.

We offered him what refreshment our poverty allowed. The following day, more at ease, he came to see us. He entered our house. There, in the presence of many of his people, I explained to him that there was but a single Creator, whose handiwork we all are; that he assigned our times as he saw fit, creating new human beings and bringing death for others, so that our own efforts could not shield us against death. I told him how foolish he was —being an Indian like everybody else who drank, ate, and had the same animal needs for food, sleep, and so forth as other people do—to so forget himself and his Creator as to term himself God. I told him he ought to admit that he was a man—in fact, less than a man because he showed less judgment than everyone else in his silly pretenses. He gave evidence of listening to me well. Denying everything that had been rumored about him, he invited us to visit his own town, where he wished to entertain us.

A few days later Father Simón Masseta and myself set out. The Indian received us graciously. We immediately raised the standard of the cross in that den of lions—for all these mountains and ravines were inhabited by magicians and sorcerers. We established a town with two thousand inhabitants. From once being wild lions' lairs, which had witnessed only drunkenness, lechery, feuds, killings, people eating one another, and continual turmoil under the sway of the devil, whose teachings lay behind all this, the territory was transformed into a paradise where God's word was heard in the church and where the people recited their prayers in their houses at the top of their voices before going to sleep and after waking up. Instead of sharpening human bones for their arrows, they now carved crosses to wear around their necks and vied with one another to learn what was needed for baptism.

The number of settlements we founded in those provinces reached a total of thirteen. Sermons were given each Sunday and catechism was taught every day of the year. Confessions were very frequent. In some of the first settlements we placed the most venerable Sacrament of the Altar. In these towns where the Lord was present, no concubinage or other vices were permitted. The people of these towns communicated four times a year, with a good preparation through sacramental confession, a discipline which they underwent eight days before. They made daily progress in the good of their souls. They were striking solid roots in the faith; the entire Christian commonwealth there was flourishing. The Sunday Masses were celebrated with figured choral music and excellent instruments. Large provinces of pagans on our borders were eager for us to enter their lands and instruct their children.

Then came the day of doom for these reductions, as well as for the prospect of founding others. Its instruments were the townsmen of São Paulo.

CHAPTER 35

The invasion of these reductions by the townsmen of São Paulo

THE TOWN of São Paulo[96] is situated in the south. It is the most inland settlement on the entire coast, sixteen leagues from the sea. It is protected by a towering mountain range called Paraná Piacaba, meaning a place from which one sees the sea. The mountains are so steep that four men could block the way of large armies. Easy access to the town might be afforded by a gradual road from the Janeiro River, if a section of the forest were opened up, but the people of São Paulo strongly resist this. It is quite fertile country; there are wheat, maize, wines, beef, and pork. These are raised there and carried for sale throughout the coast upon the backs of Indian men and women, who are forced to bear loads like mules even if they have children to raise. The inhabitants of the town are Castilians, Portuguese, Italians, and people of other nationalities gathered there by a desire to live as they like in freedom, without the constraints of law. Their way of life is destruction of the human race: they kill all those who flee from them to escape the wretched slavery they inflict upon them.

They go out for two or three years at a stretch hunting human beings like animals. Some have been out ten or twelve years. They return home to find new children born to other men who, thinking them dead, had married their wives. They themselves bring home the children they had sired in the forests. Since I will be discussing this point elsewhere, this brief description will have to suffice. These people, worse than brigands, invaded our reductions; they seized captives, killed, and pillaged altars. Three of us priests went to their encampment, where they already held many people captive. We begged them to release to us those they had captured, many of whom were in chains. They immediately began screaming, like raving madmen, "Seize them, seize them; they are traitors!" They likewise fired their arquebuses and wounded eight or nine Indians who had come with us. One died on the spot from a bullet in the thigh. Father Cristóbal de Mendoza came off with an arrow wound. They took Father José Doménech prisoner, uttering against us words to be expected from their unholy mouths: that we were not priests but devils, heretics, enemies of God, and that we preached lies to the Indians. One of them aimed a musket at my chest, and I bared my breast so that the ball would enter without resistance.

Not long after, to the beat of drums and in military order, they entered the two reductions of San Antonio and San Miguel, striking down Indians with their cutlasses. The poor Indians took refuge in the church, where they were slain like cattle in a slaughterhouse. They plundered the paltry ornaments of the church, spilling the holy oils on the ground. The Fathers at first wanted to carry out the Blessed Sacrament in their hands to quell these wild animals with its presence. And had they not thought better of it, we would have seen these accursed men perpetrate a terribly scandalous act.[97] Not only here but in other reductions as well, the Fathers asked me if we might reverently take out the sacramental Lord and hold it at the church door to stop these men. I said, "Do you want these heretics to seize the most holy Sacrament before our eyes, throw it to the ground, trample on it, and burn it?" Accordingly, we had to consume the Blessed Sacrament, exiling it from the altar where it had been venerated by people who but yesterday had been pagans and unbelievers. They entered the room of one of the Fathers, anticipating a great treasure. They found two ragged shirts and a worn old cotton cassock. Far from being edified by the poverty of these apostolic men, they made the clothes into banners and displayed them to the Indians, saying: "Look what poor wretches you have in your lands. They have nothing to eat in their own country, and come to yours to defraud you with their ruses. Look at the shirts they wear. We, on the other hand, wear fine clothes and have many things to give you. It is wrong for you to have these poor wretches in your land, and so we have come to drive them out of this whole territory. This land belongs to us, not to the Spanish king." As one of them made this speech the others went on killing.

An Indian fled from one of the marauders trying to kill him and sought refuge with Father Simón. The marauder shot him to death in the Father's arms, without confession, endangering the Father's life as well, in disregard of his venerable gray hairs. He chided the man, promising him retribution in hell. "I will be saved in spite of God," the malefactor answered; "all you have to do to be saved is believe." He now knows by experience how false his doctrine is: he was killed by three gunshots, without confession. Moreover, his body vanished after his soul. It could not be found in the grave where, in uncertainty whether he deserved it, he was buried.

I must not overlook a droll maneuver of theirs during these attacks and invasions. They bring with them wolves in sheep's clothing, great hypocrites, whose job is as follows. While the others are robbing and plundering the churches, tying up Indians, killing and hacking children to pieces, these men go up to the Fathers, displaying large rosaries around their necks. They ask for confession, talk about prayer and recollection, inquire if the sacraments are administered in the parish there, and speak of what a great thing it is to serve God, hastily telling their rosary beads as they engage in this talk.[98]

These men rounded up a vast number of people from our own villages, as well as pagans from other places with whom we had been parleying to bring them into the reductions. They gave them the plague, and many persons died without baptism, many Christians without confession. We attempted to go to baptize and confess them. I volunteered, but they refused to let me. We learned that they were about to leave and that they intended to burn the sick and disabled. I sent Father Cristóbal de Mendoza to beg them to let us baptize these people first, or else leave them alive. With their usual duplicity, they answered that they would let us know. But as they left the location—a large enclosure bigger than the square here in Madrid—they fired the huts—all of them of straw—and with bestial inhumanity burned great numbers of people.

Fathers Simón Masseta and Justo Mansilla[99] followed these bandits in the company of their parishioners, every single one of whom had been carried off. The Fathers took along five Indians who carried their two sleeping hammocks, but with their usual brutality they took these men away from them, forcing the Fathers to carry the hammocks on their own backs. The latter performed many works of mercy on the road. They would stay behind at the resting places and encampments to find sick people to baptize and confess, fulfilling the work of apostolic men. The dead who were left by the wayside they were unable to bury. After traveling nearly three hundred leagues, they reached the town of São Paulo. They sought justice in various quarters, but it is a fiction to speak of justice. The authorities did nothing but cozen them. The Fathers despaired of accomplishing anything, and turned back on the same road. The people whistled and mocked at them, the very authorities of São Paulo came out against them along with the inhabitants, calling them dogs, heretics, infamous, foolhardy to return to their country. Not content with words, they laid violent hands on Father Simón Masseta, showing no respect for his age or gray hair. The people shouted, "Seize these dogs!" As the two Jesuits sought refuge in a college of the Society there, some secular officials went ahead of them and blocked the doors, with extraordinary din and shouting. Under orders from the magistrates (there called the *camara*), they arrested them and took them to the house of a layperson where they were confined by guards who displayed conspicuous contempt for the dignity of their priesthood. There the Fathers awaited further and worse affronts for the sake of God and their sheep. There are Fathers on the São Paulo coast who profess that they never experienced disrespect from the Dutch, but instead much courtesy and consideration, sometimes even hospitality, even though they are heretics and enemies of the Society.

CHAPTER 36

More on the invasion from São Paulo

THE INHABITANTS of São Paulo grew more and more unrestrained, there being no one to check them. From 1628 up to the present day they have never ceased warring on Christians, taking them prisoner and selling them. They carried out a belligerent invasion of the reduction of San Francisco Javier, a populous town where the Blessed Sacrament had long been present. The townspeople were well informed about the cruelty of these brigands, and many fled into the woods with their wives and children. They would come out to search for food in their own fields; but there they would run into their enemies, who captured and tortured them until they told where they had left the rest of their people. These they then tracked down and brought into their palisade. On such occasions there was no offering resistance, for they would hack off a head with a saber or split a person down the middle to terrorize the rest. Uncertain whether we ought to take the Blessed Sacrament out in our hands to head off these enemies of the human race, we thought it wiser to consume it instead.

With the few people that were with us, we put up a small palisade so they would not catch us unawares. At one in the afternoon, with a barbarous commotion, they entered our yard through a small grove. We went out at the noise and brought the people inside the dwellings for protection. While the others were seizing everything in sight, one of the religious hypocrites I described earlier began a prolonged discussion with a Father about highly spiritual topics—confession and the different kinds and degrees of prayer. He wore his scapular, a form of armor widely used in those territories. It falls like a dalmatic to the feet; it is made of quilted cotton cloth and is quite strong. He had his musket on his shoulder, his sword buckled on, and a long rosary in his hands which he pretended to pray, counting the beads with great speed. As we learned later, he was doubtless tallying the captives to make sure he got his due share, a regular source of severe trouble among them. On this occasion, thanks to the diligence of the Fathers, they took few captives. One of the men seized a woman by the hair. She defended herself like a man, even encumbered by a six-month-old child in her arms. Failing to subdue her, the villain snatched the child from her breast and carried it off. The child was not yet able to eat, and one of the Fathers went to ask for it so that it would not starve to death. The man who had it refused to give it up, demanding the mother as a prisoner. She lamented the suffering of her little son. Long indeed was the time the Father spent trying to soften the brutal heart of that tiger.

One of them came out of the palisade and calmly set fire to a straw house next to the church. As soon as it began to burn, he began shouting, "Be my witnesses that the Fathers are arsonists!" We immediately went to extinguish the fire so we could save the church.

We sent all the people who escaped from there with us to Loreto and San Ignacio, the only two of the thirteen towns that remained.

CHAPTER 37

How the men from São Paulo destroyed a Spanish town and numerous villages of Indians who served them

AFTER BATTENING on the Indians, these wolves undertook the destruction of the Spaniards. Villa Rica had a hundred and thirty men. Within its jurisdiction were nine villages of Indians whose service they employed. The men from São Paulo progressively devastated the Indian settlements. Many of their inhabitants fled to the town. They then laid siege to the town itself. The Spaniards retreated into a large enclosure surrounded by a mud wall, and there put up their defense. However, they were perishing from hunger, since the raiders from São Paulo controlled the fields and prevented them from getting any food. Many of the Indians inside the fort were secretly going over to the enemy just to get food and to be on the winning side. Things came to a pass where the Spaniards themselves discussed surrendering to the enemy. To their good fortune, the bishop,[100] oblivious of the plight of his sheep, came to visit them. Seeing the ravages produced by these wolves, he arrayed himself in his pontifical garb, his accompanying clerics similarly donning their priestly vestments. Thus panoplied, they processed out towards the men. Upon recognizing the bishop, they withdrew some distance without waiting to talk to him. This afforded the people penned up inside a breathing space and a chance to prepare their escape. They fitted out their boats and transferred themselves more than seventy leagues away, descending to the town of Maracayú, the place where, as already mentioned, the herb is grown. The enemies of God remained as masters of the country. One of the townsmen of Villa Rica had made an agreement with the enemy to move with his wife and household to São Paulo. He put his plan into execution, and ascended the Paraná. He was just reaching the end of his journey when he was ambushed by Indians belonging to São Paulo. With their customary savagery, they shot him dead with arrows and took off his wife and belongings.

CHAPTER 38

Exit of the Indians of Loreto and San Ignacio in flight from the enemy

FATHER FRANCISCO Vázquez Trujillo,[101] then provincial superior, had visited the entire territory during this time. He was present at the destruction of San Javier. Grasping the situation clearly, he ordered us to arrange things in great secrecy, so that when it became necessary to move because of the common enemy we could do so safely and calmly. He undertook to get the royal audiencia in Chuquisaca to approve this.

The watch that we constantly maintained advised us that the enemy were on their way. At this the Indians determined to move—to abandon their lands in order to preserve their lives and their freedom. This move was facilitated by an official request from the authorities in the city of Guairá, who asked us to move the people because their own forces were too slight to help us against such an aggressive enemy. The request was utterly disingenuous and deceitful. The Spaniards planned to intercept us on the road and, like the men from São Paulo, steal our sheep and divide them among themselves. Subsequent events showed this, although their plan failed. The move was also expedited by the fact that the Indians had already provided themselves with canoes, since their exit would have to be made down the Paraná.

It was an amazing sight, the entire shore filled with Indians busily building rafts—these were made by joining two canoes or two large logs dug out like boats, and placing on top a well-roofed cabin that gave good protection from rain and sun. The people were all busily carrying down to the shore their furnishings, stores, livestock, and birds. The noise of tools, the haste and confusion, all made clear that the day of doom was near. Who could think otherwise when they saw us six or seven priests consuming the Blessed Sacrament, taking down the religious pictures, consuming the oils, and gathering up the vestments; likewise disinterring the buried bodies of the three outstanding missioners so that, having been the companions of our travails, they might share this final one with us and not be abandoned in the wilderness; and leaving behind our lovely, beautifully decorated churches, which we closed up tight to keep them from becoming the lairs of beasts? The spectacle was so horrendous and calamitous that heaven manifested its sorrow—not by means of comets but on earth by means of a painting, two yards high, in one of the Paraná reductions that lay more than a hundred leagues from those we were abandoning and was the place where we planned to end our journey. At the same time as we were abandoning the churches, this picture sweated drops so large and abundant that two of the Fathers were unable to soak up the sweat with cotton. They wondered at this amazing occurrence and feared some grave calamity, ignorant of the one that was befalling us. We received word of this occurrence at the worst moment of our migration, and I confess that it gave me great consolation and joy to see the Virgin so visibly showing herself the companion of our hardships and agonies. These were so acute (I speak only of my own—those of my companions were grievous indeed) that without exaggeration there were three times when I felt that for sheer grief and anxiety my soul was taking leave of me. However, taking refuge in prayer, I felt safe from death.

The same grief was experienced by two angels. Tears like large pearls were seen falling from their eyes, to show how heaven and the seven angel princes (to whom, as mentioned above, I had dedicated the great reduction of Tayaoba) mourned at seeing their reduction emptied of its people; this was officially verified by the bishop of Paraguay.

In very short order seven hundred rafts were constructed, besides the numerous individual canoes. On them embarked more than twelve thousand souls, sole survivors of this raging deluge. We had gone only two days downstream when some Indians who had delayed their departure caught up with us. From them we learned of our terrible enemies' rage at finding themselves cheated. Had they hurried a little faster, they would certainly have trapped us and taken a great catch. They arrived at the empty town. They assaulted the church doors. Meeting with resistance in getting them open (for they were solidly barred up), they smashed them to bits. Their outrageous hands might have been stayed at least by the doors' beautiful workmanship, if not by the realization that these were churches where God had for so many years been worshiped. Trooping boisterously into the churches, they assailed the altarpieces, knocking out their columns and throwing them to the ground, carrying them off in pieces for their cooking fires. They themselves confessed to certain religious that after committing this act of barbarism their flesh quaked at their own temerity. They took up their lodging in the churches and in our cells. The latter, which had never seen a woman before, they filled with Indian women.

I must not fail to mention a searching investigation of our lives which they themselves acknowledged they made. To suborn witnesses, they took as concubines Indian women whom they had stolen from our reductions. To these they gave delicacies and gifts to get them to report on our life and habits, in their efforts to dig up something. They also took great pains with the men and with the Indians most closely associated with us, conducting a rigorous investigation into our lives by means of persistent questioning. And what did they find? With shame and confusion they acknowledged their act of presumption. Indeed, they might have been edified by what the witnesses told them.

What could the people tell them? They told how freely we reprehended every vice, especially impurity. What could they tell them? That never, by day or night, had a woman entered our cells—that once when a pair of women came at midnight into the cell of a Father who was sleeping alone in the reduction, with the lustful intention of seducing him to evil, he was warned by his guardian angel in a dream of the deadly poison being prepared for him by impurity; arising aghast, he shouted to some Indians sleeping in another room and berated them for their carelessness, even though he could not see who was entering the enclosure. "Go look for them," he ordered; "two people have gotten in." The two women, who at the noise had hidden in the corner of a room, were discovered. They were sent away and, deeply contrite, went to confession the following day. What could the people tell them? That when solicited by women—even in sacred places—they brought them to deep penitence, a good confession, and the resolve to lead a good life henceforth, as indeed they did. They could tell them that, as we have mentioned, they had been offered women for household services but had explained to the pagan Indians the purity and circumspection practiced by priests and sent the women away. That they had maintained themselves for years without seeing bread, wine, salt, or meat except rarely. That they had spent long hours at night in prayer—the effects of which are better left unwritten here, along with other matters regarding the apostolic religious in that province, my intention being to mention only what pertains to the Indians. That the result of their preaching and life was the removal of multitudes of concubines, the abandonment of their paganism by countless pagans who entered the fold of the Church. The ledgers alone that we preserved (others were burned by the oppressor) showed above twenty-two thousand souls inscribed in the baptismal roll. This is what their suborned witnesses told them.

Let us now return to our fleet of rafts. It was traveling in apparent safety from the enemies it had left behind when we got word that the Spaniards living in Guairá were waiting for us at the narrow, dangerous stretch made by the famous waterfalls of the Paraná. They had built a stockade fort on the shore there to block us and take the people prisoner. Their plan was that as the boats passed they would cut down from within the fort the rowers and others who could put up a defense. With the host thus weakened, they would sally forth to the capture. I heard this report. Wondering whether it was correct, I left the people and went ahead in a light craft. I found it was true. Heedless of betrayal, I entered the palisade and protested, presenting my arguments. They stopped their ears to me and drew their swords. Five of them held their blades to my breast and tried to take me prisoner. I escaped through their midst thanks to an overgarment I was wearing.

I returned to my companions for consultation. All were in distress and grief at seeing fortune both dog their heels and block their advance. From every direction people were trying to seize them. We decided that two Fathers would go back and demand that these men give us free passage, reminding them that they themselves had admitted in their official request that they were not strong enough to help us, and telling them that the São Paulo raiders would drive them from their own lands—as they soon after did to them and to the town of Jerez, carrying off many of the inhabitants from both places, including a secular priest. The two envoy Fathers had no success. We decided then to send a further pair as a third warning, to fulfill the demands of justice. I and another religious went. I begged them to let us by, but found them even more steeled to resist. We were acutely fearful that the men from São Paulo in the abandoned towns to our rear might come dashing downstream in pursuit of us. They and the others here seemed to us two hungry wolf packs amid a flock of harmless sheep. Accordingly, where strength failed I resorted to bluff. I indicated that we were determined to get through in spite of them. I went up to a man who was there with his wife and warned him to get her away so that a woman would not be listed among the day's dead. We thereupon returned to decide our course of action.

Fazed by what they had heard, the Spaniards had second thoughts about their brutal plan. They no longer felt secure in their fort; they imagined themselves already destroyed. And when conscience tightens the cords, the truth becomes quite clear. They decided their action was very wrong and sent messengers asking us to set a time and give them safe passage out of their palisade. This was very humanely and courteously granted them. They left— more discomfited, in my opinion, at their own treacherous attempt than at seeing the prey they were so confident of slip through their fingers. We thereupon occupied the position.

At this point we were forced to abandon our canoes. The river here becomes unnavigable, the water plunging downward and creating whirlpools that make one's eyes flinch in terror. We made the experiment anyway of sending three hundred canoes over these cliffs of water to see if any could get through unharmed. Otherwise we would be forced to make a detour of twenty-five leagues overland before returning to our course on the river. However, the force of the water, the enormous drop, and the violence with which it dashed the boats against the rugged reefs below reduced them to splinters. Our plan on this journey had been to descend this river to get to the settlements which the Society had made along it.

Once past through this obstacle, we undertook to pursue our journey overland. Men, women, and children—every living creature—readied their burdens, loading their possessions and food onto their backs. The number of people was swollen by those brought down at this time by Father Pedro de Espinosa[102] from the farthest reductions of Tayaoba. Tayaoba himself was dead, having received the sacraments and given warranties of his eternal salvation.

Father Provincial had left me orders that, if circumstances allowed, I should either proceed myself or send Fathers to the province of the Itatíns over on the Paraguay river towards Peru. I accordingly dispatched Fathers Diego Rancioner,[103] Nicolás Hersacio,[104] and Mansilla, zealous missionaries. The first two of these gave their lives—if not through the tyrant's sword that was never far from their desires, then through the severity of their immense labors, a more drawn-out martyrdom about which I shall speak later. They took with them bells, pictures, and other objects too heavy for transportation overland.

When the time came for the exit of this nation of Israel, in flight like Jacob from a barbarous people, they sat on the banks of the river and recalled with emotion their present hardships, anxiety, and poverty, as they found themselves driven in flight from their own lands by persons who in justice should have been their protectors. With emotion they recalled their houses, and above all the house of God where for so many years they had worshiped, humbly served, and received him into their souls in the life-giving Sacrament. They still had the harps and musical instruments which they had used to make music to God in their homeland on festival days, their devotion swelling amid sweet motets and their prolonged sessions in church seeming short as they listened to the sound of their well-tuned instruments. Now stringless, broken, and serving but to bring back sad memories, these were abandoned among the crags of that rugged trail.

We completed our overland journey in eight days and returned once more to the river, now smoother and more navigable. We thought this would be the end of our troubles, for we fully expected to find there boats and fresh supplies of food, which would in fact have been supplied by the Fathers who had reductions a good distance from there if the news of our migration had not been too late in reaching them; instead, this proved the beginning of another ordeal.

CHAPTER 39

Continuation of the same

HUNGER, DISEASE, and divergence of opinion produced an enormous confusion. How could there help being hunger, with an immense crowd of children and so many people who could bring only a limited quantity of food for the trip, their only means of transport being their own backs and shoulders? How could there help being disease with people in such dire need that the very thought of their food running out bred hunger and as a result disease? They did what they could in these conditions. Some, with immense effort, built new canoes. Some cleared part of the forest for planting and eventually harvesting food, so that we could continue on our course. Others launched out onto the water upon rafts of cane (here reaching the thickness of a thigh and a length of fifty feet), trusting more to their skill in swimming than to the safety of boats.

One of these rafts, loaded with people, had hardly started on its way when it capsized and threw everybody off. Everyone swam free except for one woman with twin children at her breast, who began going under within sight of two of us Fathers standing there. My companion shouted to the Indians to jump in and get her. There are fishes in the river there that the natives call great serpents. We have seen them swallow men whole and throw them up again whole, but with their bones shattered as if crushed by rocks. Terror of these deservedly feared animals for a long time held the Indians back. They watched Argus-eyed for any sign of where the woman and her children were being swept by the water. Many believed they had already been devoured by these creatures. I confess that intense grief overwhelmed me. Tears streaming from my eyes, I turned to heaven and placed the blame for these woes on my own faults. Looking toward God, who to a living faith is vividly present, I said: "Lord, can it be that you brought this people forth from their own country for this—to break my eyes at this sight after breaking my heart with their sufferings? They may end up claiming they would have been better off in slavery but still alive than dead in these fishes' maws." I ran toward the spot where I estimated she would be. The top of her head emerged. They plunged in to get her, grabbed her firmly by the hair, and dragged her out. The time it took to drag her out would alone have sufficed to drown her. She came on shore amid general rejoicing. My companion and

I arrived on the scene, no less amazed over the two little children: they started laughing uproariously as if they had been through some merry game, not a dire ordeal. The good Indian woman told us of the trial she had undergone regarding her two children. Her longing to live inclined her to abandon one child to the fishes and use her skill at swimming to save the other. However, her mother's love surmounted the peril and was rewarded with the rescue of both her twins.

A raft of two fine canoes carrying some fifty persons ventured out. I gave them two Indians who knew the river, advising them that when they came to dangerous stretches they should take to land to avoid them. Trusting their boat, they plunged into a great whirlpool that sucked the raft down with all on board. Resorting to their arms and skill at swimming, they escaped with their lives. Flung in different directions by the raging water, each one bewailed his companions, thinking them drowned, until after two days they reassembled to recount their misfortunes. Eleven blessed infants had drowned, and were thus spared seeing the troubles that lay ahead. After these two experiences we took extreme care with the boats, and saw no more disasters on the river. When they learned of our migration, the Fathers came to our assistance, dispatching canoes that arrived empty and went back laden with people.

They selected a pair of sites, seemingly prepared for them by heaven, on a fine navigable stream that flowed into the great Paraná. There they built some low straw huts. In the area, at a distance of three leagues, are two of our oldest reductions. These helped out with food in these dire straits. But who had the power to feed this host of people over a long period of time, here in a wilderness where they could find nothing—who else but the Lord who with five loaves had fed another multitude in the desert? We sold our little books, our cassocks and capes, our vestments, chalices, and church furnishings, sending them to the city of Asunción to obtain seed for sowing, with which our college there and its rector, Father Diego Alfaro,[105] liberally provided us.

With the generous permission of an honorable gentleman, Commander Manuel Cabral, a citizen of the town of Corrientes and owner of a great herd of cattle on the broad plains there from which over forty thousand head have been taken over the last two years, Father Pedro de Espinosa and I went in with skilled men and horses and brought out quite a fair number of beefs. Initially, twelve to fourteen cows were slaughtered daily in each of the two reductions, Loreto and San Ignacio. This provided each person with a portion so small that it just sufficed to keep life going and postpone death. They ate old leather; they ate the horses' ropes and hobbles; at night they tore the cowhide thongs off the stockade fence at our house. Toads, snakes, any vermin they could lay eyes on, did not escape their mouths.

Disease, never slow to come on such occasions, struck. The Fathers labored tirelessly to treat both souls and bodies, toiling day and night. Some two thousand persons, adults and infants, rendered their souls to heaven, those capable of it receiving all the sacraments. While the memory of the abundance they had once enjoyed in their own lands brought their present misery vividly before them, they died happy, repeating, "Better that the body die than that the soul's faith be imperiled among those godless men from São Paulo." This was their universal consolation.

The little folk who had no one to look after them, either because of their parents' incapacity or, as was often the case, because they were orphaned, were afforded every care, being given portions of cooked food in their little dishes. As they took it back to their houses there would be chaos. They would grab at each other's food, and there would be weeping and confusion. A child trying to avoid this threat would run into another child and spill his food. Others would have their own food stolen while they were trying to grab someone else's. The problem was solved by having a Father there who made them eat in his presence.

We then turned our attention to the raising of food. We gave them seed; unmindful of the future harvest, they would eat it up. Others would plant the seeds one day only to discover on the morrow that they had been removed from the holes overnight. This we considered an even worse plague, affecting as it did the multiplication of food. After pondering the problem, we condemned the delinquents to the stocks for the whole time until the crops grew and were out of danger. With this measure their labors were successful.

God is no less provident in our own times than in olden days, and the resources of his power did not end with the manna that he gave at that time. He came to this poor people's help with a medicine against both disease and hunger. In the stream alongside the settlement they found a plant that we call sea-parsley, and they *ygau*. When full-grown it is half a yard long. It roots right on the rocks, where it grows without leaving the water. It is naturally salty, tasty, and produces good blood. Like a shrub, it maintains its peak for a limited time. Everyone went out to collect it; heedless of the morrow, they took all that they found. I confess my own lack of trust for several days as I watched them greedily strip the rocks with no prospect of finding anything on the following day. But he who is succor of the afflicted daily came to their aid with what they needed—so much so that, my pusillanimity overcome, I encouraged them to take advantage of the generosity of him who does not forget even a base little worm. Boiled with meat, this plant served as a remedy against the dysentery that was violently carrying them off. Its use brought a change in the mark of death and pallor of countenance they all bore. During this difficult time about thirteen thousand head of cattle were consumed, some of them purchased and others donated as alms. Two thousand pesos were spent on cotton, wool, and linen to clothe their nakedness, and on seed for food and planting, apart from a substantial alms that Father Diego de Boroa, today provincial, brought and distributed with his own hand.

This hardship was a great trial. I leave to the reader's imagination what my poor pen has left unmentioned. The severe summer ended and spring returned.[106] They set to work manfully. Each one opened three or four clearings. The earth began to produce its fruits, gratefully returning a teeming harvest. They filled their cribs with maize. There was an excellent crop of manioca, the common bread. Vegetables of every kind grew in abundance. We purchased a bit of livestock—pigs, ducks, chickens, and pigeons—distributing them all to the leading Indians. After this deluge, these animals filled the land in extraordinary abundance, one which they still enjoy and with remarkable generosity share with the needy in other towns. Since cotton does poorly there because of the severe frost which sometimes kills it, I took the step of buying them eighteen hundred sheep so that they could make their clothes with wool and cotton. They did not all turn out successfully, however. At the time when wild Indians killed Father Pedro de Espinosa, they also stole part of the sheep.

We all attributed this abundance to the devotion that started up of everyone's hearing Mass daily. A stimulation for this devotion were several examples related by writers on the subject. Spacious, fine-looking, easily accessible churches were built. Musical instruments were brought back—bassoons, cornets, violins, harps, zithers, guitars, and spinets. Mass was celebrated to their sound, with figured choral music by two or three choirs. In the churches we placed the Blessed Sacrament, whose feast of Corpus Christi is celebrated in poverty but with devotion and elegance. The people set up their altars, and erect arches on which they hang birds of the air, beasts of the wood, and fish of the water. In the places where the priest is to walk with the Blessed Sacrament they lay rush mats so that he will not tread the soil. They strew on the streets fruits of their harvest (in lieu of the coins scattered at triumphs by the mighty) to be walked on by the priest; these are collected later and kept for planting. In each reduction some eight hundred to a thousand persons receive Communion four times a year, excellently prepared by confession and cleansing of their souls.

CHAPTER 40

Some edifying incidents

I WOULD CONSIDERABLY digress were I to give in detail the edifying incidents that occurred during this difficult period, which lasted in its severity for three years. I will mention a few. In the reduction where we burned the devil's oracle of dead bones as recounted above, there was a living Indian who in his life and misshapen body quite resembled the devil. His name was Zaguacari, which means "handsome little fellow." His appearance belied his name, however. He was quite short; his head was fixed to his shoulders in such a way that to turn his face he had to turn his whole body; his fingers and toes were curved downwards much like those of birds; his shins were all that could be seen of his legs; his hands and feet had little or no strength. Realizing that he could not feed himself by the labor of his hands, he attempted to make his way by his intelligence and exceptional eloquence—he possessed a natural rhetoric that kept his hearers spellbound. And even though his physique should have brought him the contempt of others, his unusual freakishness engendered awe and amazement in everyone. He found a means to success: by dint of hoaxes and lies he acquired the prestige of a magician.

He later rose so high that he was thought to be God. He pretended to bestow rain, good weather, and crops. If the latter turned out badly, he was quite able to lie his way out by claiming he had caused this himself because of the people's provocation in not providing for his needs. He was so clever that he hoodwinked not only the Indians in the region but even those living far away. Even some in service to the Spanish, and longstanding Christians, who lived many leagues off, would come as if on pilgrimage to see him. The cunning fellow was very chary about appearing in public, and this heightened people's eagerness to see him. We heard about him and learned that he had his dwelling upon a very high hill and that when he died they planned to build him a temple like those already mentioned. We sent him an invitation, ostensibly to honor him. He held back. The people in the town said that if we took him away from them we would be taking away their food, since as God he provided for them abundantly. He eventually did come to visit us. We treated him well and urged him not to hesitate about coming to see us often.

Christmas arrived, and neighboring Indians thronged into the town. I decided this was a perfect occasion to take advantage of the festivities in order to dethrone this devil and pernicious idol. Sending for him and explaining what a great festival day it was, I said that he ought to delight us in his own person by playing a game common among the Christians: his eyes would be covered, and if he caught anybody while blindfolded in this way, he would be given a fine prize. He offered some difficulty but, overcome by his desire for the prize, let himself be blindfolded. We had prepared beforehand some lads who had very Christian parents to start the game off. A number of people from the reduction and from outside gathered at our house for the sport. The merriment began and the youths started teasing him, mimicking his clumsy walk, tugging at his clothes, knocking and pushing him until he was thrown to the ground. The poor fellow, determined to win the prize, kept on trying to seize somebody. The bystanders were startled to see their god thus put to scorn. Amid their astonishment, the town boys cheered him with loud shouts and laughter; but then, as they shed their earlier awe and fear of the freak, they began furiously running into him and leaving him in such a state that out of compassion I rescued him from their hands.

They played this same game with him on other occasions, the little children enjoying it so much that they began seeking him out for their amusement. We took him into our house and put him to sweeping the kitchen, courtyard, and church vestibule, to making baskets, and to attending catechism. Applying his excellent mind to the truth, he abandoned his lies and learned quite well what was needed for baptism. We gave him the name of Juan, and he attended Mass in the church daily. Distinguished people came from great distances to see him; in place of his earlier lies he now proclaimed truths to them, revealing his former charlatanry and hoaxes. In this way he did much good.

During the above-mentioned migration and turmoil he always followed us. In the transferred reduction of Loreto we always kept him in our house, where he comported himself as a Christian and even as a preacher of Christ. There he fell ill. I treated him in the house with the care demanded by charity, and he received all the sacraments with great devotion. The night he died he sent for me and said: "Father mine—for you have really been the father of my soul—I owe you a great deal. I depart, trusting in God that I will go to heaven, with gratitude to you for what you did to bring me down and keep me from being destroyed by my own foolishness. I die happy because, thanks be to God, I have received all the sacraments and feel nothing in my soul to cause me concern. The only things that pain me are my former follies, but I have confidence in God that he will give me the pardon which his mercy always bestows. Now I want to restore to you some-thing that does not belong to me; I forgot to do so earlier." He took from his breast a small purse and removed a bit of chain and a needle. Handing them to me, he said: "This is not mine. I found it near your cell and kept it until now." I must confess that I felt confusion and envy at seeing a soul, yesterday so stained, today so pure and clean that his conscience was pricked by a single pin. I aided him with advice for his departure. Making fervent acts, he closed his eyes on the things of this world with warranties that he opened them upon those of heaven.

I could recount many such deaths and changes to a better life, but brevity requires me to pass over them. I mention only a conviction that is widely held in those territories: that the number of persons who are saved is very high because they hold tenaciously to the faith and perform works with perseverance.

By now, four years of displacement, hunger, and turmoil were behind us. We decided it was time no longer just to recover the calm essential for Christian living but to advance the people in virtue. We therefore undertook to establish a sodality of our Lady.[107] We selected only twelve persons as members, those most advanced in virtue. It was launched with great musical festivities and a heavily attended Mass and sermon. On that day the sodality members received Communion, and this provoked considerable holy rivalry throughout the reduction. Small numbers of additional persons have gradually been selected for admission, and they have been the leaven for great growth in virtue. They diligently attend their meetings; they have a talk every Sunday evening and occasional conferences on how to grow in virtue, presided over by one of the Fathers; they receive Communion more frequently than the rest of the town. When the confessor sees no serious sins in their confession and inquires whether they have fallen into any, they reply that they are now members of the sodality and that it would ill beseem such persons to commit sin. This holds not only for members but also for candidates: they reply that it would be wrong, as candidates for the sodality of so pure a Lady, to foul their own souls by sins. In general, devotion to the Blessed Virgin has grown mightily, not only among adults but also among little boys and girls; they commonly call her "our Mother." I could recount a great many instances in confirmation of this holy devotion of theirs, but will pass them over for brevity's sake and because the examples I am about to give adequately make my point.

One of the many carried off by the raiders from São Paulo was an Indian girl. In Brazil she married, and then gave free rein to her inclinations. No one should be surprised that their lack of instruction produces such disorders. She heard that our faithful were going to Communion and leading Christian lives in the reductions which we had at the time in Guairá. She was fired with a desire to enjoy such a life, and besought her husband to get her out of the brutish life they were leading. They set off through dense forests, flying from the cruel treatment which their master would wreak on them if he pursued and caught them. On their wanderings they suffered many hardships from lack of food, from the journey, and from the burden of the two children they brought with them. The wife became very gaunt, feeble, and nearly overcome with exhaustion. She reached the point where she felt she could go no farther but would leave her body buried on the spot. She knelt down and with devout tears begged our Lady for strength to reach her own town of Loreto, where she promised to serve her. She was evidently heard, as the sequel demonstrated. Upon finishing her prayer she felt like another woman, strong and energetic. They thus continued their journey and, after walking more than three hundred leagues, reached the longed-for town. There Father Francisco Díaz, learning of their peregrination, got them well settled and defended her from a bandit who asserted that, as unclaimed property, they belonged to him.

She considered herself already in glory, and earnestly devoted herself to the service of the Blessed Virgin. She heard Mass daily and straightway requested Communion, the hunger for which had drawn her there. She was put off until she had been well instructed in the faith, about which she had heard not a thing—even the best parish priests baptizing in this way. She lived in the reduction for several years, confessing frequently and receiving Communion four times a year. Her husband died, and she urged the Fathers to marry her daughter so she would continue to live a pure life with a husband and not defile her chastity before marriage. Another child, a boy, she raised with great care, teaching him the fear of the Lord. During our migration from these towns this good woman was of considerable help. From her own experience she advised everyone to forfeit their lives rather than to fall into the hands of the marauders from São Paulo, whose way of life was that of animals.

She suffered much during the move, and we assisted her with food and clothing. Her son deserted her in order to escape the hardships. The good mother mourned his absence for the sole reason that she feared he would go to ruin and defile his soul with sins. Demonstrating her love for him, she told me one day, "I would rather see my son dead here from want and hunger than someplace else where he will offend God." The mother's ceaseless prayers brought the young man back. She had already been received into the sodality when she sent me word that she was ill. I visited her, heard her confession, and found nothing to absolve. I asked her if she had gone to Communion for the jubilee three days before. She said no and at the same time gave the reason. The catechism examiners—those communicating are always examined on the catechism lest failure to repeat it lead them to forget it—had disqualified her because she had gotten confused and made four mistakes. Such is the strictness with which the Indian men examine the men and the women the women; in this way they know the Christian mysteries well and observe them better.

I decided she was acting sick in order to receive Communion on the grounds of illness, a pious fraud that has often been practiced on us. I asked her if she wished to receive Communion. She replied that she thought that her illness was brought on by her pain at seeing her friends worthy to receive the Lord whereas she was rejected for her sins. I told her to have herself brought to the church in a hammock as they do for the sick. Deeply consoled at hearing me generously offer her Communion, she made the following reply (and let it put some to shame): "Father, I will use a staff and go on my own feet to receive my Lord and my God." I confess that this touched me and moved me to considerable devotion. She received Communion and returned to her bed. A few days later, having received all the sacraments and making acts of fervor, she concluded her life.

Women came to wrap her in her shroud, and three young men from the sodality came to wake her through the night (an office entrusted only to members of the sodality). Midnight came, when they noticed that the deceased woman gave signs of life, moving and struggling to get free of her shroud. They approached, released her, and found her alive. The first thing she said was, "Call the Father." They told her that I was in another town nearby. "I am sorry that the Father is away," she said, "for I had much to tell him for his consolation. Call Father Juan Agustín;[108] I will tell him." While they were sending for the Father, she asked one of the men who were waking her for a rosary and little metal Christ he had around his neck. She took it with great devotion and reverence and began kissing it and pressing it tightly to her heart. Word ran through the town that Isabel had risen from the dead, and since her good life had given her a good name, many people came to her house. She addressed the members of the sodality in this fashion:

"My children who belong to the sodality of our holy Mother and Lady, it is for your sake that I have returned to my body. I actually died, and I am going to live now for but five days more, since I come only to give you good news on the part of our Mother and Lady, the Blessed Virgin. She is very happy with this sodality and very pleased with those who live in it. She tells you to carry it forward. And I beg you for my own part to keep well before your minds your duty to pursue virtue, give good example, love one another, and put into practice the counsels which the Fathers give you."

Father Juan Agustín arrived, and she went on:

"As soon as I passed from this life I was taken to hell. There I saw a terrible fire that burns without giving light; it is fearsome. In it I saw some who died and had lived in our company, persons we all knew. They suffered many torments. Then I was taken to heaven, where I saw our Mother, so beautiful, so shining, so lovely, so revered and served by all the blessed. In her company were countless beautiful and shining saints. Everything here is trash, filth, and ugliness; everything there is loveliness, beauty, and wealth. I saw the dead members of our sodality, brightly shining and robed in glory. When they saw me they gave me a thousand congratulations, chiefly for being a member of the sodality. They send you great messages, especially that you should carry forward this sodality and be true Christians."

The good woman progressively sent for everyone in the town, men and women, exhorting them to have love and charity, to go to Mass, to do good works, to give whatever alms they could to the poor, to fulfill the commandments of God. She spoke wonderfully to them about the ugliness of sin, the beauty of virtue, the horror of hell, the fearsomeness of the judgment and the strict accounting exacted by God, and the beauty of heavenly glory. Though she sent for everybody else, she did not call her son, apparently to punish him for his negligence in not requesting admission to the sodality. Begged to summon him, she refused to do so until the last day. Then she sent for him and said, "I did not want to see you because you do not belong to the sodality. See that you immediately ask the Fathers to receive you. Never become separated from them; serve and love them always; they are our true fathers. Avoid offending God so that you will deserve to go and enjoy the blessedness yonder."

All this he did quite well. He immediately urged us to receive him, and he serves the Fathers with his person and lives like a religious. Among the women who came to see the good woman, there arrived one whom she told to get out. At the time we did not know why, for she seemed to be living a good life. It came out that she was living badly. Brought to her senses by this rebuff, she made a good confession, changed her way of living, and is today a splendid example.

When this good woman had fulfilled her mission, and the five days she said she had to live were over, she took her leave amid the copious tears of all and fell asleep quite peacefully and calmly in the Lord. She continued clasping the rosary and crucifix so tightly that after death they could not get them away from her even with great effort. The effects that she left behind her were marvelous. Out of a commendable desire to imitate her, not a person in the town failed to go to confession. Her memory is still green today.

Eight or nine months after her burial, when someone else who had died was being interred, they brought up her body. The flesh was intact, supple, and free of ill odor. We placed her in a more fitting location. A religious heard of this case and with great devotion begged me to send him the rosary. The Father received it and valued it highly. In his reduction many children were perishing from disease; none survived. An Indian reported to him with deep anguish that his only son was dying. Feeling compassion and unable to do anything else for him, the Father gave him the rosary, without saying whose it had been, for him to place upon the child. A short while later the father returned to tell him that his son was now healthy and well.

CHAPTER 41

A similar case

A SIMILAR incident occurred in this same reduction. Among the little girls there was one who was raised in the catechetical school, which she attended regularly. At eighteen we married her to a young man who had been raised in our own house. I can report of both that they never lost their baptismal grace. The lad died shortly afterwards—with excellent warranties of his salvation, for I had raised them and guided their souls up to the moment of death. A little while later the girl fell sick. Having received all the sacraments, she called me on the eve of her death and spoke as follows: "Father, I am now dying happy and consoled for I have nothing to cause me grief. I beg you not to bury my body in the cemetery but in church, in front of our Lady's image. And I also ask you to pray to God for me. I promise that when I am in heaven I will pray for you." At midnight she expired. Those of her house and some members of the sodality held the wake. She had been wrapped in her shroud; three hours later she gave signs of life—whether she had actually died, as she herself said, or had suffered a seizure. The members of her household came and unbound her. She asked that I be called. I had been eager for her to keep her promise to me, and so as soon as I heard the lamentations from her house at one o'clock in the night, I had gone before the Blessed Sacrament to keep my own promise of commending her to our Lord, and was eagerly awaiting daylight so I could say Mass for her. They sent for me. A large part of the town were already at her house with wax candles in their hands. Although they questioned her, she replied, "Let the Father come, and then you will hear what happened to me." I found her quite cheerful and not at all looking like a corpse or someone with an illness from which she would die any time soon. She was holding in her arms a wooden cross about three quarters of a yard long, and her countenance was joyful as an angel's. She had me sit down beside her and said:

"Father, I passed from this life tonight. The first thing I saw was a band of fierce devils that came out to meet me. They were carrying hooks which they tried to seize me with. But a beautiful angel who was with me protected me and drove off the devils with a fiery sword. The angel guided me to hell to see the frightful fire suffered by the damned. I heard the loud dogs' howls, bulls' roars, and snakes' hissings that are made by the devils. I saw how they beat and tortured the souls there. I recognized some among them who had lived in our midst, but nobody from the sodality."

She mentioned to me two women she had seen in that place whose evil life had been a cause of great concern to me and whom I had been on the point of expelling from the town when they died about two weeks earlier.

They were newcomers from the forest and not much given to coming into church. This good woman had not known of their deaths before dying herself, and professed as much. She also mentioned a young man who had been raised from childhood in our school but had profited very little. I had taken him to a pagan town to be a teacher but he behaved very badly. After chastising him severely, I removed him. He returned to his own country and died, and although he made his confession it was presumed that he died ill prepared.

The woman went on: "From there the angel took me to see the glory of the blessed. I saw God on a beautiful throne surrounded by numberless blessed ones." I asked what God was like, what form he had. She replied: "I do not know what he is like, nor can I express his greatness. There are no words to describe it, and nothing in this life to compare with it. Fire is the only thing I can use: he was something infinitely more blazing than fire. He does not burn one; rather the sight of him makes the soul rejoice and exult. More I cannot say. I also saw our Lady, but how can I describe to you her beauty—nothing can compare with it—or the joy in which those blessed souls were?" From time to time she would repeat: "Oh, Father, what lovely things I saw there! Everything here is ugly and contemptible in comparison. This world has no people, it is deserted in comparison with what I saw there. Just the angels that I saw are more numerous than the sands or the leaves of the trees in the forests here. I recognized many people there from here in the reductions. Among them, in great glory, were the three Fathers who died in Guairá. I saw Isabel (the woman we mentioned as having risen from the dead) and she said to me, 'Sister, take a good look at these things so that you can describe them back there to the people on earth.' I was then sorry at what she said, because I realized that I had to come back here and it grieved me to leave those lovely things. But she saw my pain and went on: 'Do not be sad, for the Mother of God wants you to go and report all this to our relatives so that they will be encouraged to serve God and not grow weary in pursuing virtue. You are going to come back here this very day, never to leave this life again.' This is why I have come, Father. And now I want to return to that blessed life. I only wish that all the people in these towns without exception could die today and go with me today to see what lovely things I saw—what lovely children, what dances, what festivals I saw. The dancing was by the little children who died in these towns after baptism. Among them I saw my son, who died at four months, and I saw my husband." Here she mentioned by name many whom we had reared in our school and catechism, giving quite singular particulars about their predestination. She went on: "Father, do not grow weary of teaching these relatives of mine the way to heaven, so that they may win salvation. The good you are doing is incredible. Oh, if only they did not sin! Oh, if only they loved God with all their hearts! Oh, if only they obeyed his commandments! How happy they would be at the hour of their death."

She sent for the members of the sodality and urged them to persevere, telling them that the Virgin was very pleased with them and with their holy exercise. A few days earlier a girl had died who had been reared from childhood in great recollection. She had gone to confession weekly; and having guided her soul throughout her life I can affirm in all truth that she never committed a mortal sin. The woman stated that she had seen this girl in heaven in great glory, and that the girl had told her: "Tell my parents not to mourn my death, for I am alive and in the glory that you see. Tell them to continue the life they are leading so that they will deserve to come here and be with me." This girl's parents have been, and now are, singularly exemplary persons. The woman exhorted the town's caciques to give good example and especially to assist the Fathers in working for the good of her relatives' souls. Calling one of her sisters, she said: "Sister, I charge you with responsibility for our mother's instruction. Go over again with her the elements of our faith, for I want you to know that I saw many old men and old women in hell."

It was a most inspiring spectacle to see a girl who before marrying and after being widowed had always been reserved and shy about speaking now transformed into a preacher and apostle to her people, as well as to see the people holding lit candles and shedding copious tears of emotion. I confess that this produced in me a desire to die at once and to serve God very sincerely, together with a remarkable affection and love for the realities of heaven. It had the same effect on everyone, as their actions showed as soon as she breathed her last.

She went on talking for ten hours. I was quite amazed to see her uninterruptedly preaching and announcing the kingdom of God. The hour arrived for her to pass to eternal life—as may be taken for granted from her blameless life.

She said: "Father, now is the hour for me to go to that homeland of mine where the true life is lived. Remain with God and do not forget my soul, for I shall not forget you there in blessedness." I asked her if she had anything to confess. She replied that the only thing she regretted was still being in this life. She crossed her arms over the cross, which she had never let go of, and lost her power of speech. I asked her if she would remember me and her relatives in heaven. She nodded her head to say yes and thereupon gave up her soul as if in a gentle sleep. Her face remained beautiful as an angel's. Far from her appearance inspiring dread, its angelic comeliness and beauty seized our hearts, a sure warranty that she was on her way to her longed-for homeland. I confess that even five years after this took place she is still present to me and inspires me with her memory. As I write these words I feel deeply moved and fired to imitate her.

When, shortly thereafter, the people of the town celebrated Holy Week, it turned out that not a man, woman, or child failed to go to confession. I carefully asked everyone which of the good woman's words or actions had impressed them most. Each person readily recounted some detail that had stuck in the memory. Some spoke of the glory of heaven, others of the pains of hell; others of relatives of theirs who already enjoyed God and had been seen by the good woman. In the streets at night people were seen taking the discipline, many lashing themselves at the door of the church. In sum, the event was a great spur to everyone, particularly the members of the sodality. They talked of nothing else for many days, to their remarkable benefit.

CHAPTER 42

An account of other individual cases

A DEVOUT ELDERLY woman fell ill. Reaching the hour of death, she had received the sacraments and was in her last agony. I did not think she would last a quarter of an hour. Her voice hoarse and her breast heaving, she remained in this condition for more than a month. She would often send for me but had nothing to confess. This caused considerable wonder. A devout Indian told me why he thought death was not taking her: he suspected that she was not a Christian. The reason for the uncertainty was that she was a newcomer and had joined us during the migration of the towns already described, claiming to be a Christian. I discovered that she was not and baptized her. She was in full possession of her senses and answered all the questions well. Once she received the sacrament she expired.

A prominent cacique, a man of great virtue, was asleep. Someone came and woke him and said, "Look what is beside you." Looking, he saw a deep pit full of fire, in the midst of which there was a blazing bed with someone on it who was tossing, turning, and shrieking. "Do you know the person you see?" he said. He replied that he did not. "Look carefully, I know you know him." He took a good look and recognized the person: it was a prominent cacique who was still alive and a relative of his. The visitor said: "The bed you see is prepared for him and for others who refuse to reform their lives. You are not ignorant of the sins of this man." Father Francisco Díaz, to whom he reported this, wisely warned him not to reveal to anyone the person's identity but to tell what he had seen in general terms.

The vision was not an empty one. A short time later, as the cacique who had been seen in flames was standing at the door of his house, he noticed that his room was on fire. He went in to rescue a chest with all his possessions, and God allowed the fire to blaze up so that it shut the door on the wretched man. He cried piteously for help. People came, but the fire prevented them from entering. Trapped in the blazing room, the wretched man lay on the ground and tried to cover himself with a cowhide. They partially extinguished the fire, and when the flames receded they found him still alive, on a bed of fire just as the other man had seen. He was black as a coal; though still alive he could no longer speak or give signs of contrition. He had been a man of notorious vices. What most vexed us about his scandalous behavior was that he would resolve from time to time to reform but would soon return to the fire of his lust. In fact, I had decided that if he died I would bury him at the door of the church with a special marker as a warning and example.

This was not the end of God's justice toward this dead man or of his mercy toward the living. A young man of good life who belonged to the sodality had been away from the reduction and so knew nothing of the vision or prophecy about this dead man, nor of his death by burning. While wide awake he saw a figure next to him who said, "Pay attention to what I will show you." Suddenly he saw before him the burned cacique, horrible and terrifying in appearance. He was seated upon a hideous devil, black as an Ethiopian and on fire. "Do you know this poor man?" asked the figure. "Yes, I know him well," replied the young man. "Then be sure to tell your town what you have seen. This is why I have shown this to you, as an example to those who give free rein to their vices and leave no room for God's mercy." The young man, quite terrified and nearly speechless, recounted to us what he had seen. It did a lot of good, which is God's purpose in backing up our preaching with incidents like this.

A devil was vexing a young man in the sodality with doubts about the sufferings of souls in purgatory. Our sermons and stories failed to satisfy him. Two beautiful-looking persons in white appeared to the young man when he was half awake and said, "We have come to teach you what the sufferings of purgatory are like." They placed him in a terrible fire and said, "You must stay here for just five days and then we will take you out." So excruciating were the torments he felt that he was convinced he had already been there for years. "How you have deceived me," he complained to them; "you have kept me here for many years!" "You are wrong," they replied; "not one half of a half of a quarter hour has gone by yet. This is to let you know what the pains of purgatory are like." Thus was his doubt resolved.

CHAPTER 43

Further individual incidents

OUR LORD has willed to let them understand how pleased he is with their devotion to the saints. An Indian belonging to the sodality had devotion in preserving the little papers on which were each of the saints he had been assigned since becoming a member. He had saved eleven of these, and kept them in a small bag, together with a scrap of a lined Agnus Dei and a bit of blessed wax. He went to his blacksmith's job one day, and hung his relics up where, together with the bull, they happened to fall down into the charcoal. Unaware of this, he threw the charcoal onto the forge. Alerted by the smoke given off, they stirred the coals and found the bag completely burned, but the papers, wax, and Agnus Dei unharmed, no more disintegrated than if they had been in water. Wondering at this wonder, they brought it to me.

Two of us priests were on a trip to visit a town. Exhausted, we stopped in a deserted place for the night, but a grave uneasiness kept us from sleep. We agreed to go on by night since the way was good and there was a moon. We met the dawn within sight of the settlement, having walked all night without the least distress. While we were still in sight of the town, some inhabitants of the place came out to welcome us. I inquired whether there were any sick people. They said no—only that an old lady had died the day before and they were getting ready to bury her. We arrived at the town and I asked for the Indian woman's house. They told me not to bother going to see her since she was already dead. "Let us go," I replied; "I will say a few responsories for her." I entered the house. It was so murky that nothing of her could be seen. I asked aloud, "Where is the dead woman?" The woman answered, "Here I am, Father. I am not dead; I am waiting to go to confession to you." I heard her confession with great consolation to myself. Her confession over, she lost her power of speech and handed her soul to the Creator, who so greatly values those souls of his who were redeemed by his blood.

Irked at being despoiled of his tyrannical spoils, the devil tried his hand to see if he could reestablish himself by means of the magicians' bones we mentioned earlier. A young man of quite good life had been ill for months. While his parents were with him about one o'clock in the afternoon, he saw before him a naked Ethiopian carrying in a little basket the bones of a dead man. The young man asked who he was. The other replied, "I am one of those that were burned by your Father there" (as recounted earlier). "Well, what do you want here?" asked the young man. "I have come to see you," the devil replied, "because I want you to be my friend." "Get away from here," the young man answered, "I do not want your friendship. And if they burned you, how do you dare come back?" The devil came closer and closer, and the young man kept invoking the name of Jesus and telling him to go away. With soft words the devil kept trying to get him to listen to his impostures: "I am the one who really loves you people. I have come desiring to teach you the truth, for these Fathers do not tell it to you. I am the one who gives you all that you have, for I am your God." "You lie," cried the young man; "you are the devil." As he said this the devil entered his body. The young man cried aloud, calling to God for help and telling the devil to leave him. The numerous bystanders, and his parents themselves, were dumbfounded. Although they had not seen the devil, they heard what he said, both outside and inside the young man. They heard his own voice in his mouth and the devil's in his belly. The sick man asked them to call me. At the time I happened to be having an attack of fever, and they declined to summon me. He was so tortured by his evil guest that he begged his father to flog him hard: this would drive the beast out. Love made him refuse, but the mother, deciding that this would help, seized some cords and flogged her son. He kept telling his mother to lay on strongly and the devil to get out of him. At last, after repeated demands and replies, the devil went out, leaving the young man a wreck. When my illness was over I went to see him and heard his confession; his conscience was perfectly clean. At midnight, when he was sure that those in the house were asleep, he arose from bed—having been incapable of this for several months—and took a discipline at the doors of the church. One of his father's vassals followed him as he went out. When he saw him severely flogging himself, he gave the alarm. He was so weak that they carried him home in their arms.

I must not forget another occurrence in this same reduction a few months later. A prominent cacique became ill, a man who had been of great assistance to us before the migration of the people at the time when we burned the bodies as already described. He had been in bed for over a month, when he left his room as best he could to enjoy the clear summer night. Hardly had he gone into the street when he was surrounded by five shapes in rich and fragrant apparel. He was afraid, but they reassured him that they were good spirits and asked him if he had gone to confession. He replied that he had done so at the beginning of his illness and now felt nothing to cause him concern. They answered: "We already know that you live a good life and always go to Mass. Do you remember the bones that the Fathers burned?" "Yes," he replied. They went on: "Did you believe the things they said?" "I never believed such a thing," the Indian replied. "You did well," they said, "for they were devils, enemies of your good and lovers of our harm. Tell the people here to live well and to listen to the teaching of the Fathers, for they teach you the truth. However, you have people among you who are like a comb with broken and uneven teeth: some are progressing in virtue, while others fall short. We guard this town and drive off the devils, who mainly urge you to evil at night. Do you pray the Virgin's rosary?" "Yes," he replied. "We ourselves are honored to wear it around our necks," they said; "look, touch this rosary."

By now delighted with their good words and quite without fear, the Indian touched the rosary and a cross, upon which he smelled a fragrant odor which clung to his fingers. "How long has it been," they asked, "since you went to see the Father?" "Three weeks," he replied; "I have not gone to see him because I cannot stand up." "Well then, go to see him tomorrow; from now on you will be well. Tell him everything you heard here, that he is not to weary of teaching you people and that we take care of protecting you. Be sure that you go and tell him this as soon as day breaks. We shall be in his cell before you and will hear what you say to him." I had hardly left prayers in the church to go to my cell when I spied him at the door. I was surprised to see him since I knew that his illness kept him to his bed. He told me the whole story, and how he was truly recovered. To prove it he began working on a job that was underway in the church.

I will conclude these things which the Lord and the most holy Virgin have done among his people. I omit many, satisfied with having briefly recounted these to the Lord's glory. He does marvelous things with simple, plain, guileless people, for he is a lover of simplicity. "His conversation is with the simple."[109] Moreover, as mentioned earlier, with a new Christian people he employs means that are new—actually, ancient means that are still needed for watering tender plants like those of the Indians so that they will grow in virtue and increase in grace. I will give just one more good example, of evildoing rather than of edification, that is pertinent to my intention.

Certain persons, who base their living upon the blood they suck from these poor Indians and who take the part of the raiders from São Paulo, seeing that we had delivered these people from their hands and refused to let them seize them, wrote letters to various persons—prelates, bishops, and lords —and even spread rumors here at court that I (whom they charge as the culprit) had removed Indians from their own lands and carried them off to foreign regions, causing them all to die along the way. They complained loudly of this mistake. I received letters from bishops and magistrates censuring my blunder. Even since I have been here at court, lords of the Council to whose ears this report had come have questioned me about this calamity. Although I have satisfied them—or rather, although the truth itself has cried aloud—the following brief statement may serve as a reply.

The royal audiencia of Chuquisaca accorded us ample permission to move the Indians. The measure was carried out with their full authorization. While the move took place before the approval arrived, it arrived shortly thereafter. Besides, who would imagine that anyone in such a crisis, when he sees the knife at his throat, ought to await permission before fleeing? Natural law itself authorized them to escape slavery and preserve their freedom, even their faith and eternal welfare, which they would have altogether forfeited, as others have done, if they had delayed their flight for even a couple of days.

It would have been a more Christian action to write to court that the raiders from São Paulo had taken prisoner sixty thousand souls from our reductions, of whom fewer than a thousand survive today, the rest having been killed by sheer flogging, toil, and misery. But how were they to make such an accusation when they themselves were accomplices to the crime? In order to demonstrate that their reports were false and that the Indians they claimed I had killed were alive, I petitioned a certain governor to receive the tribute from these Indians for His Majesty. I even proposed Don Cristóbal de Aresti, bishop of Paraguay, and Father Diego de Alfaro, rector of the college in Asunción, as mediators. Despite all these efforts I never succeeded in obtaining my wish. The reason why is obvious and I shall not trouble myself to explain it. Indeed, it would indeed have been a Christian action had they reproached me for offering tribute from a people living in exile after all the terrible sufferings described above—had they advised me to petition His Majesty graciously to grant them the freedom and exemption from tribute which their affliction deserved, so that they could reap the benefit of their loyalty in departing from undoubted enemies and taking refuge in the protection His Majesty accords to this poor, oppressed people. But let us resume our narrative, and trust that the truth will defend itself.

CHAPTER 44

Death of Father de Espinosa at the hands of unbelievers

FATHER PEDRO de Espinosa was a native of Baeza, a son of parents who were true servants of God; they had four sons, all of whom they dedicated to the Society. One of the sons, who went to the Indies to labor for souls, wrote his parents from Panama to raise his brother Pedro with care, for he was to follow him and die at the hands of pagans. Father Pedro himself, at prayer while still in Spain, had the impression that he was being dragged on the ground by Indians—and he found himself actually on the ground—and that they were trampling on him and tormenting him. Both of these presages were to be fulfilled.

He went to the Indies, where he performed apostolic labors in Guairá. He had responsibility from its start for a reduction of barbarous people, whom he tamed by his long-suffering and patience. The town had two thousand householders, and thus a population of nine to ten thousand souls, who had been gathered together through our efforts. I could say much of his exceptional virtues.

He labored indefatigably during the above-mentioned migration of the towns. For years he walked on foot, though a man of delicate constitution, and crowned his labors with a happy death. Charity and obedience had bidden him take some sheep to the reductions of Loreto and San Ignacio to clothe the poor, because of a shortage of cotton caused by the frosts. On his return trip with the sheep, a group of bestial pagan Indians came upon him at midnight where he was camping in the wilderness and there clubbed him to death. As the servant of God commended himself to Jesus and Mary, the Indians railed at him for invoking such false gods and untruthfully calling on them for help. The Father upbraided them for their unbelief. They immediately stripped him naked, on an extremely cold winter night. As the good Father commended himself and offered his soul to the Lord, the barbarians, irate and annoyed at seeing him so eager for the God whom they denied, smashed his head. They left him naked to the tigers, who completely devoured him; we recovered only one arm and leg for burial.

His death was deeply mourned and bewailed by the Indians. By his preaching he had brought them life; he had civilized them, instructing them in carpentry and tailoring, which he had acquired by his native talent. The very night he was killed, he appeared to a great friend and helper of his in the conversion of the Indians. With joyful countenance he said to him, "Ah, my brother, remain with God; I am going to my rest in heaven." Two days before his death God our Lord revealed the Father's peril to another great friend of his, and on the day itself revealed the murder to him, along with the manner of their killing him, even though it occurred many leagues away. A blessed life and a blessed death!

CHAPTER 45

General observations

FOR A better understanding of the reductions mentioned earlier and those described below, I shall here set down a number of general remarks applicable to all the reductions and settlements. It is not my intention to speak of the virtues and achievements of the laborers in this vineyard, men who left their native countries, families, and comforts and penetrated into foreign lands, sacrificing themselves to hunger, nakedness, and even the sword (as we shall see), renouncing the acclaim they would have garnered here in Spain for their teaching, preaching, and other distinguished activities —lures that can bring down the highest-flying falcon. Nor do I wish to compare this spiritual conquest with other splendid ones. This conquest is completely lacking in outward splendor; it has only the interior splendor of countless souls.

And if in Japan there are martyrs by the sword, in those territories there is no lack of arrows for the same; moreover, I find less there in the way of houses and palaces, civilization, silks, Japanese costume, variety in food and luxuries—not that the apostolic men in Japan possess these things, although the sight of them does afford attraction and interest. In those territories clothing and costume are what nature bestows on human beings at birth, so that the Fathers have to make strenuous efforts to cover what might offend modest eyes: they are obliged to toil incessantly at providing the people with wool, corded cloth, and cotton. To promote the raising of cotton, the Fathers have demonstrated to the Indians in their own persons how to break the soil with a plow, an innovation for them but now quite successful.

Nor is it my intention to speak of those who labor in colleges and cities of the Spaniards. They are so shorthanded that the largest college has only five Fathers, others three, some no more than two. They are also under obligation to attend to the instruction of Spaniards, Indians, and blacks—all in their own languages, according to the Apostle's weighty admonition: "Unless I know the meaning of a word, I will be a barbarian to the person I am speaking to, and he to me."[110] Moreover, in a given Spanish city there are normally Indians speaking a variety of languages, and the Fathers have to know these in order to instruct them. There is not a single Father who, in addition to his native tongue and Latin, does not know at least one foreign language. Many know two or three. Books on these languages are presently being printed here at court. It has cost considerable toil to work out the language of the blacks and put it into a form for printing; this too has been done successfully. For in the numerous fleets of transports that enter Buenos Aires with these blacks, it has been verified that there are always cases of fraud regarding their baptism. This problem is met by the zeal of the rectors themselves and the older Fathers. They go to the ships and to the sheds where the blacks are packed together like sheep and where their diseases and stench drive even their owners away. There the Fathers treat their souls and bodies, and annually reap a copious harvest.

It is the power of the gospel that I seek to set forth. Its potency is manifested by gentling lions, taming tigers, transforming wild beasts into human beings and even angels. To give an idea of the toil and hardships of those who labor in this vineyard and create the towns—of which I shall make simple mention—would require rehearsing here the Apostle's litany of his hardships in the second letter to the Corinthians, which, while describing the saint's own experience, is equally valid today.

At this point I will review the various practices and customs which have been established by dint of our constant preaching, along with some other comments, so that I will not need to repeat them for each reduction.

Nature has shown herself quite miserly towards the people there in denying them metals that are elsewhere abundant (this despite the fact that some persons were led by their lust for these metals to assert that the people did possess them, and to send reports to that effect here to court; I refer the reader to chapter 80 of this account for a reply—not my own but that of a governor who did all he could to uncover either the mountain of gold or the truth of their imaginings). She has shown herself generous in disburdening them of idols and false worship, with the result that they readily embrace Catholic truth and remain solid and persevering in their allegiance to it. We purchase their good will at the price of one-pound wedges of iron. These are the implements they depend on for their living; formerly they used stone tools to cut the bushes in their fields. When presented with an iron wedge worth four to six farthings in Spain, a cacique will come out of the forests, mountains, or other hidden dwelling-places and enter the reduction with his vassals, amounting, with their dependents, to one or two hundred souls, who, once properly instructed, receive baptism. The rest aspire to fishhooks, needles, pins, and beads of glass and other materials.

They all raise food, and each man has his own plot. When past eleven years of age, boys have a plot of their own. Upon these they very coopera-tively assist each other. They neither buy nor sell, for they freely and unselfishly help each other in their needs, and show great generosity to people passing through. Accordingly, there is no theft; they live in peace and without quarrels.

Throughout the year they hear Mass at daybreak and go to work from church. This holy preparation is very successful. While the sacrament of confession is received from the start, Communion is put off for a number of years, more for some and fewer for others. For while their capacity for learning matters of faith and mechanical arts is well known, the resistance among the older people is considerable.

Those who are qualified receive Communion four times annually, when they have a public festivity with a preparation by sermons and pious stories, fasts, disciplines, and other penances. Those who belong to the sodality of the Blessed Virgin, and some who do not, go to confession weekly; the less zealous every month. In confession they dredge up the tiniest faults, such as being ungrateful for what God has done for them, inadvertently taking a mouthful of meat on Friday and then spitting it out when they remember, not going to Mass on work days, and the like. Even when they have been well instructed about erroneous conscience, they continue in this fashion. Although at times off the point, their concise way of representing their whole interior life prevents tiresomeness, and their simplicity is pleasing. They continue mentioning things they did while still unbelievers; even though this is not matter for the sacrament, their sorrow over what they did is edifying.

They celebrate the main feasts with more devotion than splendor because of the poverty which they share with their churches. Disciplines to the blood have had to be restricted, for many have been endangered by the cold and their lack of covering. Their emotion at hearing the Passion is so strong that not infrequently, impeded by our own tears arising from those of the people, we have ended our sermons without finishing our train of thought.

They are highly capable in mechanical matters. There are excellent carpenters, ironworkers, tailors, weavers, and shoemakers. Though they possessed none of these skills before, the systematic effort of the Fathers has made them masters of them, not least in effective cultivation of the earth with the plow. They are remarkably attached to the music in which the Fathers instruct the caciques' children, along with reading and writing. They celebrate Mass with elaborate music for two or three choirs. They play musical instruments with great skill: bassoons, cornets, oboes, harps, zithers, guitars, rebecks, clarinets, and other instruments. This greatly contributes to attracting pagans and making them eager to bring us into their lands to form and teach their children.[111]

Drunkenness has no place among them, for their own wines are too weak to produce it. Any lapses against chastity that may be discovered are met with effective correction and exemplary punishment from the care and zeal of the caciques, fathers of families, and constables. They patrol the town at night and anyone caught doing anything suspicious is chastised. Concubinage is not even dreamed of, since the punishment for it would be perpetual exile. Efforts are made to get them married early, before sin can anticipate them.

They have erected hospitals for treating the poor, the men separate from the women. The Fathers have taught them how to bleed and frequently practice it themselves; they have appointed infirmarians who do their job diligently. They have other practices of this sort which give shape to an excellent civilized commonwealth.

Spaniards have not penetrated this area. It was conquered by the gospel alone and it was our desire that the Indians be under His Majesty's protection (which in fact they are, as can be seen from his royal letters patent cited in our final chapter) and pay their just tribute to him. There have not been wanting persons to report to this court that we are committing rebellion with the Indians and will not let any Spaniard into their towns. It will be clear from chapter 80 that this is not the case. We may well be unwilling for the Spanish to view them with their own eyes; although they would find much to be edified by, I fear they would not much edify the Indians.

Many among the Spanish are eager for His Majesty to hand the Indians over to them in *encomienda* after the ten years of exemption granted them by His Majesty following the reception of baptism, thus to impose upon them the unparalleled yoke of personal service—the measure devised by Pharaoh for oppressing the people of Israel—which in the Indies has caused the death of countless people without hope even of eternal life because of their want of instruction, their continuous occupation (as His Majesty puts it in his royal letters patent) in this diabolical personal service denying them the time to acquire and practice it. Furthermore, these persons have attributed the issuance of the royal letters patent not to His Majesty's Christian zeal or to his obligation to protect a people destitute of all human protection, but rather to what they call the interfering obstinacy of the Society. In this way they turn this most Catholic measure of His Majesty to our discredit, endeavoring to persuade the high officials here at court that we exploit the Indians in Paraguay for our own profit.

I bear authenticated evidence to the contrary. If I be required to present it here from persons of unimpeachable credit, I offer as witnesses Doctor Francisco de Alfaro, auditor on the Council of Finance, who is a man of extraordinary experience of the Indies, having visited numerous provinces and left them most just laws which were ratified by His Majesty, especially for my province of Paraguay; and also the most worthy prelate of Rio de Janeiro, Doctor Lorenzo de Mendoza. The latter's diocese is close to the province, and he is fully aware that in reality our provincial superiors in Paraguay have laid out over two thousand pesos on wedges, knives, and other objects of barter, and on corded cloth, linen, wool, and cotton for the Indians, as is clearly itemized in the authenticated report that I present. These moneys came from the inheritances of our own religious and from the alms which the same prelate, before taking his office, helped to beg in Potosí and the province of the Chichas. Of this I have his testimony. All of this was applied by superiors to the garnering of those poor souls, whose poverty is so great that many are unable to pay even two pesos of tribute imposed on each by His Majesty. And it has happened that at the very time when I was sending my cloak and my cassock, my Bible, concordances, and other papers, and even the altar chalices and ornaments, to be sold in the Spanish towns for the wool and cotton that I ordered from Santa Fe to clothe the poor Indians, reports were being sent that we exploited the Indians for our own traffic and profit.

There were times when I visited the Fathers in the reductions and found them without a shirt on their back and disguising their penury with a bit of linen around their neck. Others were sleeping on a cowhide, having giving their little mattresses to the sick. They had spared not even their poor blanket, tearing it up to clothe the poor. The provincials themselves have provided extraordinary examples of this. When Doctor Lorenzo de Mendoza, prelate of Rio de Janeiro, who has been commissioned by the royal council to examine this narration, reached this point in the text he made the following marginal annotation in his own hand:

> When Fathers Simón Masseta and Justo Mansilla arrived in Brazil from the province of Paraguay, following their flocks who had been seized by the townsmen of São Paulo and seeking justice for them—of which they found not a whit—the Fathers of the Society of Jesus in

Rio de Janeiro themselves told me on several occasions that they were astonished to see the almost unbearable poverty that the Fathers of the Society of Jesus in Paraguay suffered for the conversion of pagans, and of which these two apostolic men gave evidence.

Thus far the prelate's words.

We would indeed deserve censure if we exposed ourselves to the frequent risk of death incurred in those parts for the sake of temporal interests. It would also be the height of imprudence to forsake the religious advantages of a college for the extreme stress of life among pagans if our purpose were any merely human interest. No sensible Christian will see anything wrong in our teaching the Indians how to farm so they can procure what they need to cover themselves (this is all the patrimony they can aspire to), lest nakedness be an excuse for not coming to church to hear God's word, as sometimes happens. Indeed, one ought to consider them bound to do this as shepherds of that flock.

I freely acknowledge that my objective is to preserve the Indians from personal service. My purpose herein is the common good of both Indians and Spaniards. The arguments for this are given by His Majesty in his royal letters patent which I shall place at the end. It is not my objective that they should be idle—that would be a blameworthy objective indeed. Rather, I desire that they pay His Majesty the tribute which their poverty allows, for they will have plenty of struggle to support themselves and their families. If His Majesty vouchsafes to use these tributes to reward the services rendered by Spaniards, it will be justly done and no one will object; indeed, we ask and petition that they be compensated with these tributes. But to place the Indians in their power—the personal service would furnish them a knife for butchering the sheep of Jesus Christ like the sheep in a slaughterhouse.

CHAPTER 46

The Society's reductions in the province

THE PARAGUAY province today has twenty-five settlements of Indians under its care. I have already spoken of two of them; I shall now discuss the others. I shall start with two reductions on the Paraguay River. These are daughters of Loreto and San Ignacio, from which they set forth to begin a great harvest offered by extensive provinces of pagans belonging to the Chiriguanas and other nations, peoples who have defended themselves by force of arms and even captured flags from our Spanish, which they still hold and display as trophies today, from the time of the viceroy Don Francisco de Toledo.

The task was undertaken by three fervent members of the Society: Fathers

Diego Rancioner, Justo Banciur,[112] and Nicolás Hernacio. They chose two sites for their apostolic labors. Many peoples have come to hear them and returned to their own and the neighboring territories with highly favorable reports. This has produced a desire to have them in their own towns. Their proximity to the pagans is such that they are only three leagues away from a nation called the Payagás, whose untamed ferocity has been the death of many Spanish. These people have become very friendly with the Fathers, whom they honor with the name of crossbearers because of the crosses we carry in our hands. They ask for religious, and on their account so do many other provinces, such as the Guatos, Ibitiriguaras, and Hill People, who live in rough mountainous country. Besides these provinces who already know about the Fathers, there are many others deeper in the interior. For lack of manpower the scythe has not been put to this harvest, particularly since death's scythe has taken the lives of Fathers Diego Rancioner and Nicolás Hernacio—carrying them off in the flower of their hopes: for although they had toiled apostolically in Guairá and its provinces, they considered they had done nothing.

Father Rancioner was a Fleming. The son of a great commander against the rebels, he himself had served in the war. He was singularly endowed with learning. His ordinary bed in the missions was of cowhide on the floor, and his life's actions were of the same tenor. Father Nicolás was a Frenchman. He left the palace of the king of France, where his noble father, allured by the hopes that so often fail, had placed him, and went to the province of Paraguay at word of the riches of souls there. He there labored untiringly for their benefit. I am a witness to his extraordinary deeds, which modesty here passes over. I will only mention that his usual bed was a board on the ground. In his illness he exchanged this for a bit of straw. Death took him alone and without a companion, by an illness so terrible that his intestines were visible through a hole that had formed in his side. His food was as luxurious as his bed.

He was visited by the fierce barbarians mentioned above—for virtue tames wild animals. Finding him so destitute of food, they brought him some of their dainties: bits of roasted snake, which they consider quite a delicacy, and fishes roasted for several days—fire for meat and fish substituting for their total lack of salt. He told two young men who had joined him in his work that he would end his life on the same day that St. Francis Xavier ended his, for this was what he had prayed for. This was not his only resemblance to the saint: like him he died in utter dereliction, deprived of the sacraments because there was no priest. But his life was such that he merited such a death. Father Justo Mansilla straightway went to take charge of the two reductions, where I left him alone with the prospect of a vast harvest of pagans. May the Lord grant that the owner of this vineyard, His Catholic Majesty, may send laborers into it.[113]

CHAPTER 47

The reduction of San Ignacio on the Paraná

O N THE great Paraná River there are seven settlements.[114] The first
is San Ignacio. It was also the first to be founded in the province by
members of the Society. Its founder was the Venerable Father Marciel de
Lorenzana, whose life (as already mentioned) has been written. The people
here could not be conquered by force of arms; this man conquered them with
the gospel alone and with the charity and patience of Christ. This being the
door through which the Christian message was to be communicated to
countless pagans, the common enemy tried to shut it lest he be robbed of his
prey. He stirred up the pagans further in the interior to act for him, urging
them to kill not only the Father but also those who had received him.

Those with the Father were few at that time, their enemies numerous.
Firmly resolved to hold fast to the truth of the gospel, they asked the Father
to baptize them, so that as Christians (they were all catechumens) they might
fight with courage. As the enemy drew near the Father hastened their
baptism, baptizing them four at a time. They begged him to hide because of
the danger. "I must be the first," he said, "and your captain in this war. I
trust in God that we shall win." In the end they were victorious. The number
of people who came to settle there grew, so that they built the splendid town
that can be seen today. They dedicated it to St. Ignatius, who has proved a
true father in difficult situations: apart from the common help that he
renders throughout the towns to women having difficult childbirths (of which
a long account could be given), I will mention just a few samples of the
saint's patronage.

A young man was expelled from the sodality of the Virgin (which has
grown mightily there) for an offense that called for such a punishment,
although in fact the accusation was false; in addition he was arrested. He felt
outraged and insulted. Exploiting this situation, the devil led him from one
abyss to another by tempting him to hang himself in despair. He determined
to do so, so frenzied that if his feet had not been held fast in the stocks he
would have voluntarily sacrificed himself to the devil. As he lay awake at
midnight brooding on his plan, a light came in the door. He thought it was
a friend of his. It was indeed: it was St. Ignatius. Shedding rays of light from
his face, and greater rays of zeal for the young man's soul, he drew near to
him and said in a loving voice, "God protect you, son." Placing his hand on
the young man's head, he said to him: "Do not worry; you are innocent and
will soon be freed." With that the saint vanished. Delivered from his
temptation, the young man cried aloud. People came and found the doors
locked and the lad weeping bitter tears of repentance for having succumbed

to despair.

A woman was held tightly in the grip of an oft-repeated sin. The saint appeared to her, reproving her great disregard of her own soul, by which she was on the way to eternal perdition, and getting her to make a good confession, abandon the vice, and follow the path of virtue.

Another woman was in the grip of an illness and had received the sacraments for departing from this life. Her family already bewailed her imminent death. They placed upon her breast an image of the holy Father. She immediately opened her eyes; embracing the saint, she experienced his help by its effect, for she was straightway cured.

No less here did the sovereign Virgin demonstrate her pleasure with her sodalities. A woman who wanted to be admitted undertook an examination of her soul in order to cleanse it by a general confession, this being a requirement for admission. While struggling with her examination one night, she fell asleep and dreamed that she saw the Virgin and heard her reminding her of certain sins of her youth which were now long past and had never been confessed—through forgetfulness or poor examination. Awaking, the woman realized that the reminder had been correct. Repentant, glad, and grateful to the Virgin, she confessed her faults.

CHAPTER 48

The reduction of Encarnación at the place called Itapúa

WE BEHOLD in this town today the holy Apostle's transformation from Saul into Paul. These were the people who waged savage war on the previously mentioned reduction for receiving the gospel. Their conversion was undertaken by the holy martyr Father Roque González,[115] of whom I shall speak later. He broached its resistance with apostolic zeal and subjugated it with the sword of preaching, by dint of labors, struggles, and patent risks to his life—the usual price of pagan peoples. His fellow in these vicissitudes was Father Diego de Boroa, whose not inferior zeal is proven today by his having won and gathered entire flocks into the sheepfold of the Catholic Church. The incidents they encountered while rooting this unruly people in the faith deserve a lengthy history, which will one day be published. The desire instilled in this people by God stirred them to accept the yoke, but they were deterred by their own inconstancy and desire to live in their own bestial fashion with numerous women—a common obstacle. However, the constancy of these two men won out, breaking down the fear with which certain magicians and sorcerers—who are a deadly plague—intimidated them. They dedicated this town to the sovereign Virgin, of whom we may rightly say, "She brings healing to the nations of the globe."[116] Her help, deeply trusted in, was demonstrated by experience. She healed the wounds of that sick people, who flocked eagerly to the saving waters of baptism and the preventive medicine of matrimony, holding fast to the anchor of prayer, to which they are much given, and to devotion towards their patroness. Her sodality has been started and flourishes today, with frequent confession and Communion four times a year.

A Father asked a member of this sodality if they felt any desire to go back to their old untrammeled way of life. "No, Father," he replied, "for since we have become the Virgin's slaves such thoughts have been wiped out, and we see such a transformation that we do not recognize ourselves. From the beasts we once were we now see ourselves rational human beings."

We have seen fine examples of extraordinary resistance to the sin of unchastity, the people accepting any pain or hardship in order to avoid it. A man asked a woman if she was alone. Knowing his depraved heart, she replied that she was not alone, that God was always with her. As the lecherous man attempted to seduce her chastity, she said, "Do not waste your time. As long as God is present I will never offend him." Another woman, similarly solicited, took the rosary she wore down her breast and placed it on the lecherous youth, saying, "See, I am a slave of the Virgin; do not trouble me." Others reply, "Look, I go to Communion; sin should not enter where God does."

We have often seen them on journeys, after rowing all day on the river, kneel down under the trees and recite the rosary. We have come upon them in this holy practice in the middle of the night. They come with questions about the faith raised for them by the devil, in order to be guided by the Fathers. They ask questions about the next life, glory, eternal punishments, and how to grow in virtue. In sum, they spur each other on to lead orderly lives—even lives of high perfection, as will be seen from the following example.

It is customary for them to marry immediately upon coming of age so that they will not suffer harm through want of this remedy. One young man in the sodality married a girl his own age, a maiden of excellent qualities. On their wedding day the chaste youth addressed his wife as follows: "If you are pleased to agree with my decision, I will know that you love me and that you have truly chosen me as your husband. I want you to know that it is my wish to preserve my body clean so that my soul will also be pure. I have never gone to a woman and I wish not to lose this jewel. If you are willing for us to live out our lives chastely as brother and sister, it would be the strongest proof of your love you could give me. You have heard what the Fathers tell us about purity, about its beauty and its reward. You have also many times heard of the ugliness of the vice, which drags those who sink themselves in it to unbridled license like madness. It will be wise for us, then, to dedicate ourselves to the perpetual service of the Virgin, mother of purity and lover of those who imitate her in this noble virtue. Consider this well, for the time of this life is short and that of the other everlasting; fleshly delight is short-lived, its punishment endless. And while marriage is lawful and good, the Fathers tell us it is better to live in purity. I realize that the Fathers warn us all that our perfection consists in marrying as soon as the appetite for pleasure dawns, before the night of sin can seize us. We have complied by marrying in public; we are now brother and sister in secret."

Who would not be attracted to this desire by sweet, chaste arguments like this? The chaste virgin, his wife, promised to be his sister always. They lived this way for a long time with no one knowing of their resolve. The Lord harvested this ripe fruit for his heavenly table; he sent the young man an illness from which—attired in the robe of grace by means of the sacraments, and having told his angelic resolve to Father Juan de Porras,[117] whose zeal and vigilance has brought this people to a high degree of perfection—he died with the warranties afforded by such an act and such a life. I can testify that we who knew and dealt with this young man recognized in him warranties of no ordinary virtue.

The Father considered the good endowments of the maiden widow, and suggested that it might be wise for her to marry in order to avoid dangers. She replied that, having preserved her purity with her first husband, she would preserve it the better by not taking a second one. The Father insisted, apprehensive about the foes arrayed against this virtue. She answered that it was her intention and firm resolution to die as she had lived; but that if he, as her father and confessor, deemed that for the good of her soul she ought to marry, he should reflect about it carefully and commend it to the Lord, and then order her to do what was best for her. This example is not far from those left us by an Alexis or a Calybites[118]—all the more so if we turn our eyes to the pagan life which this people led only yesterday, when the universal idol of them all was the flesh.

Newborn babies were dying in the reduction. What caused the most grief was that some died before or at the moment of birth, thus departing unbaptized. The people took St. Ignatius as their patron and vowed to celebrate his feast with great spiritual festiveness and to go to confession and Communion on that day. Pregnant women and those giving birth immediately experienced the saint's protection, for since that time we have seen a great increase of babies. I shall not take time to recount the saint's miraculous intervention for women in difficult childbirth, for it would take a large volume.

CHAPTER 49

The reduction of Corpus Christi

THIS PEOPLE'S way of life when they were pagans was no better than that of those in the previous reduction. They were brought into the reduction by the unremitting labor of Fathers Roque González and Diego de Boroa. Since it was on the feast of Corpus Christi that they had penetrated this stronghold, where the devil had amassed great spoils, they dedicated the town to the Lord under that title. There were many magicians who suc-cumbed little by little to the truth. The entire people were baptized. They have started the sodality of the Blessed Virgin, they go to Communion four times a year after good preparation, and they are making good progress in catechetical instruction. Though all of them live quite firm in the faith, there did remain one holdout, a sorcerer who, a Christian in outward appearance, was a devil within. He himself gave it away as follows.

A devil complained to a certain person that they would not let him into a particular town. Despite his attempts to inveigle them into evil, they repelled him and resisted his solicitations. He said, "I have a great friend in Corpus Christi who does not act like that. He listens to me closely and looks after my interests with care." Learning of this, I wrote to the Fathers in charge of the town, and in their sermons they spoke in lurid terms of the reasons for complaint they were giving to the devil. The Lord willed that this magician and sorcerer quickly be exposed. His mother and wife having fallen ill, he deprived them of the sacraments. When they asked him to send for a Father, he never did so, deceitfully telling them that they were not going to die and the Father that they were already well. They eventually died deprived of final assistance, and he was subjected to a severe punishment.

CHAPTER 50

The reduction of Concepción de Nuestra Señora

THIS PLACE was reached by the voice of the outstanding Father and holy martyr, Roque González. Like a ringing trumpet it thundered through those forests filled with pagans, with its eloquent preaching in their own Indian tongue. Even more did he win them over by the example of his holy life. Although, once having brought together here lions and tigers from that wild forest, he was eager to move on to neighboring provinces, his zeal was delayed for some years by the obduracy of certain magicians who blocked his way like furies. He very gradually instructed the people of this town, assisted by Father Alonzo de Aragona,[119] an Italian and a man of outstanding marks of rare virtue, who later concluded his labors with a blessed death. Like the others, this town was a seedbed of sorcerers. They were defeated by the divine preaching. However, one remained so obstinate and stubborn that though he became a Christian he remained a minister of the devil still. He pretended to go to confession, but always did so mendaciously. He repeated these false confessions for many years, until the Father of lights gave him light.

There appeared to him a saint, by all indications St. Francis Xavier, in surplice and stole and with a book in his hand. He said, "Why do you not grieve for yourself, wretched man? Make a good confession and get out of your filth." Then came his master the devil, blazing with fire but even more with wrath, to terrify him with fearsome gestures and scare him away from the advice he was being given by the saint. The saint, however, easily drove him off. Terrified by the devil and caressed by the saint, the Indian made a careful examination of his own impostures and confessed them with great sorrow. The saint reappeared to him after his confession. He praised what he had done and urged him to prepare to receive the life-giving Bread of heaven, which he should ask the Fathers to grant him. He had been a Saul; he is now a Paul by the fine example of his life, by which he preaches and undoes his former frauds.

There was a young woman whom the devil had been unable to vanquish with his temptations when she was in good health. In a clear and visible shape, he tried to provoke her to consent in a sin of impurity. The more strongly to bind her, he promised that at her death he would take her to his own delights. Assisted by a Father to whom she confided her temptations, she received the sacraments and fell asleep in the Lord.

An Indian was in his final agony, after preparation by all the sacraments for departure from this life. There appeared to him a venerable man in bishop's regalia (with which he was not familiar). He spoke to him as follows: "Son, see the danger you are in, the agonies brought by death, the boldness and daring with which the devil tempts, afflicts, and drives sinners to despair. You are now experiencing this. It will be good for you to become a herald of these perils. Accordingly, you will soon recover from this illness; see that you publish this to your people and tell them that the way to heaven is hard and that they should give a mind to their own salvation and go to church, the place where God hears them, and there beg a remedy for their needs." The man called his confessor and told him this. The dying man's claim was attested by his sudden recovery, but even more by his diligence in carrying out his mission, benefiting both himself and—by his words and example—everyone else.

So well established is the sodality of the Virgin in this town that its youth flourish in the greatest purity, modesty, and reserve, of which excellent examples have been observed.

CHAPTER 51

The reduction of Nuestra Señora de los Reyes

T HE SOCIETY forged this reduction from various Indian nations which speak different languages, although they can communicate in the common language, Guaraní.[120] It is located on the boundary of an untamed nation called the Charrúas, a people of gigantic size. Their dwelling place is whatever the night brings; they roam the countryside like wild animals, pursuing game and fishing in the lakes. They do not farm and have no idea how to. Some have joined this reduction. They are drawn to the port of Buenos Aires by the whiff of wine, which they buy with the horses they catch from the almost innumerable ownerless herds in the wild. They will exchange a good horse for four to six reals, at times for two reals or even a loaf of bread or a drink of wine. We have seen them there, in the presence of prelates and governors, overpowered by wine and sprawled on the ground. It is heartbreaking to see this disorder; if only the energy applied to other matters were put into their conversion, settlement, and baptism, I have no doubt they could be domesticated.

On another side of this reduction is a further nation called the Yaros, who also live like animals with no fixed places. Like the Charrúas, they are very warlike, using stone balls which they hurl with astonishing accuracy. Eighty Indians from the reduction once went out to round up some of the ownerless cattle which are so numerous that they fill the countryside for many leagues, there being nothing to prevent their increase. The Yaros surrounded our Indians. The latter, seeing that the others held the advantage, offered peace; it was refused. Our men brought into the safety of a meadow of tall grass a group of children they had taken along for an outing. The battle was engaged; forty of our own Indians and many of the enemy were killed. The latters' strength forced the survivors to retreat to the meadow. The enemy set it on fire. With the dry grass burning on all sides, there would have been no escape from the peril had not the flames been quenched by a heavy rain sent by heaven, which enabled our men to get back to their town. It turned out that on the day they set forth they had all gone to confession and Communion. Many returned from the trip to be reconciled, furnishing us warranties of their eternal salvation.

This trial was followed by that of plague. Everyone fell ill, with the sole exception of a ten-year-old girl. Her escape was attributed to the fact that upon awaking every morning she would kneel, make the sign of the cross, and implore our Lady to protect her from the plague.

The zealous efforts of Father Diego de Salazar, an old missioner, have established harmony among the various nationalities and types in this town.

He devoted his attention to the young people, so that they would not grow up with the bad habits of their parents. There was an Indian who consistently avoided sermons and instruction in the faith. A child went past him, so small that it could barely walk or utter articulate speech. The Indian asked, "Child, where are you going in such a determined way?" The child replied, as though with an adult mind, "I am going to hear the word of God that the Fathers preach in the church; I do not want to be left outside with the animals." These words pierced the man's heart. Lessoned by a child, he followed its example and persevered in coming regularly.

An old man—they tend to be very obstinate—fell ill. The Father visited him and invited him to go to confession, but he replied he had nothing to confess. At the same time he requested to be taken to his farm. The Father returned and forbade them to take him. Sitting down, he urgently and lovingly insisted that he cleanse his soul through confession. Seeing the Father's determination and fearing that he could see inside him, the Indian began to disgorge his sins. He demonstrated true sorrow and repentance, and, receiving absolution, delivered up his soul (to judge by this warranty) to God.

What I shall recount next did not occur in this place but is relevant nonetheless. There are old people who believe that the breviary talks to the Fathers and informs them about hidden things. One of these persons committed a crime. The caciques subjected him to punishment to make him confess, but he obstinately refused. A Father came and asked him to confess for the sake of the common good, but he refused. It chanced that the Father then recited one of the day hours, and said when finished, "Son, confess the thing they say about you." The Indian answered, "Your book has already told you." Grasping what the Indian meant, the Father replied, "This book tells the truth." "Well then," said the other, "since the book has already told you, I might as well tell the truth." He thereupon confessed and the problem was taken care of.

The Indians from this town found a little pagan girl lost in the forest and in danger of being eaten by wild animals. In good health when baptized by the Father, she immediately grew ill and flew to heaven, as if predestined.

CHAPTER 52

The reduction of Santa Maria la Mayor

THE PEOPLE of this town were conquered by Father Diego de Boroa at the cost of great trials and persistence. They were located at a place that was impossible for the Father to enter unless they cooperated in bringing him in, on account of a rugged mountain range and the two huge rivers that encircle it. They expelled the Father several times with indignation and anger, and on occasion planned to kill him. But the Father's courage, charity, and zeal subdued this stronghold of the devil.

As his companion he had an old and fervent missioner, Father Claudio Reyer[121] from Burgundy, known for his talent in instructing the Indians. The Indians realized the good they possessed through having received the Fathers, and gratefully welcomed the faith and civilization just as in the other reductions. They rid themselves of the common obstacle of concubines in order to do so. In fear of the brutal invasion from São Paulo, the town transferred to a better site, where they live in peace and very much as Christians, devoted to the Virgin, whose sodality there is truly exemplary.

A sodality member's son, less than a year old, was fascinated by the sight of babies being buried with flowers and garlands on their heads. He several times asked his father's permission to die, and even lay on the ground and acted dead—as if practicing. Pressed by his son for permission, the father replied, "Son, if God wishes for you to die, his holy will be done." Hearing his father's approval and acceptance, the child said, "Then, father, I am going to die." He lay down on his bed and died, with no previous illness.

Physicians declare, not without reason, that the imagination can have an effect. This was verified in the case of an Indian who was resting with his wife while on a journey. Two deadly vipers, frenzied by their poison, came out of a cave and attacked the pair. The Indian killed the snakes, but was quite shaken by the sudden occurrence. Out of curiosity, he cut the animals up to examine their death-dealing instrument. Having done this, he went on his way. He was so obsessed by the venomous vipers that, during the night, he screamed in his sleep that the vipers were killing him. His wife awoke and found his pulse already gone. A Father came and found him in his agony; informed of what had happened, he applied the usual antidotes as if the man had really been poisoned. The man quickly recovered consciousness, although he remained unwell for six days and was left as weak as if he had been through a grave illness. As he himself acknowledged, the panic from his dream of being killed by snakebite had brought about the illness.

CHAPTER 53

The reduction of San Francisco Xavier

THE PEOPLE of the region where this town was founded were gathered by the gospel through the usual effort of hard work, gift giving, and perseverance. All were baptized. Some of them held on to their previous evil way of life, but secretly. To these the devil sent one of his ministers from the north, where, as we shall see later, are the seedbeds of these wicked people. The man disguised his coming under a cloak of devotion, as if to hear the word of God. Father Francisco de Céspedes,[122] then in charge of the reduction, gave him a loving and hospitable welcome. The man gathered around himself the bad elements in the town. So that they could plot without disturbance, they built him a house away from the town, where he gave them his talks. His theme was the usual one, carnal liberty: "Let us live like our ancestors. What do the Fathers find wrong in our having plenty of women? It is surely folly for us to forsake our elders' customs and good way of life and submit to the new practices these Fathers want to bring in. I think the best thing we can do about this evil is for us to kill the Father here."

His audience applauded him with celebration and dancing, convinced that a great prophet had arrived among them. The Lord willed that a young man of good inclinations and virtue was present at this talk. He immediately went to tell the Father, though without mentioning the plot to kill him. The Father took them by surprise; they fled from his presence to avoid recognition. The magician, who alone remained behind, left rebuked but not amended. Shortly thereafter the latter seized his bow and arrows and, with a numerous escort of malefactors, went in search of the Father, uttering absurdities against him like a possessed person and blaspheming our holy faith. In the dark of the night, the Father managed to escape this brute's rage through rear courtyards; otherwise he would certainly have been killed. They dealt the young man who had warned the Father a blow with a club, leaving him for dead. The noise drew the good people of the town, and they went after the Father and brought him home.

The culprits fled to the forest, taking with them the dregs of the town's people including a number of children who went along with their mothers. Armed with charity and escorted by strongly Christian people and another Father who had come to assist him, the Father pursued the fugitives' tracks and overtook them. The ringleaders of the uprising we sent to the reductions of Encarnación and Nuestra Señora de Loreto on the Paraná to be worked on by the people there, who were so strongly rooted in the faith. The magician who was the main ringleader went to Loreto. Far from forgetting his evil devices, he there attempted to puff himself up and gain ascendancy. The people of the town, particularly well grounded in the faith and Christian manners, reported his absurd efforts to me. I had him punished and made him attend catechism with the children, where he learned the essentials. He soon fell ill, and after numerous sessions on my part spent working with him, he died with warranties of eternal salvation.

The remainder were removed from this life by the plague, confessing their past errors. It was much observed that the plague seized on them alone and bypassed the rest of the town, who kept their health and life. This town continues very advanced in virtue.

CHAPTER 54

The reduction of Asunción[123]

THE FLOCK assembled here by the efforts mentioned above is today shepherded by Father Cristóbal de Altamirano,[124] well known for his tireless labor and discretion in taming lions. His exertion in tending to bodies and souls during a severe epidemic brought him close to the point of death. He would visit the sick clinging to two young men. There were times when he would collapse exhausted in a faint to the ground, his fall broken by the rain which ran in rivers through the streets. A Brother who was with him took his pulse; detecting signs of mortal illness, he begged him to take to his bed. However, because he was spurred by zeal for his sheep to succor them in this severe crisis, he was consoled by the Lord with the sudden gift of health and strength, so that he was able to exercise his zeal without difficulty. When there were no healthy people left in the town to help them, the Father and Brother carried the dead to burial on their own shoulders and dug the graves. They cooked food for the living and distributed it personally. The Indians said gratefully of these actions: "When we were pagans we used to die like dogs and run away from each other. Now that we are Christians, the Father of us all has sent us this help for our souls and bodies."

The devil appeared one night to a lad whose life was already in death's hands. He said: "You have come to your life's final end. Your sins are so great that God's justice will not admit you to penitence, so you might as well give up the idea of confessing. What will the Father say when he sees how you have neglected your soul up till now? Besides, you will lose the good name you have with him. Take my advice and forget about your sins."

The mother of mercy and refuge of sinners, the sovereign Virgin, came to him. She put the devil to flight and said to the sick man, "Son, take courage and go to confession; my Son will forgive you." The youth boldly arose and, though the members of his household thought he was out of his mind and tried to stop him, he fearlessly went to the Father and begged with tears to go to confession. The Father was disconcerted at seeing him; thinking the same as the members of his household, he told him to leave. But the young man replied, "Look, Father, I am going straight to hell; I have committed many sins." He told the Father what he had seen and made a good confession, whereupon he recovered the health of his soul and, not long after, that of his body.

Unfazed by the harm to his reputation, he made public what had happened and how the Virgin had been good to him. This won the Virgin many devotees and induced many to hope for pardon, inducing all to turn their backs on despair.

CHAPTER 55

The reduction of San Nicolás

THE APOSTOLIC man Father Roque González strode with a giant's courage through this barbarian wickedness, opening a breach for the holy gospel and drawing ever closer to the glorious palm of martyrdom. He found the people of this place, while quite reclusive, not unwilling to hear his message of the Christian faith. He established his town there under the patronage of St. Nicholas, whose favor has been evinced by this people's extraordinary Christianity. Despite their steadfastness being assailed by difficult periods of famine and disease, the deep roots which the faith has struck in them have kept them solid and stalwart. This was well illustrated in a Christian woman. She gave birth and, seeing the marks of death on her newborn baby and having no one to summon the Father, herself carried him to the baptismal font, where, as soon has she had washed him, he flew off to heaven, leaving her joyful at having given eternal life to one who, had she waited an instant longer, would have died to the vision of God forever.

Devotion to the Virgin in her sodality is very strong, as can be seen from many exemplary actions.

CHAPTER 56

The reduction of Candelaria

THE DESIRE for Christian instruction attracted to this town an outstanding group of Indians who rapidly received the garment of grace in
baptism and grew in virtue and in devotion to the Virgin, dedicating
themselves as her slaves and establishing a very devout sodality. Heaven
harvested the ripe fruit of numerous babies who passed to rest in their flower,
as well of as adults who, having made a general confession and being
provided with the sacraments, we trust bear them company.

The practice of the Christian religion is universal, so that anything not in
accord with it is noticed. Some fifty Indians went on a journey. They passed
a crag to which they had superstitiously ascribed a secret power when they
were pagans, having been taught this by the magicians, and to which they
would pray for good fortune on their trip. Now as they went by they all made
sport of their former delusion. Only three of them surreptitiously observed
their earlier rite. On their return trip they all fell sick, and the three died lest
they repeat their pagan act, while the others returned out of danger.

An irreligious youth always avoided going to Mass, even on days when the
Church requires it. He was a stumbling block to the others, taking them into
the forest. One feast day, overcome by a strong temptation, he took another
fellow out with him and would not let him go back for Mass. The following
day, also a feast day, he again wanted to keep him away. However, his
companion, regretting the day he had missed, decided to make this one and
so left him. He had gone but a few steps when he heard his tempter screaming for help. Turning to look, he saw him in the clutches of a fierce tiger
which was furiously rending him to pieces. He fled from the peril and told
what had happened. The people came and discovered that a good part of
him had already been eaten by the tiger—a manifest punishment and
example to the rest.

CHAPTER 57

The martyrdom of three religious of the Society of Jesus

OUR TRAVELS have now brought us to the place where three apostolic men were made victims, sealing their faith with their blood and giving the lie to the unbelief of the pagans. These were the Venerable Fathers Roque González, Juan del Castillo, and Alonso Rodríguez.[125] Moreover, if the first of three species of martyrdom is patience in adversity and hardship (as St. Gregory declares: "Spiritual martyrdom is of three kinds, the first being genuine patience in adversity"), I maintain that these outstanding men did not undergo martyrdom once only. Rather, they did so on every occasion they had for the most genuine patience, and such was every step they took among the pagans, each pagan being one more occasion of martyrdom.

Father Roque González was a native of the city of Asunción. He was the son of parents noble by their virtue and by their blood, and he fulfilled his devotion to both these claims upon him. In this Father shone the rays of grace which the Father of lights poured into his soul as a child so that he might enlighten countless souls as an adult. He was brought up in our own house (which was more his home than his parents' house was) on the milk of prayer, in which he persevered until it formed him into a perfect man. When he sang his first Mass, they placed a palm in his hands (which his modesty declined) betokening the perfect purity which he preserved unblemished amid the occasions of sin. It was a foreshadowing of the palm which heaven had prepared for him by martyrdom. He declined the honors which the bishop repeatedly offered him in his cathedral[126] by recourse to the Church's having a vow to refuse dignities.

He entered the Society in 1609. After a few months as a novice, he was made a missionary, a task proper to our professed members. So manifest were his virtue and zeal that he was entrusted with the Society's most difficult mission; he there initiated his martyrdom among barbarous peoples. He went to the Paraná, where we have already outlined his zealous labors. He filled the Uruguay territory with reductions. When these heroic accomplishments failed to satiate his heart, he launched upon another which brought him the crown of martyrdom.

Near the reduction of Candelaria, where we last left off, there was a cacique named Cuarobay. Once he was won over with trifling gifts, his good will eased the Father's entrance into his land, which was called Caró, or "house of wasps." Even the name of the place corresponded to the Fathers' blessed destiny: it was indeed a house of wasps, for their stings hastened his steps to the crown.

In this area lived the greatest cacique known throughout those regions.

He was held in awe because of the evil arts, tricks, and magic with which he kept the people deluded. His name was Nezú, "Awe." Father Roque won him over. This cacique, desiring—whether falsely or sincerely—to keep the Fathers on his lands, built a church for God and a house for the Fathers. At this time Father Juan del Castillo[127] was making good use of his gifts and fervor in San Nicolás. He was from Belmonte, a son of noble parents. Father Roque brought him along to take possession of the church which Nezú had constructed. They there raised the trophy of Christ our Lord's victories, and the two of them remained there for some days.

A recent arrival in the reductions there was Father Alonso Rodríguez,[128] a native of Zamora and a man adorned with virtues. His zeal led him to urge Father Roque to take him to the Caró reduction, and he obtained his wish. It did not take him long to sense a change from the affection the people had originally shown him in their town. Nezú reversed his steadfastness and treated Father Castillo with insults, a result of the rage with which the devil burned at seeing himself stripped even there of his dominance. Through a bad Indian who had apostatized from the faith, the devil won over Nezú's friendship as a means to obtain his victory, kindling his spark of hatred toward the Fathers with such arguments as this: "I see our age-old freedom to roam through valleys and forests being lost. These foreign priests are penning us up in towns, not for our good but to make us listen to teaching opposed to our ancestral practices and customs. And if you look carefully, Nezú, you are already starting to lose the awe that is owed to your name. For if today the tigers and other wild animals of these forests are subject to you and do incredible things in your defense, tomorrow you yourself—as you already see in others—will be subject to the voice of these strangers. The women you now enjoy in accord with our customs, and who love you, you will see despising you tomorrow and becoming the wives of your very slaves. What spirit is so strong as to put up with such offenses? Cast your eyes through all these towns whose inhabitants' lack of spirit has allowed these wretched men a foothold, and see how their power has dwindled. They are no longer men; they are women subject to a foreigner's will. If this evil is not cut off here, if you give way, you will see all the peoples who live between here and the sea made subject to them, to your own disgrace and shame. You, the true god of the living, will find yourself miserable and humiliated. This can easily be prevented if you employ your power to kill these wretched men." Nezú's flame, fanned thus from hell, blazed up—particularly since he possessed two sheds filled with women, whom he kept like two herds of unclean animals at the beck of his pleasure.

CHAPTER 58

Nezú plots the death of the Fathers

THIS COUNTERFEIT god and slave of the devil, possessed by a raging anger, plotted the death not only of these three Fathers but of all the Fathers of the Uruguay. He sent a mandate to all the caciques, ordering them all to kill the Fathers in their lands; he would do the same in his own. He scolded them for their readiness to accept the Fathers' teaching, and for cowardice if they did not carry out his command. He threatened to order the tigers and wild beasts of the forest to come raging out and tear to pieces anyone who did not comply.

The Fathers were so unaware of this treachery that Fathers Roque and Alonso were planning to celebrate a festival for the dedication of the town of Caró.[129] A large troop of scoundrels had gathered there. The saintly Father Roque, after celebrating Mass and making his thanksgiving to the Most High with his usual devotion, started to fasten with his own hands the tongue onto a bell—something those barbarous people had never seen before —in order to enliven the festival with its ringing. Hardly had Carupé, a leading cacique, seen him engaged in this activity when he signaled one of his slaves, who had been instructed beforehand, to kill him. This vile slave of the devil—his name was Maranguá, "vile," and he lived up to it through this vile deed—raised a mace. It was of wood but had the hardness and appearance of iron. He dealt the Father a savage blow on the head, smashing his skull. To the bell's striking and chiming, the Father's soul soared joyfully heavenward. We have the bell to this day as a relic, even though they removed a good part of it to make arrowheads. They vented their cowardly rage upon his saintly body, pounding it with bludgeons and sparing neither face nor head.

They trooped off to the hut where Father Alonso was. At the shouts of the mob, he and his death came simultaneously to the threshold. An evil cacique seized him and commanded one of his servants to kill him. They rained blows upon him. The mastiff who held him, fearful of being hit by a stray blow himself, let go of him. With filial love Father Alonso moved towards the corpse of his already dead father, saying over and over: "Sons, why are you killing me? Sons, what are you doing?" He wanted to offer the sacrifice of himself in church, where he had so often celebrated Mass and offered himself as a sacrifice in fervent prayer. But even here his wish was not to be, for death took him on the very threshold. To sate their fury upon this tender lamb, the tigers split his body in half at the belly and pulled his thighs asunder. They dragged his venerable remnants around the church and then threw him inside, pausing like a tiger that licks its bloody claws after the hunt.

They went on to pillage the furnishings of the church. With pagan impiety, they plundered the altars and dressed in the priestly vestments, which they tore up and divided among themselves. The chalice and paten they broke into pieces and wore as ornaments around their infamous necks. The cross, raised as a trophy by faith, was cast down by faithless paganism and consumed in fire. Especially deep was our sorrow at the execrable havoc they wrought on a painting of the Virgin. It was a beloved possession of the holy Father Roque and the companion of his travels. He would raise it in a town and then, once the town was well established, move it to another. He thus rightly called it the *Conquistadora*, and he ascribed to its presence the success of his undertakings—conquests in which it was present for both gain and for loss, since, the image perishing together with their bodies, they now enjoy immortal glory in heaven.

I say nothing of what they seized in the way of religious treasures, since there was little to be had. Instructed by now in how to battle with corpses, they did abominable things to a pair of crucifixes, which they smashed and tried to reduce to ashes along with the Fathers' sacred limbs. Heaven, however, preserved some quite large fragments, which serve today for our inspiration and consolation.

Many of the people, innocent of the plot and guiltless of the crime, were profoundly distressed over this massacre. While their love for their religious Fathers called for vengeance, their fear of the parricide's fury withheld it. A venerable old man, a prominent cacique, who had been seized by a longing to be a Christian, inveighed against them severely and vituperatively for this atrocious crime. He held up to them the kindliness, love, and gifts—the greatest of all being the Catholic faith—with which the Fathers had attempted to enrich them. Their rage and fury abandoned all respect for his venerable gray hairs; they closed in upon him and brutally clubbed him to death—a blessed death indeed; for, with Christian defiance in the face of evident danger to his life, he defended Catholic truth even though he was a pagan—not, as we may believe, without a supernatural impulse of faith. The same reproach was expressed by two boys who were stricken with filial grief over the slaughter that had been so suddenly wrought on their beloved Fathers. These too they seized to kill, but they escaped with their lives. They also saved the lives of the Fathers in other reductions, traveling over secret paths to tell them of the death of Father Roque and his companion.

The news reached Nezú. He straightway sent a troop of conspirators to Father Juan del Castillo's hut to kill him immediately. They brazenly asked him for wedges (the iron axe heads they use), fishhooks, and other articles. The holy man had been unconcernedly rendering God his tribute of praise in the canonical hours. He distributed to them what he had. They repaid his generosity by binding his arms and dragging him through the streets with shoving, cuffing, and blows, and telling him, "You shall now die at our hands like Roque and Alonso, and not a trace of your evil seed will be left."

The Father begged them to take him to his brothers still alive so that together they might make up a single holocaust. An evil Indian replied by stabbing him three times with a sword. Others followed with arrows and stakes, piercing his face and eyes and saying, "Here you must die, you sorcerer dog!" "You will not kill my soul," the holy man answered; "it is immortal. I gladly let my body suffer to confirm the faith of Jesus Christ which I have always taught you." They dragged him three quarters of a league over rocks so jagged that the stones soon stripped off his clothes, his modesty suffering more from the nakedness than from his wounds. He so longed for the consummation of his martyrdom that when the rope they dragged him by nearly came loose he said to them, "Tie me again, for I am glad to die."

The executioners wearied of dragging him, though the holy man did not weary of his cruel torment. They then dropped two heavy rocks onto his head. The holy man received them pronouncing the sweet names of Jesus and Mary, to whom he entrusted his blessed soul. They left his body for the birds and beasts to batten on. But though the place was a den of tigers, these acted humanely, in reproach of the barbarians' beastly savagery. The latter disregarded the beasts' example and, all unwittingly, offered his dead body to heaven through fire as a living holocaust. To appear as a priest, even if a false one, Nezú donned the priestly vestments and displayed himself to the people. He had the babies brought before him and with his own barbarous rites attempted to erase the indelible character impressed on their souls in baptism. He scraped their tongues which had tasted the salt of the Spirit of wisdom; he also scraped their breasts and backs to rub off the holy oils by which they had been prepared for the struggle.

They then attempted to complete their victory by killing the other Fathers, who, at the news of these events, already suffered martyrdom by the sword of sorrow that had been plunged through them. Firm in the faith, the Christians took a stand in defence of their faith and of their Fathers, displaying so much valor that they killed a number of the enemy.

The next day the Caró returned to check on the pyres where they had left the venerable remnants of the two holy men the previous day. They heard the following words coming quite distinctly from holy Roque's heart (as concordant witnesses have testified): "You have killed one that loves you. You have killed my body and broken my bones, but not my soul, which is now among the blessed in heaven. Many sufferings will come to you because of my death, for my sons will come to punish you for maltreating the picture of the Mother of God." This should have sufficed to bring them to reason, but, rendered deaf by their bestial brutishness, they said, "This charlatan is still talking." They opened his loving breast and removed his heart. Though cold, it burned with flames of charity. The murderer Maranguá immediately pierced it with an arrow. To dispose of every trace of the martyrs, they lit a huge fire and threw the two bodies and the heart into it. The latter, however, remained intact. The fire of charity overcame the flames from the wood, and the heart was left like gold refined and purified in fire. It is today preserved in Rome, together with the arrow. [130]

The towns joined together to exact punishment, which was exemplary. Nezú was soon forced to flee through the forest. He took refuge in a pagan town where he lives today. We have invited him with the peace and truth of the Gospel, our desires warranting hope of winning him over so that his poor soul will not be lost. We now have all of his vassals in a fine settlement called San Javier, and the accomplices in the holy men's deaths live deeply repentant and ashamed.

CHAPTER 59

More on this plot and on the Caró reduction

AN ACCOMPLICE in the martyrdom of these holy men was a famous cacique named Tambavé. As his booty from the inhuman crime he took a horse which the venerable Father Roque had ridden. The horse displayed its grief for its missing master by refusing to eat—even when, to test their suspicion that it was acting this way out of sorrow and grief, they persistently offered it hay and grain. It would go up to houses where Indians were celebrating the holy men's death with festivity and games to the odor of wine; there, as if possessed of reason, it would neigh fearfully. The Indians went outside to look, and were convinced by the animal's perseverance to admit that it acted this way from grief. This was further confirmed when they noticed that whenever Father Roque's name was mentioned tears streamed from each of its eyes. The witnesses themselves affirmed that there was no doubt of this, because they tested it repeatedly. Additional confirmation was furnished by the fact that the horse never allowed an Indian to mount it. When an Indian dressed in the Father's cassock and pretended he was the horse's holy master, he was easily able to subdue and even mount it. It grew so thin from its fasting that the Indians could see it was of no use to them, and that they were being reproached even by a beast, and so they killed it.

If this was one testimony to the martyrs' heavenly glory, no less so was their executioners' conversion, which they effected from heaven by their prayers. Many were deeply remorseful and confessed their foolhardy deed with sorrow. I will mention only one of these: an Indian named Tambape, who from being a cacique and lord became a servant of the Fathers, assisting them in works of charity towards the sick, whom he served with all love, and in other lowly tasks. So powerful was his preaching of Christ that, having become a Paul, he contributed to the conversion of many pagans who today enjoy baptism and the Christian faith. So well disposed was he when death took him that he confessed his sin aloud, praying for pardon to the holy men he had crowned in words of such deep emotion that it touched his hearers' hearts. His advice to his vassals just before his end gave evidence of his dying zeal that they all serve God and shun the fictitious wiles of the sorcerers. Strengthened by the sacraments, he now rests in peace.

This town has steadily been growing in virtue and banishing vice, the children acting as teachers for their parents. I will give but one notable example of this. A woman was secretly living an unchaste life. The only witness was her two-year-old daughter, who was so young that the woman had no fear of her guilt being exposed. Offended by her grave sin, the child told the lascivious mother: "I want to die so that I will not see your impure deeds. Amend your life; I will beg forgiveness for you in heaven." The child was seized by a sudden illness and began approaching death. As she saw at what a pace her daughter was nearing death, the mother took seriously what she had treated as a joke. The child soon died. The mother turned to the remedy of confession and penance and today lives an exemplary life, awaiting the fulfillment of her daughter's pledge.

A young man found himself in an occasion of looking at obscene things. He remembered hearing in a sermon an exposition of Christ our Lord's words: "If your eye scandalizes you, pluck it out,"[131] and with his fingers he inflicted a hurt upon his eyes which left him ailing for several days. One of the Fathers chided him for this, but he replied, "I would rather lose both eyes than offend God!" When seriously tempted, this young man would use a pin or a thorn to pierce his arms and thighs, a deed which in a perfect religious would be remarkable.

Despite the many sweet-smelling lilies, there is no lack of thorns. An Indian was living in notable neglect of his soul, regularly missing Mass on feast days. One Saturday in Lent the devil put him in the way of wild game. He concealed it during the day and gorged on it in the middle of the night, saying, "God cannot see me, he is asleep now." God did see him that night— and the following day as well, when, upon the man's absenting himself from Sunday Mass, he was punished in an exemplary way. The Father noticed that he was not in church and sent into the woods to find him. As the man entered his house death suddenly overtook him: he fell dead on the threshold, his soul leaving behind a body so malodorous, swollen, and ugly that it inspired both horror and salutary warning.

The sodality of the Virgin is very advanced in this reduction, and our Lady bestows her mercies upon it. One of its members was teaching his daughters, five and three years old, how to recite the rosary and other devotions. The elder took so much to heart repeating Hail Marys on her knees that she was scolded for excess. Our Lady showed how pleasing this service was to her. The two sisters were together at the door of their house, even there continuing their prayers, when they suddenly saw beside them a lady in shining white clothes with a lovely child in her arms. She took hold of the child who was so devoted to her, telling her sister, "Do not be afraid; I will return your sister to you." The sister was startled and amazed; the strangeness of the woman, whom she had never seen before, made her run inside to tell her mother. The mother anxiously searched the neighborhood for her daughter, and her distraught husband looked everywhere throughout the town.

They returned home shedding bitter tears of sorrow for the loss of their daughter. They again asked the child for clues about the woman who had carried off their beloved daughter. She kept saying, "A very beautiful lady took her away from me." At the height of their distress, they beheld the little girl come in the door. They asked her about the person who had stolen their beloved treasure, and she told the same story as her sister—that the beautiful lady had taken her away, making her the companion of a very pretty child who was her son, to a lovely garden where she showered her with pleasures and kindnesses and told her that, instead of the necklaces and trinkets which she wore around her neck, she ought to wear her rosary; also that the lady had taught her a little song in praise of the Virgin, which she carefully rehearsed. The little girl sang the song charmingly. "This woman," she said, "surpasses other women. Her clothing was like the sun, she has sweet, loving words. I do not know why she brought me back here; I feel lonely without her son. How I wish I could have stayed with her forever!"

Astonished and no less delighted, the parents gave her some food, but the child, who had tasted that heavenly food, found it disgusting and would not even try it. The next morning her parents brought her to church, and when she saw a beautiful statue of the Virgin with her holy Son in her arms, she cried out, "That is the lady who treated me so kindly." The people were no less amazed than edified. The child continues her devotions, as do many others moved by her example.

The souls in purgatory have repaid the continual devotion with which the people offer disciplines and other penances for their sufferings. The town was once ablaze with flames; the houses being of straw, there was no human way to prevent the raging fire from consuming them all. The people made a vow to offer Masses and penances; when they finished their vow the fire died down, to the wonder and amazement of all.

CHAPTER 60

The reduction of San Carlos

ONCE WELL grounded in the faith, the Indians themselves serve as hunters to gather in these flocks. A person who formerly ranged the forest unsubdued is today, pacified, our Fathers' helper in tracking down others; and thus the spiritual conquest goes on. A host of pagans joined this town and with time were progressively baptized. Within sight of the town was a mountain range peopled by rational beasts living in paganism. Their swineherd was a great magician; he stubbornly barred their steps and ears to the word of the gospel. Though the ordinary people wanted to hear it, he obliterated their desires by threatening them with tigers and serpents, the usual fabrication of these sorcerers.

Father Pablo Palermo,[132] who was in charge of this conquest, tramped back and forth through the forest and assembled an abundant flock of four hundred Indian men—with their dependents, a total of some sixteen hundred persons. He won over the magician by love and with gifts which, though of slight value, are able to crack such hard rocks. Once among Christians, the magician found himself no longer obeyed by his people, his tricks and frauds undone. He feared he would be forced to give up the covey of women he had freely enjoyed in the hills. Angry with the light, he fled in the darkest night into the forest like a stallion with his herd of mares, so anxious was he to keep them. But his attempts were in vain. Making a great effort at flight, he went so deep into the mountains that the Father's diligence proved unable to find him; but divine justice found him and punished his rebellion with a disease from which they all died—although from amid these thorns heaven plucked many flowers: numerous infants who flew to their eternal rest beautified by the first grace of baptism.

Among those who survived from these bands was an ancient of eighty years who had grown old in impure vices. The Father undertook to baptize him, but the usual difficulty of the women arose, and he fled to the forest to avoid having to give them up. The conscientious Father's zeal found him out, yet his soft and loving words, in addition to gifts, did not suffice to soften this hard old man; he fled once more at the summons of the devil, who twice appeared to him and got him to run away. The souls in purgatory changed his heart in response to a novena of Masses offered for them by the Father. The fortunate old man fell sick, and within a few days of his coming back acknowledged the danger to his soul and body, and his own obstinacy and hardness. He dismissed the women and earnestly requested baptism. Cleansed of his old leprosy, and with fervent acts of sorrow and hope, he fled from this life to life everlasting.

A longing for holy Communion softened the hardness of a long-standing Christian who had kept a certain sin secret for many years out of shame. The example he saw of those who went to Communion made him eager to taste the Bread of life. Seeing his own life lost and ruined, he made a long and careful examination of conscience and cleansed his soul by a general confession. The Lord showed his pleasure at the man's receiving Communion by thanking him in a dream for his efforts and warning him never to hide any sin from his confessor, since confessors were his vicars on earth for the salvation of sinners. His avidity for more grace thus whetted, he continues to lead a Christian life, never failing to attend Mass daily and make his confessions.

CHAPTER 61

The reduction of San Pedro and San Pablo

THIS SETTLEMENT is rather recent. Some four thousand persons have been baptized, and the remaining pagans are preparing to receive the sacrament. They all give evidence that this reduction will be a place of splendid Christianity.

CHAPTER 62

The reduction of Santo Tomé

THIS IS a quite prominent place. The people roundabout call it Tape— "the city" par excellence. The town is so large that the province is named after it, commonly being called the province of Tape. Though new to the faith, the people there equal the most long-standing Christians and are rapidly being baptized. There are now nearly six thousand Christians. Their conversion was almost miraculous, for they were a stiff-necked people. Heaven overcame their savagery by means of tigers. These ranged in packs through their clearings, farms, and forests, killing many people, mainly pagans who rebelliously avoided the Fathers. It once happened that a band of Indians attacked by tigers put up a palisade, where the tigers besieged them for four days and prevented them from getting out. As a result all the pagans started coming into the reduction, and this affliction was ended by a novena of sung Masses.

During an abundance of food, they forgot themselves and began roaming the forests again, the pagans no longer concerned to receive the faith nor the Christians to live in conformity to God's law. The tigers immediately returned and wrought even greater havoc. The natives came to their senses and returned to their duty, realizing that the animals' behavior went beyond what was natural. The tigers were gotten rid of by means of prayers and petitions.

This ought to have confirmed their amendment, but inconstant nature, abetted by peace, food, repose, and forgetfulness of the familiar scourge, relapsed once more into its crimes. A number of magicians, who had cast away their magic out of fear, secretly became more pernicious than ever. But those instruments of divine justice, the tigers, returned to wreak even worse ravages. More than two hundred traps were set, baited with dogs and deer, but not a single tiger fell in; they would extract the bait without falling into the traps. The people recognized their fault and implored mercy; mutinying against the magicians, they forced them to renounce their diabolical frauds. Having thus come to their senses, they have been delivered from these ravages.

One unbelieving Indian had a pair of concubines. He was baptized and married one of them. Three years later he asked the Father to marry him to the other, saying that he had married the first only temporarily. When he learned that this was impossible, he seized the girl and fled to the forest. Father Luis Arnot,[133] who has labored faithfully in the cultivation of this people, made zealous efforts to find him. The woman he found alone and nearly dead, having been lost by her lover. They found the man as well a good distance away. Restored to health in the town, the two fled a second time to live among pagans—an old wound heals late or never. Once more the sheep were rounded up. The first wife died, and the man married the concubine; though they had little joy of each other, for death soon claimed their lives.

A woman tried to seduce a modest young man. She seized him in an out-of-the-way spot and tried to compel him. He tried to urge her to chastity and purity, but when he saw that his arguments had no effect he took a stick to her and got away.

A lustful young man lewdly attempted to seduce a chaste girl. She did her best to avoid him. He caught her alone and tried to force her to consent in his sin. Helpless and weeping, the girl said: "Look, I go to Communion and receive God; do not do me this offense. You should be afraid that God will punish you severely." The man was suddenly seized by an inward panic that left him trembling and powerless to pursue his attempt; thus the chaste woman got away.

CHAPTER 63

The reduction of San José

THIS TOWN was founded by Father José Cataldino, from Italy, an apostolic man who has labored zealously and ceaselessly for more than thirty years in the conversion of pagans. Almost three thousand souls have been baptized in this town. When at its peak, the town was struck by a malignant plague. With no one to till the ground, there was no food; but this was compensated for by the charity of the Father and of his companion, Father Manuel Bertot.[134] Heaven took the first fruits of numerous infants who died. Many adults were lost, going into the forests and dying without the water of baptism. One old man left the town with his wife and daughters, all of them unbelievers except for the youngest child, who was a Christian. The old man died suddenly; the mother was returning to the town with the intention of being baptized but within a few days followed her husband in death. The children were eager to approach the baptismal font, but two of them were too weak to travel. Amid the distress they experienced—the eldest at being still a pagan and her sisters at the prospect of death—the eldest took charge of the other two. She would carry one on her back for some distance and then return for the other. Sustaining this effort, she walked for two whole days, finally entering the town with one of her sisters on her back. The Fathers sent out for the other. They had the girls treated well, and washed the two sisters in baptism. They thereupon flew to heaven, the youngest, who was already a Christian, following them five days later.

During this difficult period the town resorted to the universal refuge of devotion to the Virgin through recitation of her rosary, which they did in common on Saturdays in the church. With this they have experienced great prosperity.

Father José had a miraculous experience. He was riding from one town to another on a nervous horse. At a bad place in the road the horse stumbled and threw its rider. The latter's foot caught in the stirrup and the skittish horse galloped over a rough stony field, kicking and dragging the Father. The stirrup strap broke under the Father's weight. He is sixty-eight years old. His companion came up, thinking him dead or badly injured, but found him sitting up and so unharmed that on reaching town he said a Mass of thanksgiving.

At the crisis of a difficult childbirth they did not have the image of St. Ignatius, who in these parts is an outstanding miracle worker. His place was taken by his holy and venerable son, Brother Alfonso Rodríguez.[135] The devout woman was given the latter's picture by the Father, and no sooner had she received it with faith and reverence than she brought her child to live birth even though it was thought already dead and sure to cause the mother's death. It is no wonder that in such illustrious occurrences the father should let so saintly a son take his place.

CHAPTER 64

The reduction of San Miguel

REPORT OF the gospel reached this town, and its dwellers, avid for so great a blessing, walked many leagues in quest of Fathers. The first to set foot here was the holy martyr, Father Cristóbal de Mendoza; he begot them in Christ and reared them on the milk of the gospel. It has about five thousand persons, today all of them Christians. After the saintly man's martyrdom, Father Miguel Gómez[136] tended them. He was witness to a presage of the sufferings that were to be undergone by this whole Christian community shortly afterwards.

The Father had a painting of Christ being clothed after his scourging. He noticed that it was sweating copiously from the knees down. The sweat was also visible on the footsteps, and on the pricks of the scourges and on the thorns. When taken up with cotton, the sweat would flow again at the same rate. There was sweating at the same time on a picture of our Lady of the Assumption and on a picture of St. Ignatius in the township of Espíritu Santo, from which the Indians living in those townships had gone out to make war. We were assured of this by the Fathers of our Society. We remarked earlier that the same thing happened in Guairá with a picture of our Lady, a clear token of heaven's grief at the offense given by the raiders from São Paulo and the other townships—and as a consolation for us, since we see heaven seconding our grief in our distress.

Many incidents took place here; I will mention one. An old woman, an unbeliever, felt her death near. Leaning on a cane she set out for the town, intending to become a Christian. She was so weak that she fell to the ground at every step. An Indian took hold of her and carried her on his back to the Father. The latter straightway baptized her, as she answered the catechism with her voice intact; she then immediately lost it and discharged her blessed soul. The same has happened to other old people who, even in good health, were baptized and suddenly died.

God is marvelous in his mercy. He demonstrated this to us very clearly in the case of an Indian who had been an accomplice in the death of the saintly Father Juan del Castillo. He ran away and came to this territory to get away from the Fathers and from the faith, which molested him because it opposed his sorceries and trickery. Father Cristóbal de Mendoza discovered him here, but he immediately fled with his pagan dependents. He went deep into the mountains and there, by dint of arguments and magic, deterred many people from baptism. The zealous Father followed him, won him over, and brought him back to this town in order to have him nearby and tame him. The convincing reasons given by the Father compelled him to request the waters of baptism, which, after proper catechizing, he received to his own and everyone's great consolation. During the short time that he lived, he gave tokens of his predestination. He fell ill. When the devil saw that he had slipped from his hands, he attempted to win him back by powerful incite-ments and temptations, which the valiant Indian resisted. The devil appeared to him in visible form and complained of his ingratitude; he promised him health and a long life if he would return to their old friendship. Together with alluring promises he threatened him with terrible punishments, mounting a very dangerous assault. The doughty fighter requested the holy oils, and once anointed proclaimed that he had no more fear of the devil.

A fit seized him in his final agony; he appeared to be undergoing a terrible struggle. Covered with sweat he kept repeating: "God the Father, God the Son, God the Holy Spirit, forgive me my sins so that this devil will leave me. I confess that I have been a great sinner and a very bad man. May your mercy pardon me so that this evil spirit may see you helping me and be frightened away." Gripping a cross firmly in his hands, he said to it piteously: "Good Cross, holy Cross, be my strong helper so that I can get rid of this devil who has laid hold of me." Those present, amazed, felt conflicting emotions of sorrow and consolation at seeing him tormented yet conquering; others felt warned by the scene. He turned to them and said: "Live well and be good Christians, for though God delays, he does punish in the end. And you, Christ Jesus, be my helper against your enemies and mine so that they will leave me." His gestures indicated that he was trying to break free of someone who held him fast; he kept crying for help in his agony, which lasted a good while. He came to himself, now free of the devil, and recounted his suffering, which had been diabolical. He thanked the Lord for giving him victory, and begged pardon of all for deceiving them with his magic; with heartfelt acts and colloquies, he slept in peace.

Less fortunate were the following. A foreign Indian came to this reduction and was upsetting the people with evil words and worse example. Falling ill, and resentful at the Father's admonitions and urgings that he be baptized, he had himself removed from the town to a farm. The Father followed him there. Fleeing further, he had himself carried into a dense forest, saying that the bells and the Father's arguments were driving him out of his wits. The Father's charity found him out, but neither his gifts nor his loving words sufficed to soften the Indian's stony heart; he would even turn toward the wall to avoid hearing his words. Stubbornly determined to die an unbeliever like his ancestors, he died unhappily.

Another old man, grown old in sins of impurity and unwilling to purchase baptism at the price of his concubines, fled to the forest with them and a small son. The Father sent after them to help them, but divine justice had already seized on them, suddenly killing them all.

CHAPTER 65

The reduction of San Cosme and San Damián

THE FATHERS' zealous efforts succeeded in gathering here, from different forests and mountains, approximately five thousand souls, who are progressively being baptized. Many were convinced to return to their old dwelling places by the magicians' persistent opposition to the gospel. Those who let themselves be persuaded experienced due punishment, dying unexpectedly in their paganism. Ranging the forests, the Fathers rescued many for heaven at the cost of hardships. A severe plague broke out, and they assisted all with food for body and soul. Because of the widespread disease, the land was bereft of those who tilled it. Lest it remain idle and there be no seed for sowing and for feeding the needy, the Fathers worked the land themselves, bringing in abundant crops with which they fed the sick and attracted the people who had taken refuge in the forests.

Because of its oddness I will mention an unusual case, the first such that we have seen among these people. An unbelieving father had his own daughter as a concubine. She forsook this crime through baptism, which she received with deep sorrow for this enormous wickedness. Shortly thereafter she died with good warranties of her eternal salvation. Love for his concubine daughter remained alive in the father; overwhelmed by sorrow at her death, he went off to his farm together with a little son of his. The two fell out over a trifle, and the irascible boy, unmindful of his duty as a son, killed his own father with a club. Heaven was thus avenged through this brother, son, and brother-in-law.

As the Father was distributing the usual food among the poor, he came upon two women who were exceptionally emaciated. He suggested baptizing them the next day, but they went several days without returning. The Father himself went to look for them in a forest where he learned they had gone. Their good fortune found them prostrate on the ground and at the point of death. He catechized them and gave them baptism, and they straightway gave their souls to the Creator.

A fervent young man, told that one of his brothers was dying in the forest, sought him out and carried him on his back to the town. He did the same for his mother, who was in the same peril far away. Well prepared by baptism, they both died soon afterwards. The young man so battened on these works of mercy that it was his delight and recreation to convey the dangerously ill on his back so that they would not die unbelievers—thereby conveying eternal life to many and a rare example to all.

Altogether the opposite was another Indian who, unmindful of his own mother and his children, abandoned them in the extreme necessity of a protracted illness. He ran off to the woods and did not attend the catechism class to which he was obliged in order to become a Christian. The Father sought him out, brought him back, and tried with gifts to get him to amend. But, his mother having died without baptism because of his heedlessness, heaven also permitted that he and his wife should die without baptism, meeting a sudden death in the forest.

One Indian compelled God to forget him because he was so forgetful of himself. He would run away from church and catechism to roam the forest in quest of animals, for he was devoted to hunting. The Father always intended to look for him, but kept forgetting to. The poor fellow fell sick in the forest. A relative went to ask the Father to visit him, but, even though spending the whole day in the priest's presence, never managed to tell him. The Indian left, resolving to come back the next day and let him know; but that very day the sick man died without baptism, forgotten as he had forgotten himself.

CHAPTER 66

The reduction of Santa Teresa

FIVE THOUSAND souls have joined this town of Santa Teresa as a result of the fervent efforts of Father Francisco Jiménez,[137] who spent his time not only preaching the gospel but also working the land, cultivating large areas and instructing the natives how to till the ground with a plow. Report of this gathered in great flocks of souls. An old man's people abandoned him on the way, since he was unable to walk and in addition was ill. Anxious to be baptized, he crawled on his hands and feet over a rough track for three days. The Father went out to find him; he received baptism and died. There is a large population of unbelievers throughout this region. An Indian from this reduction went to one of their towns and there fell sick. When he told them of the charity of the Fathers towards the sick, they at once abandoned their houses and joined the reduction; they received baptism and some have died with warranties of their salvation.

The Father ranged through the forests, rivers, and ravines there and discovered a great number of unbelievers, who received him with notable love. They asked him to designate sites for starting towns, but this proved impossible because of a lack of Fathers. He did baptize two hundred and fifty infants, and about a thousand souls followed him to settle in this reduction.

CHAPTER 67

The reduction of Natividad de Nuestra Señora

ABOUT SIX thousand souls have been settled here. By now some twenty-six hundred have received baptism and the rest are in preparation for it. The report of this sacrament led one Indian to come to this reduction with his wife and four children. All of them fell ill because of the length and severity of the trip. The Father visited them and the good woman received him with these words: "You are very welcome, Father. I have come to this country from my own in quest of baptism. I find myself poor here, but it does not surprise or grieve me since my only purpose in coming was to receive baptism." The husband said the same. After being properly catechized, they were baptized by him that day and on the following day took flight to heaven. The Father took charge of the four children, three of whom followed their parents shortly after being washed with the water of eternal salvation.

There is no place where the gospel does not meet with resistance from those ministers of the devil, the magicians. They attribute death to baptism and in this way try to deter people from the sacrament. One boy became sick, and his unbelieving parents, convinced by the magicians' deceits, hid him a considerable distance from the town. The boy kept begging to be brought to the Father so that he might be made a son of God by baptism, but without success. However, some Indians were moved by his appeals and brought him to the Fathers' house, for the boy would not go to that of his father and mother. He was baptized and the next day departed for heaven.

The same thing happened to a very elderly lady who by means of entreaties got herself brought to the town. Seeing her there very distressed, the Father asked why. She replied that she was afflicted because she was still an unbeliever and weighed down by all the years she had spent serving the devil. The Father consoled her and baptized her, whereupon her afflictions vanished, and the following day she reposed in the Lord.

Each place here has its own peculiar customs. Lamentation for the dead is a universal practice, with special vehemence in the case of more noble persons. However, in this place it was also usual for a woman to strip naked, seize a bow and arrows, go out into the street, and shoot arrows at the sun in token of her rage against death, whom they strive to kill with their wishes. The Fathers strove to prevent these unseemly actions, but it was neither feasible nor right to push the people too hard since they arrived only recently. A leading cacique grew ill and devoutly received the water of baptism. As he neared death he ordered all his people not to perform these ceremonies when he died: they should not lament him as though dead but rejoice over him as a living person on his way to everlasting life. This blessed cacique died, and the whole town complied with his dying wish; from then on the keening ended and the pagan rites hitherto in use disappeared.

CHAPTER 68

The reduction of Santa Ana

ABOUT SIX thousand people settled here, and in a short time some twenty-six hundred were baptized. A great cacique came to live here. His name was Ayerobia, meaning "I trust" (at baptism he was given the name Bartolomé); his name well expressed his longing for salvation, and it was confirmed by outstanding deeds. He undertook the task of spurring negligent pagans to receive baptism. He would seek them out, take them into his house, feed them, instruct them in the faith himself as though he were a long-time Christian, and present them, already prepared, to be given the sacrament by the Father. He devoted his efforts to beautifying the church, doing carpentry work. On hearing of the invasion by the raiders from São Paulo at the reduction of Jesús-María, where they killed and seized many people, his heart was pierced with grief at seeing men who claimed to be Christians throw up obstacles to the evangelization of the pagans. Armed with confession, he set off to support his brethren, and during a skirmish in which he killed a number of Tupís,[138] who are like bandits brought along as auxiliaries by the townsmen of São Paulo, he himself was killed, leaving his name alive with trust that he is saved.

Another cacique imitated him in his life and death. He displayed his zeal in rounding up the rabble of magicians and sorcerers, getting them to come to catechism, and bringing them en masse to church on Sundays, with the zeal of a genuine and faithful Christian. As such he too, like the other, died in the war.

I do not wish to pass over a rather droll, though really edifying, story. A virtuous young man, stirred by the Fathers' sermons on chastity to ardent love for the virtue, vehemently begged to be castrated. Edified by his zeal, the Fathers explained to him the impermissibility of this and the way he should act in order to be chaste.

Faith demonstrated its effects in a miraculous incident. An Indian was lethally bitten on the foot by a poisonous viper and collapsed as if dead, emitting quantities of blood from both feet, and also from his eyes, ears, nose, mouth, and other parts of his body, just as if he had been wounded by the snake in each of these parts. He confessed and, receiving the oils in his final agony with great devotion, begged with no less devotion and insistence to be taken to church so that he could behold the holy sacrifice of the Mass at his departure. So great was his devotion that the Father was overcome and said

Mass in a suitable place nearby. The sick man heard the Mass and was cured immediately.

Overcome by shame, another man concealed a filthy sin in confession. He immediately fell sick, the symptoms such that he appeared on the point of breathing out his soul. The confessor arrived; attributing his bodily symptoms to an evil in his soul, he urged the man to make a good confession. The Indian took warning and made a good confession. Already while making it he began feeling better, and upon reception of absolution found himself in good health. But he soon proved forgetful and relapsed into his crime. Divine justice once more visited him with a mortal sickness. The poor man, repentant and weak, resorted to the proven remedy of confession. His soul was healed, but not his body: within a few days his life was over.

An old man was drawn to this place by divine predestination. He traveled more than forty leagues from his own place to this one, passing safely through the territory of pagans whose occupation is to kill strangers. He presented himself to Father José Oregio,[139] an Italian. The latter, seeing the pilgrim's perfect dispositions, immediately gave him instructions and administered baptism to him. The old man was overjoyed at seeing his wish fulfilled, and on the following day, while talking, finished his life.

Less fortunate than he were two persons who took up residence here, a husband and wife, unbelievers of advanced age. While the whole town fervently attended instructions in order to receive the gift of baptism, these two alone would slip away at the first sound of the bell; not even when warned by the example and admonition of their own people would they submit. Informed of their case, the Father went in person to invite them. He showed them the way to the church, since in all that time they had not even seen its threshold. Had divine predestination accepted them, this would have been a good start. They, however, returned to their previous obduracy and continued to absent themselves from the town when the others prayed in the church. Punishment came on them as they entered their own house, sending them a sudden quaking with symptoms such that they collapsed on the spot. Although the Father rushed to them, death sped even faster, exiling them from this life and from paradise as well.

CHAPTER 69

The reduction of San Cristóbal

THE HOLY gospel already enjoyed so much credit among the pagans of
this district that a desire to have it in their own lands united them here
from a variety of places. What elsewhere the Fathers had to do themselves
by dint of great efforts, the Indians here did quite of their own accord. They
put up a house to receive and lodge the priests, they chose children and sent
them to the Christian towns for instruction in the faith so they could serve
as their teachers later on, and they also brought able Indians to learn
carpentry with a view to building their own church. The man behind all this
was a very respected cacique endowed with an inclination to the good. He
received the name Antonio at his baptism, which he requested very earnestly
and which cost him several journeys. For a long time the shortage of priests
made it impossible for them to attend to these people. However, through the
zeal of Antonio and many others who imitated him, a planting was begun
here, and although it was not yet irrigated by waters from the fountains of
the Savior, they made excellent preparations for the latter to flow freely by
banishing magicians, who offered zealous opposition with their false teachings,
and by reciting all the prayers at the top of their voices in their houses,
having as their instructors their own children who had been pupils of our
Fathers. Antonio himself, though already of advanced age, became so well
versed in Christian doctrine that he was able to teach it and spread it with
great success.

Their insistent requests to be given a Father were finally successful. They
welcomed Father Juan Agustín as if he were an angel, vying with each other
in revealing their concubines and begging baptism with exceptional eagerness.
In a short time nine hundred and fifty persons received the sacrament. So
faithful were they that one cacique, who had exchanged all his concubines
for baptism, upon one of the latter's returning to his house some months
later, with Christian zeal instructed her thoroughly and sent her away again,
asking the Father to correct her. Such are the effects of divine grace. They
caught a magician who, in a diabolical rage at seeing his sham arts discredited, was attempting to persuade some simple Indians to forsake their Christian
freedom and retain his own fictitious freedom. They put down this magician's
diabolical zeal with an exemplary punishment, exalting our Catholic law and
the gift they had received from the Fathers.

These sorcerers are so stubborn that it takes a long time to soften their
obduracy. One of them had a brother in his house who was sick. They urged
him to take him to the Father; but upon hearing this, the sick man, taught
by his brother's lies, refused. He straightway experienced his punishment,

shrieking, gesturing, and writhing like someone possessed; he spewed foam from his mouth and followed it by discharging his unhappy soul without baptism.

An Indian, unmindful of what he had promised at baptism, lived licentiously and never went to Mass or gave other indication of being a Christian. He fell ill; although in danger, he attempted to conceal it to escape confession. He had a fit—not dying as he claimed—in which he saw himself taken by frightful ministers before the tribunal of God, by whom he was harshly chidden for his faults and given as a punishment to suffer the pangs of his illness for many days, at the end of which he would die. He came to himself, repented, and confessed his sins. His sickness went on for many days, he himself being grateful for the mercy of his kindly Judge. When the time of his penance was completed, he departed (as we trust) to enjoy the fruit thereof.

The zeal of this Father led him to remote habitations in search of the sick, of whom he baptized a great number. He once penetrated so deeply into the forest that he got lost, his guide unable to find the way back. But a soul's predestination guided them: they came upon a hut where they found a tender infant that was hastening towards death. The Father baptized it and it immediately departed for eternal life.

Getting lost another time, it was to find his mark: he happened on a woman who was already being mourned as dead. Realizing that she was still alive, he made her a daughter of God by baptism, whereupon she died so as to live forever.

CHAPTER 70

The reduction of Jesús-María

THIS REDUCTION was given shape by Father Pedro Romero, of whose zeal and concern I have already spoken and could say a great deal more. Though kept busy as superior of all the reductions by constantly visiting and consoling his brothers, he labored in all the reductions for the cultivation of the Indians. At this place two thousand families gathered, amounting to ten thousand souls. In order to attend to his principal responsibility, he left in his place the outstanding Father Cristóbal de Mendoza, who was crowned with a martyr's halo. As a veteran and expert in gathering peoples to the Christian religion, he instructed the settlement there with great success, heaven inspiring him with an ardent zeal to convert the great flocks of pagans shepherded by the devil throughout those valleys, mountains, rivers, and ravines.

He learned of some Tupís who serve as traders and brokers for the townsmen of São Paulo. In Portuguese they are called *pombeiros* and in our Spanish *palomeros*, "pigeon hunters," from their resemblance to cock-pigeons that are trained to collect and steal pigeons from other cotes. The natives call them *mú*, or "contractors." They divide up districts and each one at his post has his crew and exchange table for buying Indian men, women, and children. For this purpose the inhabitants of the coastal towns in Brazil send them axes, cutlasses, knives, and all sorts of hardware, old clothes, hats, jackets, and a thousand knickknacks to be used for buying souls just as here one would send to buy a flock of sheep or a herd of cows.

Although they claim to be Christians, these *pombeiros* are the very devils of hell; they are the workshop of every kind of evil and sin, the customhouse of drunkenness and the foulest sins. They have their houses full of pagan women purchased for their impure deeds. They incite the pagan Indians to wage war on each other, to seize and take each other prisoner, and bring them for appraisal and sale. The Indians' need for this hardware in farming makes them seize one another—at times they will even hand over their relatives and the dwellers in their own houses for an axe or a cutlass, which is the going price. Thus, the brawniest among them will throw their arms around anyone unable to resist and take him prisoner, saying, "Now you are my slave!" Submitting, the latter lets himself be taken to the *pombeiros*, where he is treated and works as a slave. I learned of one story which, although droll, is nevertheless sad.

An Indian was taken captive in the way described. Unable to ward off the violence done him, he was about to be handed over in perpetual slavery to these infamous publicans. He saw that they were buying and selling a lot of people, himself among those being sold. (These *pombeiros* exist also in Angola for the transport of blacks, installed there by those who have a monopoly on the trade in blacks.) The wretched man was wondering how he could buy himself free, when he noticed a fellow who had just sold someone going away and decided he was strong enough to seize him. His longing for liberty gave him added strength; he charged at the fellow, tied him up (seizing the money he had made from his wrongful sale), took him to the *pombeiro*, and handed him over as a slave in exchange for his own liberty, thus going free. To keep from ever being in a similar predicament, he betook himself to the safety of our reductions.

When several lots have been assembled, they send word to São Paulo and the other coastal towns, and boats and canoes come up which transport them at a considerable profit. Costing originally two or three pesos, they bring fifteen or twenty pesos in the towns, and if taken to Rio de Janeiro can be sold for forty or fifty cruzados.

The saintly priest caught some of these *pombeiros*; getting their prey away from them, he set them free and dispatched them to distant reductions for instruction there. The Father and his companion, Father Pedro de Mola,[140] traveled the entire area, discovering pagan towns and bringing them word of the Christian religion.

They learned that a famous cacique, a great sorcerer and magician, was proclaiming himself the god of the whole country (a common insanity of these wretches) and was having himself worshiped by the simple people there. The Fathers wanted to win him over; to gain entry they sent the Antonio mentioned above, a man of faith and confidence. He was quite well received by Yeguacaporú, as this sham god was named, because he thought that Antonio had come to acknowledge and worship him as he had done while still a pagan. After a long discussion in which Antonio shrewdly and prudently engaged him, he told him that the Fathers would like to see him and assured him that he would not find their converse unpleasing. Yeguacaporú responded: "How do you expect me, the god and lord of all creation, the creator of lightning, the producer of life and death, to humble myself to go and see some beggarly foreigners who, to my despite and discredit, preach to this barbarian people that there is only one God and that he is in heaven? I am the one whom these men ignorantly proclaim to my discredit. I will take my just revenge and right this situation by killing all these priests so that they will cease from the frauds by which they attract ignorant people to themselves. And you, why have you let yourself be so blindly led astray?" Antonio replied that the Fathers had never done him any harm, but instead had conferred many benefits upon him and his vassals. Whereupon they changed the subject, and Antonio came back. What I have here recounted about this magician should be kept in mind later, for he played a great part in the martyrdom of Father Cristóbal de Mendoza.

The province of Caagua is renowned for its large population. Despite its remoteness, word of the Fathers had flown thither and they sent messengers requesting them to come to their lands and teach them. After consultation with God on the matter in the prayers and sacrifices of the Mass which they offered, it was decided that the Father should make a short visit to their country and, in view of the shortage of Fathers, keep their hopes alive with the expectation that, once available, they would definitely go there.

Along the route was a mountainous region inhabited by magicians who would come out on the paths like tigers after prey. The priest reached this area, and was received by these men with apparent hospitality. He informed them of his Christian purposes. A devil named Tayubay, a very great sorcerer, had retired to this lions' den. He had attempted to prevent the entrance of the gospel in San Miguel by means of his lying mischief, but the people in the town brought him bound to Father Cristóbal, who kept him in his own cell for an entire day trying to correct him with kindness and love. This kind of devil, however, is overcome only by chastisement; humiliated and discredited, the wretched man migrated to this lions' den, where he freely practiced his lying arts. These men plotted to kill the Father, but wanted to consult the above-mentioned Yeguacaporú first. With feigned love they urged the Father to return there, where he would find all the people of the area assembled so that they could all enjoy his teaching and instruction. Unaware of the treachery they were plotting, the Father promised to return, in the assurance that he would win these people. He thereupon took his leave and reached his planned destination of the Caaguape. There he was welcomed with love on the part of all. He remained there several days informing them about our faith, to which they all listened with delight.

While the Father was traveling onward as a herald of life, Tayubay was plotting to bring about his death. He gave his people a lengthy discourse, the gist of which was to avouch himself and his teaching, give the lie to that of the Father, and disparage the way of life of the Christians, who cravenly abandoned their wives in submission to a foreign teaching. He said: "Learn from my own case. See how I am in exile because of this priest, and how the ancient practice of our ancestors is cast into discredit." With that he went off to consult the sham god Yeguacaporú. The latter commissioned him to kill the Father; they all agreed and laid an ambush to await him.

On his mission, the Father's heart was filled with a consolation as ample as was his hope for the conversion of that extensive province of pagans. Giving thanks to God, and distributing to the good and loving people what gifts the general poverty there allows, he bade them farewell, leaving them with the initial sweetness of the word of God and a yearning that he himself or other Fathers would return.

CHAPTER 71

Martyrdom of Father Cristóbal de Mendoza

THE FATHER began his return trip, cheerful and satisfied with having won the good will of so many people, quite unaware of the treachery being mounted against him by the magicians. He was detected by the sentinels and word was sent of his arrival. Certain of them came out to welcome him, leading him with deceptive words to where the bulk of them were. At two o'clock in the afternoon he reached Villarroyón. There he was forced to stop by a cloudburst. The few people in his escort scattered to take shelter from the rain in little straw huts, as they usually do. They learned of the plot; some of the Father's companions rushed back to warn him, but were intercepted by the enemy before they could return and help him. Those who were still with him were few, the enemy many. Their commotion and cries rent the air and shook the earth, and the suddenness of the attack broke up any order that the few people in the Father's escort might have kept, although they did offer scattered resistance.

The Father jumped on a horse, encouraging his friends with remarkable valor. His constant concern had been the baptism of unbelievers, and so even now, with his life obviously in danger, his sole care was to protect them, both by bravely driving off the enemy and by urging the unbelievers not to put their lives at risk. He could have saved his own life, but to give eternal life to a catechumen who had been pierced by an arrow and was in his agony, he moved closer to the enemy in order to baptize him. And though he failed of his purpose because of the barbarians' resistance, he did not fail of his merit.

At the height of the Father's efforts to protect his own, he found himself in a mud hole: his horse had fallen in and was unable to get out. He shouted to his people to head into the woods and save their lives. Seizing a shield from an Indian, he fended off a rain of arrows that fell upon him. He was now alone and abandoned by his men, who had escaped into the forest. So many arrows stuck in the shield that their sheer weight kept him from protecting himself with it. As he tried to pull them out, he exposed his body and was immediately struck by an arrow in the temple. Now stunned, he was cruelly clubbed on the head twice and pierced by a pair of arrows, his body collapsing to the earth.

The barbarous mob let loose at him; trying their strength on his sacred body, they beat him with clubs. One pernicious magician cut off an ear as a trophy. They stripped him of his clothes, leaving him nothing. Finding an image of Christ round his neck, the pagans reenacted the mockery of the Jews. The rain that had occasioned his death prolonged his life to increase his merit. They intended to burn his body, but to get out of the rain they left it there for the following day, postponing until then the opening of his belly —for according to their fantastic custom unless the killer opens the dead man's belly he himself will swell up like the dead man and die.

I recall at this point that at moments when our lives were in danger this holy man told me that he hoped for a short, quick martyrdom so that he would not have to stare death in the face for long. This was not granted him. His life was prolonged by a protracted death, so that a long suffering would be followed by a long reward and so there would be no doubt of his martyr-dom. Late in the dark of night he recovered consciousness, to find all his friends gone, himself stripped naked and stuck in a bog, his head split open, a wound in the temple, his back pierced with arrows, his whole body bloodied. The dauntless martyr arose and, half dragging himself, went a short way looking for shelter. But how was he to find it there in the open? I leave to the imagination how the holy man spent that entire night.

Day had scarcely broken when the beasts emerged from their houses, like tigers from their lairs, to sate their rage on the prey they thought already dead. The trail of blood led them to the martyr, now stretched on the hard earth. They opened their sacrilegious lips with insults against him and horrible blasphemies against God: "Where is the God that you preached? He must be blind since he does not see you, and powerless since he cannot free you from our hands." The saintly man chided them for their faithlessness, now admonishing them with love to forswear paganism and embrace the law of the Christians, now threatening them with the severe punishment that God visits upon the rebellious—though he seem to take no notice and wait, his hand falls all the heavier. They ordered him to be silent but he continued. With a sword blow to the mouth they knocked out his teeth; these were gathered up by a boy there who served his Mass, and we preserve them today as relics.

The saint went on preaching and they went on beating and bludgeoning him. They cut off his lips, his remaining ear, and his nose, parodying what the saintly man used to tell the Christians when expounding the catechism. They put him over a pole and carried him to a grove of trees to die. As if his mouth were still whole he spoke to them of how glad he was to die and how great was his love for their souls, which he longed to wash in the pure waters of baptism. "My soul," he said, "will go to enjoy God; you will only kill my body. Oh, if you only knew the good that I proclaim to you, which your ingratitude does not deserve!" Wearied of torturing the saintly man, they pulled out his tongue from under his beard and with bestial ferocity began flaying his entire chest and belly, which became one mass with his tongue. He kept his eyes fixed on heaven, as though beholding the path along which his soul was to travel with great strides towards the crown. They broke his chest open and tore out the heart that burned with love for them. Piercing it through with arrows, the obdurate sorcerers said, "Let us see if his soul dies now." He at last brought his apostolic preaching to an end with this splendid martyrdom.

The fire refused to cooperate with their wish to reduce his holy body to ashes. However—so that he might pass to eternal rest through both fire and water—they flung him into a stream. The beasts returned to their homes and, not sated with the flesh of the loving Father, ate two sons whom the holy man had begotten in Christ and whom they had seized the previous day. Licking their lips in their innocent blood, amid great festivity and an abundance of wine, they ground with their teeth a bread which will be served at God's table for endless ages.

CHAPTER 72

Punishment wreaked on the parricides

THE DEGREE of love which all had for the saintly Father became evident in their grief. More than fourteen hundred Indian warriors immediately set out to avenge him. The Fathers charged them to harm no one but only to recover his holy body. The enemy were well prepared and launched a violent onslaught on our men. Driven back at first, our men reassembled in much greater numbers and at the second encounter executed a cruel slaughter. All those who had martyred the Father died. A renowned cacique from San Miguel, named Guaybicang, took the treacherous Tayubay alive. He asked him where the Father had died; once shown the place, he killed him on the spot, smashing his skull with a war club. It was ascribed to a miracle that, while many of the enemy died, not one of our men was killed; though many were badly wounded, they all recovered. They removed the body from the stream and it was received back in the town amid the universal lamentations of the Indians and the envy of the Fathers.

Father Cristóbal was a native of Santa Cruz de la Sierra, from the noblest stock in the town; his grandfather had been the first governor of the province. His name before entering the Society was Don Rodrigo de Mendoza; as a religious he took the name Cristóbal. He was a true despiser of himself, a humble and tireless worker in the conversion of unbelievers and a man of great generosity towards the poor, of which we saw outstanding examples. One night he dreamt that a poor man asked him for alms. Having nothing to give him, he took off his outer clothing in his sleep and threw it to the poor man of his dream. It would take long to recount all his heroic deeds; time will make them known in a long history.

CHAPTER 73

Hindrances to the gospel raised by the magicians, and the death of more than three hundred infants through hatred of the faith

THE GREAT sorcerer Yeguacaporú relished the killing of the saintly Father Cristóbal de Mendoza which had been perpetrated at his behest. He attempted to do the same to the others, but was stopped in his tracks by a miserable death. He did not want for successors to his charlatanry and magic. They built temples, erected pulpits, gave their sermons and baptized. The form of their baptism was to say "I unbaptize you" and wash the person's entire body. Their sermons were aimed at disparaging the Christian faith and religion. They threatened anyone who accepted it, or did not abjure it once accepted, that the tigers would eat them and that fearsome ghosts would come raging from their caverns with long stone swords to take vengeance, along with other nonsense of the same sort—all things capable of striking fear in those simple people.

They pretended that echoes are the voices of these monsters, who await the sorcerers' command to come out and destroy the Christians. Their group was joined by a woman whose gigantic stature emboldened her to declare herself goddess of the sun, moon, and other planets, whose light was under her control. She urged the destruction of the Christian towns and promised that she herself would remove the light from them in battle while her own followers remained in bright light. Every one of them has a hundred such inanities.

There is a region or province of people possessed by the devil. The devil really dwells in them; they have been given the name of "berserkers" or "mindless men." They do not farm but live on game, and when none is available, as is often the case, they live on human flesh. They roam the fields and woods in packs like mad dogs. They will burst into a town and fall like wild animals on the flock, seizing any children they can for their food. Possessed by the devil, they range the countryside at night like drunks or madmen. They eat burning coals like cherries; this is hard to believe, and I confess that I myself thought it a fabrication until I was disabused by actually seeking one of them chew burning coals in front of me as if they were lumps of sugar.

At times they enjoy quiet, but the evil spirit will suddenly mount so fierce an assault inside them that finally they become possessed. Taking their bows and arrows and roaring with eerie ferocity, they seize, slay, and scatter people like wild bulls. When the frenzy abates, they quiet down and themselves confess they do not know what it is that drives them interiorly. We captured one of them; it turned out he had already eaten his wife and children, and they caught him in the act of eating his father. He looked and acted like a tiger. A few of these have been brought into our reductions, where they seem to live quietly. Were heaven to help us with more religious, we could get this entire prey away from the devil.

At numerous points in this account we have seen that the devil tries to attract souls to himself by imitating our actions. An invention of his was to forge a religion from twelve chosen sorcerers. These won over more than seven hundred men. From among these they chose dancers, singers, and charlatans whom they sent on the sly into our towns to frighten the people away from baptism with their fables. They did a great deal of damage among the newly converted. The Fathers worked zealously on the problem, taking steps in their towns to gather in the new people; Father Francisco Díaz labored at this.

These seven hundred brigands, disciples of the twelve magicians, wrought havoc in the area upon the Christians they captured, even eating them out of hatred for the faith. An old Christian from one of our reductions covertly detected them in a devilish act: they threw a tub of boiling water over a Christian baby, gleefully celebrating his cries and writhing and then celebrating their banquet with his flesh. It has been calculated that these wolves ate more than three hundred infants out of hatred for the faith, besides many adults who suffered the same lot. A good number of the faithful took arms to repress their temerity, for they were already planning to sack our reductions and eat the Fathers. There were two battles, our faithful always coming out victorious and many of the unbelievers being killed or captured. One of these they brought in firmly trussed up; seeing himself so, he cried aloud that he was a friend of the sun, who at certain times came down to see him. At this nonsense they dragged him off and handled him so severely that if we had not gotten him away from them he would have been killed.

These cloudy days were followed by light and tranquillity. After these wars the crops, now ripening, promised an abundant harvest, had it not been for the shortage of workers which clouded our hopes. The unbelievers living nearby, now disenchanted, were submitting to the truth; those far away were asking for it; and the gospel, victorious, now seemed free from enemies. A tally of this harvest—from the registers we snatched from the flames—shows that by 1636[141] there had been gathered into the granary of the Church 94,990 souls who had accepted the faith and baptism.

But who would have imagined that Christians—unless they were heretics —would wage war against the faith of Christ? At this time the townsmen of São Paulo, Santos, São Vicente, and other coastal townships of Brazil were preparing a further invasion to destroy our peace, seize and kill Christians, burn temples, wound and injure priests, sack churches—to burn off virtue, uproot the Christian religion, and sow a crop of loathsome vices.

CHAPTER 74

Events preceding the new invasion of the province of Tape by the raiders from São Paulo

IT IS nothing unusual for God to give signs and portents of grave and momentous events. Eusebius declares as much in the first book of his *Evangelical History*; similarly Josephus in his *Jewish War*. Christ our Lord in his gospel gives the signs of the Antichrist, foretelling the loss of many—even the elect, were it possible, being in danger. But woe to him who causes these scandals! I shall now give the signs of this persecution which we experienced, and the loss of many who seemed elect will be clearly seen. Let the giver of scandal rejoice in his prey, but beware of the terrible blow that threatens him: "Woe to those who now consider matter for laughter what in the future they will bemoan!"[142]

I mentioned in chapter 2 the precautions taken twenty years earlier by the Divine Majesty in sending members of the Society to the province of Guairá to gather in the predestined before the Antichrist could harass them. I there detailed the signs that were given. The devils mentioned in chapter 17 indicated the same: they appeared in the guise of men from São Paulo and the Brazil coast, taking their appearance and carrying their muskets and arms, even professing themselves to be their friends. The devils we described in chapter 28 as being burned cried out that they would summon their friends in São Paulo to ravage the towns and avenge them. Of course the devil is a liar, but not infrequently God makes him tell the truth; and we see this in the outcome.

When the people of Loreto and San Ignacio fled their lands to escape the cruel persecution, an image of our Lady sweated copiously. As indicated in chapter 38, a pair of angels shed tears: religious of the Society who were present saw them falling in distinct streams from the corners of their eyes. The angels themselves shared in the travail, for we had dedicated the reduction of Tayaoba mentioned earlier to the Holy Angels. Their protection had delivered me in that province from more than three thousand Indians besieging me in a palisade that I built to defend myself. They thus showed themselves our companions in travail and in sorrow. This took place at the destruction of the province of Guairá.

As the first sign here in the province of Tape and the hill country, I will mention the following. Five years earlier, when the whole land enjoyed complete peace and it was considered impossible for numerous evident reasons that these men could invade, a person to whom heaven had disclosed the destruction they would wreak there wrote a note to a friend who was working in that ministry. It said: "Within five years those evil people will come there. As a proof that I wrote this and that it will unfailingly come to pass, preserve this note until they come, when I shall ask you for its return." This was fulfilled to the letter. When the two met during the invasion of these wicked men, he asked his note back from the other. I held it in my own hands.

St. Ignatius and St. Francis Xavier one day sweated copiously in one of these reductions. On this same occasion, the Christ at the Pillar mentioned in chapter 64 sweated this time as well. It is worth noting that the footprints depicted by the painter between the pillar and the spot where Christ our Lord went to put on his garments likewise sweated, to bring to our minds the tracks and footsteps of these monsters who strode cheerfully to their own destruction and eagerly towards that of the pagan and Christian Indians—as well as the painful steps which the Lord walked to redeem us all.

As these furies were setting out from their own townships, an image of our Lady in their own land, as well as another of St. Ignatius, likewise sweated. I learned that there were religious who ascribed this to heaven's sorrow over their wicked practice, which is condemned by holy and learned men, although supported by many ignorant persons.

And if these signs which God gave as a loving Father for amendment and correction do not suffice, let us turn to those given by way of punishment. In the township of São Paulo eighty-three Spaniards have died calamitous deaths. The man mentioned in chapter 35 who imprisoned Fathers Simón Masseta and Justo Mansilla suddenly fell dead. The other man who heaped them with insults and laid violent hands on them, and stirred the wrath of God by his horrendous blasphemies, died of triple bullet wounds. A few days after he was buried in church, they opened his grave for another burial and found nothing but the trace of a single shoe—he had been taken off, clothes, shoes, and all, without passing through purgatory. The man who set fire to the church of Jesús-María with burning arrows, as described earlier, shortly afterwards died such a disastrous death that his accomplices themselves made it public and attributed it to heaven's punishment.

I do not wish to pass over one fact that everyone deemed miraculous. Three months before embarking at the port of Buenos Aires, I sent ahead the first mailing[143] of the reports on the crimes of the São Paulo raiders which I had drawn up for submission here at court. The ship that carried them was wrecked in a furious storm. But that human justice might remedy these grievous evils, and God's justice manifest its desire that this be done, the latter not only preserved the papers but brought them from the stormy seas to the shore of the seacoast at Lisbon. There they were found, to the amazement of those who beheld them—heaven having concurred not only to keep them from being torn to pieces by the waves or spoilt by the sea water, but also to ensure their arrival here at court at the very moment when discussions were being held on what to do about the evils that had occurred earlier. Many people doubted the seriousness of these, but with the documents confirming the existence of fresh evils, the truth was vindicated.

In Lisbon there are many witnesses to this incident. Moreover, there arrived here at court a few months ago a worthy gentleman who had been on the ship, entrusted with a packet of letters for His Majesty. As a precaution against danger from enemies, he had removed the packet from his chest to keep at hand and send to the bottom should the ship be boarded by enemies. This was why he happened to have the king's packet by him when the ship sank, and managed to swim away with it. He says it was a marvel that the papers in question were saved, for apart from the fact that many people drowned, nothing was able to be saved from the ship.

As a conclusion of the punishment meted out by God to these men, let it suffice to mention the fact that they usually die in despair of eternal life—

God punishing them in this life with a fearful darkening and letting them
sink from one abyss of evils to another. For as they set out to make prisoners
of persons who are free (and declared such by the popes, with a reserved
excommunication against anyone taking away their freedom[144]), to kill
enormous numbers of them, to carry off their wives and daughters for their
own foul purposes, to banish the gospel and the Blessed Sacrament from their
churches—at that very moment they go to confession and Communion as if
they were starting on a pilgrimage to Compostela.[145] This is their way of
living until death; and when death assails them they receive all the
sacraments, in their wills and legacies consigning great numbers of free
persons to perpetual slavery.

CHAPTER 75

Invasion of Jesús-María by the raiders from São Paulo

WHEN NEWS came that the men from São Paulo were descending on
this reduction, the Indians began to build a small rampart. They were
unable to finish it because of the rapidity of the enemy's approach. On the
day of St. Francis Xavier in 1636,[146] as the feast day was being celebrated
with Mass and sermon, a hundred and forty Castilians[147] from Brazil,
together with a hundred and fifty Tupís, all well armed with muskets and
garbed in scapulars (a sort of dalmatic stuffed with cotton which covers the
soldier from head to foot and lets him fight safe from arrows), entered the
town in military formation to the beating of drums and the waving of flags,
and began shooting. Without waiting for parley they attacked the church,
firing their muskets; the townspeople were assembled there and its wall was
part of the unfinished rampart. Two of our Fathers and two of our Brothers[148] were present. Finding they were in grave danger from the bullets, the
Brothers and Indians undertook their just defense, the Fathers encouraging
them.

They battled for six hours, from eight in the morning until two in the
afternoon. One Father took a bullet wound in the head. One of the Brothers
had his arm shot through, while the other had a miraculous escape: a bullet
hit a medal he had around his neck and did not go through but instead
ricocheted and wounded his hand. Our Christians did all they could, hoping
for reinforcements from some people they were expecting; the women and
children on their knees implored God's help with many tears. One of the
religious, badly wounded and exhausted, took cover behind some timber. The
enemy saw him from the field and shouted: "Let's kill that dog!" They all
aimed; when the bullets were counted later, there were more than five
hundred. Even the miscreants were astonished at this.

Seeing the courage of those inside the walls and the large number of their own casualties, the enemy tried to make a breach through the palisade of the fort. A manly woman saw this; she dressed as a man and fell with a spear she was carrying upon one of the Tupís who was already opening the way for the others; she ran him through and left him there dead, blocking the entry of the others.

The enemy decided to burn the church. I confess that I have heard them say they are Christians, and even on this occasion they were wearing their big rosaries. Doubtless they have faith in God, but their actions are those of the devil. Three times they shot fire-arrows which were extinguished, albeit with difficulty. But the sun was very strong, and on their fourth try the fire took irreversible hold on the thatched church. There was confusion and shouting, the children crying and shrieking, the women moaning, and the panic general.

The enemy was jubilant and thanked God at seeing the church on fire. The rampart was small, the fire large, the sun's rays burning, the danger from the enemy evident. Eventually the reasonable decision was reached that they would do better to place themselves at the mercy of a rational foe—if they deserved such a qualification—than to be burned in that pyre. They opened a small gate and flocked out like sheep leaving their fold for the pasture. The savage tigers, as if possessed by the devil, rushed to the gate and cut them down with swords, cutlasses, and sabers, severing heads, chopping off arms, hamstringing legs, impaling bodies, and killing with the most barbaric ferocity the world has ever seen those who fled from the fire only to encounter their sabers. But what tiger would not have shrunk from bloodying its claws on those tender babies who clung unsuspectingly to their mothers' breasts?

Without exaggeration I state that here was displayed the cruelty of Herod —indeed far, far worse: Herod spared the mothers and was satisfied with the blood of their infant sons, whereas these were satisfied with neither, nor were the rivers of innocent blood sufficient to slake their insatiable ferocity. They tested the steel of their sabers by splitting children in two, opening their heads and hacking apart their tender limbs. The cries, shouts, and screams of these wolves, together with the pitiful cries of the mothers who were pierced by barbarous swords and by grief at seeing the dismemberment of their little children, created a hideous bedlam.[149] After this brutal slaughter they went in after the Fathers, who were being burned by the fire and the blazing sun, utterly unprotected. The insults and injuries they heaped on them are best left unsaid by a pen more restrained than were their hellish tongues. Nor were they moved to compassion at the sight of the wounded; on the contrary they put them under heavily guarded arrest. Rushing to rob what the fire had spared, they did not spare the sacred vestments, which they tore into pieces, carried off as trophies, and brazenly displayed in their own country, sworn testimony of this having been presented in the Council.

With difficulty obtaining permission, the Fathers emerged to see if among the bodies there were any still alive; to these they administered the sacraments. One had feigned death so he could escape in the darkness of the night; while practicing their archery, the boys who were with these barbarians put several arrows in him, which he endured in order to save his life.

They seized the choirboys. To put their instruction to the public test, the Castilians promised them women, whom they shamelessly allotted them. But the lads did not even lift their eyes to look at them. Their brutality toward their own pagan Indian auxiliaries was such that they ordered those who had been wounded by our people to be dragged to a lake and thrown in to drown, and thus be damned in their paganism. The choirboys went to catechize and baptize them, an action that would have been more appropriate for the pair of chaplains, one a religious and the other a secular priest, who were attached to this army.

Negotiations were made to ransom the wife of a leading Indian who escaped while she remained a prisoner, and some choirboys as well. However, they went off with both prisoners and ransom, together with five hundred head of cattle which were kept by this town for the support of all the others.

Decency has made me pass over many things in silence, but I must mention the following. The leader locked up in a room with himself the good-looking women—married, unmarried, or pagan—from this and other towns they ravaged, and spent the nights with them like a buck in a pen of she-goats. His purpose, apart from pleasure, was to win their affection, thus imitating what the *pombeiros*, or thieving cock-pigeons, do by attracting to their own cotes what they plunder from others. It was here that was made the investigation of our lives of which I spoke earlier, and these were the witnesses.

Word spread that the Fathers were dead, and Father Juan Agustín came from his reduction to give them burial. He secured their freedom and took them off to recover from their wounds, which were not a little dangerous.

CHAPTER 76

Invasion of the reduction of San Cristóbal

THE REDUCTION of San Cristóbal was four leagues from that of Jesús-María. Father Juan Agustín de Contreras was in charge. He had been in the devastated province of Guairá, and when he saw the brutalities they were already starting to perpetrate, he moved all his people to the reduction of Santa Ana, only three leagues away. The Father had hardly left when they invaded, pillaging and laying waste the food supplies. Sixteen hundred of our warriors assembled to hold off the enemy until the reinforcements that had been requested from other towns could arrive. In Jesús-María the Castilians already had a stake fort or corral for assembling their prey, twice the size of the plaza here in Madrid. They set up a church there, where the two chaplains said Mass—whether for rescuing souls from purgatory or for capturing the living I cannot say. The fugitive secular priest, who had been publicly denounced for leaving his curacy without permission, was under excommunication by his bishop. Both said Mass in the wilderness, using the privilege given those who convert Indians and settle them in reductions— deeming there to be no difference between settling them and subjugating them by violence.

Our sixteen hundred Indians were in San Cristóbal, where they celebrated Christmas by hearing Mass with what little joy their deadly enemy allowed them. Under the assumption that the Spanish would remain inactive that day, at least following the example of the brutes—"the ox knows its owner"[150]—and refraining from violence on such a blessed day, the people scattered in search of food. But as St. John rightly said of the Jews, "His own did not know him."[151] The raiders from São Paulo thought quite differently: the great festival was a perfect opportunity to catch the people hearing Mass in church, unarmed and intent only on their devotions. They put their plan into effect.

When our men realized this, they mustered and fought defiantly for five hours; it would have lasted longer if night had not taken away the daylight. Even with such unequal weapons—the Indians having no covering and only frail cane arrows while the Spanish were well protected and armed with muskets—they twice forced them into a forest and nearly took their flag. Many died on both sides, until night separated them. The Spanish had seized the area of the church, which they immediately sent up in flames—not the sort of action one would have expected on such a holy day.

CHAPTER 77

The reduction of Santa Ana retreats to that of Natividad; cruelties of the enemy

NEWS OF these events reached me at a considerable distance. Traveling as rapidly as I could, I arrived that same Christmas day at the reduction of Santa Ana. There I found a terrible panic. We spent the whole night in the consultation that was required to meet these calamities. The conclusion was to move the people from this town and from San Cristóbal to Natividad; it was a fairly strong position because of a river that would hold up the enemy, and lay only four leagues away.

The number of the refugees was huge. The river passage was fortified with a good rampart which afforded a sufficient defense against the enemy's seizing our boats as they ferried across the quantities of people who arrived daily in flight from the enemy. Our soldiers wanted to attack the enemy's fort, but we dissuaded them from this obviously risky project. It would be better to await the enemy in the open, where they had taken control of the cultivated land. Here our men were able to operate more effectively: laying ambushes in the woods at every step, they succeeded in killing many without danger to themselves. Already many of the enemy were afraid to go out and forage, sure they would be killed. This tactic eventually succeeded in forcing the enemy to raise camp and leave us.

Our provincial, Father Diego de Boroa, attempted to parley with the enemy, as though they were capable of reason. Several of us Fathers went with him. We found twenty corpses in San Cristóbal, cruelly hacked and bullet-ridden; we stopped to bury them. We found a little pagan girl, about seven years old, lost in the woods; she had two cruel wounds, a long one on her face and another on the head, both covered with maggots. She told us her calamitous story as follows.

"I was with my parents and your children. The men burst upon our houses and divided us among themselves. My little brother and I were taken by a different master, and to this day I have heard nothing of my parents. Finding ourselves both orphans and slaves, we ran away hoping to find you so that you could protect us as our Fathers. They chased us and in a terrible rage gave these wounds to me and another on the neck to my little brother that left him unable to move his head. Then they left us for dead. I came to my senses and realized that my little brother was still alive. I ran in panic into the woods, carrying my little brother in my arms. I was with him for three days, without food or drink and sustained by the hope that he would recover consciousness and we would be able go on. But, with him at his end and myself as you found me, I abandoned him still alive, though I was torn with grief. I tried to carry him on my back, but I could not." We treated her body and her soul as well through baptism. At every step we stumbled across corpses—beheaded, pierced with arrows, or hacked to death.

We reached the palisade they had put up in Jesús-María, where the first battle took place. It had been a fragrant flowerbed of pagans who had become Christians, whose promise for the future seemed secure but now that they are in captivity is considered doubtful. We were met by a terrible odor from the dead, the stench so overpowering that we were unable to tally them. We found only one woman alive, but she was unable to speak and a swarm of flies were sucking on her. We prized her teeth open with a knife and gave her a drink of wine; then she could talk and said, "Oh, they have taken away my mother, my brother, and all I possess!" She made her confession and then gave up her soul. She might well have been burned to death along with so many others, but it was her good fortune that her hut lay aside from the rest and was not reached by the fire. No one will ever be able to form an idea what I myself am incapable of writing down. Here we did not find, as elsewhere, bodies of people hacked to death or with their throats cut, women split open by sabers; here we found rational human beings—children, women, men—who had been roasted alive. We saw one woman roasted to death with her twin children, who had been burned as they clung to her.

These murderers have the common practice, when departing with their booty, of burning the sick, the aged, and those unable to travel, for if they remain alive, those who leave will remember them and try to go back. We spent many hours carrying the charred bodies to a trench, into which we threw them one after another. The spectacle was such that four hundred Indians who accompanied us, stricken at the sight, turned on their heels and left us.

We found another woman who had miraculously escaped sword and fire. They had tried to take her prisoner, but she resisted stoutly, saying that she wanted to die as a Christian among the Fathers. They dragged her and beat her, but finding her unyielding they gave her a deadly wound on the head, smashing her face with a rock. To make sure she was dead, they tried to burn her; but the fire showed itself merciful, to the shame of their inhuman fury. We found her nearly gone, but with human support and the divine support of baptism, she preserved her freedom and her life.

Many who have traversed the forests there have assured us that they were strewn with the corpses of people who had fled and been hunted down with sabers, swords, and cutlasses. And if these actions are a disgrace to Christianity and to the gospel itself, which falls into discredit and repels the pagans, what a disgrace to Christianity will it not be that Christians have befouled the very altar where the life-giving sacrifice of the Mass had so long been celebrated! They disfigured the altar and used it for their filthy purposes. It broke our hearts to see this irreverence.

The number of people they took away is not known, but some indication may be given by the tithes they paid the church: they gave five hundred persons to the religious as his share, just as a cattle herder pays a tithe of his sheep or cows. The secular priest got two hundred.

These events, in sum, constituted my motive for coming to the font of justice and to His Majesty's feet. I consider this a blessed task, confident as I am that the necessary measures will be taken so that those sheep, enjoying the meadows allotted them by nature (that is, their own lands) may exercise that freedom which is common to all, and, expressing their gratitude through whatever tribute their poverty permits, may live protected by the powerful arm with which His Majesty (may God grant him increase) defends his own vassals.

CHAPTER 78

Exhortation of the bishop of Tucumán to our congregation[152]

I F WELL weighed, the perilous responsibility of a bishop is beyond what can be borne, all the more so when it is over pagans—and the bishoprics of Paraguay, Tucumán, and Buenos Aires are surrounded by provinces of them. Consequently, in order to fulfill his duty and put his zeal into action, his excellency the bishop of Tucumán was obliged to employ the zeal of our Society, which is testified to by the 94,990 pagans it has united to the Church through baptism, not counting those it has baptized from 1636 to the present time. This zeal of his he displayed in an exhortation which he presented to the congregation, as follows:

Fray Melchor of the Order of our Father St. Augustine, by the grace of God and of the Apostolic See bishop of the cathedral of Tucumán, member of His Majesty's Council, etc., to Father Diego de Boroa, provincial of the Society of Jesus in the province of Tucumán, Paraguay, and Buenos Aires: greetings in our Lord Jesus Christ.

Your Reverence will surely know, as indeed you must and as the two of us have discussed many times, the great need in this province for evangelical ministers to preach and administer the holy sacraments to our sheep, particularly the Indians already converted and baptized, and to call those outside the Church to the knowledge of God and his holy gospel—the shortage of workers in parishes of those already baptized being such that there is today one mission with more than thirteen hundred persons in a single reduction that has no priest to give them instruction or hear their confessions, nor is there anyone qualified in the entire bishopric. There are other missions which have a priest but comprise such vast distances that a single priest cannot possibly do justice to them.

Furthermore, we have become aware of many irremediable shortcomings in certain territories, as we have already reported to His Majesty and of which we are informing His Holiness. Likewise, there are within the boundaries of our diocese hundreds of thousands of souls yet to be converted to our holy faith. In some provinces there has been a beginning of evangelization, and we have come to know in practice the people's good natural qualities.

Wherefore, inasmuch as we realize that Jesus Christ our Lord shed his blood for each and every one of these pagans and converts, and that through the commission bequeathed to him by his Father he has deigned to entrust this church to our small person so that we should see to the preaching of the gospel and to the making known of him, his name, and how he created and redeemed us and gave us a law by which he will judge us, adjudging us reward or punishment according to our deeds; inasmuch, further, as we are bound under mortal sin to preach the above in order to ensure that the converted may preserve their baptismal purity and those who are not may be called to receive it, and are bound, where unable to do this personally, to entrust the task to worthy persons and omit no means or effort so these wretched unbelievers may know God and attain blessedness; in view, moreover, of our assurance regarding the Society of Jesus and its zeal in attending to the honor of God and the conversion of souls, and in view of our own experience in this regard, namely, that in the time of our predecessors the Church in this bishopric was well served by said religious assisting them in the missions and preaching to unbelievers, and in general throughout the towns attending to the spiritual needs of all sorts of people at all hours of the day or night, we ourselves having experienced all this in our own time as well; and inasmuch as your Paternity has promised us to continue this work—we therefore urge you in the name of His Majesty, the patron of these churches, and in the name of God, the Lord who alone can adequately repay what this great labor deserves, and in our own name beg and implore you to perform this service to our Lord and to his Church.

And inasmuch as your order has assembled in congregation here in this city and will then be distributed throughout these dioceses, we ask you to choose the most capable men and assign them to preach the holy gospel to unbelievers both where it has not yet been preached and where it has begun to be preached, so that they may go forth as evangelical preachers to make known the name of God. I have similarly charged other laborers to go around the missions, valleys, plantations, and frontiers wherever there are people already converted and baptized, to hear their confessions, to preach, and to administer all the sacraments including that of matrimony, doing the work of parish priests or pastors; and from this moment we appoint and approve as such those whom your Paternity shall approve and appoint for these same responsibilities, conferring upon them whatever necessary faculties in law we ourselves are invested with for said purpose, thereby disburdening our own conscience with that of your Paternity.

CHAPTER 79

Letter of the same bishop to His Majesty

S IRE: *Through a royal letter addressed to my predecessors, Your Majesty commands me to inform him regarding the need in this diocese of Tucumán for members of religious orders to aid in the preaching of the gospel and the conversion of the Indians, so that, the Royal Council of the Indies having been informed on these matters, provision be made to meet this and similar needs. After more than three years since my arrival here as bishop, and after traveling nearly three hundred leagues throughout the four quarters of the diocese, personally making visitation in three of them, I can report the following:*

The boundaries of this province extend four hundred and more leagues. It has eight populous cities and many smaller places with at least twelve to fourteen thousand inhabitants, many of them already baptized but lapsed from the faith, for with the lack of instruction this nation easily reverts to its ancient customs and idolatries. There are other areas with more than fifty thousand people, where the preaching of the gospel was begun by religious of the Society of Jesus but abandoned because of the evil behavior of certain Spanish who made an armed invasion to conquer the territory; it is called the Chaco, a land with large populations of docile people who wear clothes and are settled in towns.

In the areas already Catholic, there are more than eight mission centers[153] with no priest at all to teach or hear confessions; nor is it possible to obtain any, for there is barely a single priest in each of the Spanish towns—where there is another it is question of a man who was ordained when old and sick and had not studied. I am hardly able to send priests even twice a year to make the round of these missions. I cannot be everywhere, with the result that many souls redeemed by the blood of Christ Our Lord are damned, souls that are under Your Majesty's protection and my responsibility.

In the reductions which do have secular priests, there are a great many irremediable shortcomings, for they are poorly equipped to understand their own duties and even less to instruct others. The religious orders are quite short-handed in the diocese; the Franciscans have few members, barely enough for their own choir obligations. It is really the Society of Jesus that discharges Your Majesty's and the bishop's obligations in conscience. In the cities, they attend day and night to giving instruction and hearing the confessions of the sick, and in particular to the Indians and blacks, with great and exemplary charity—for the secular priests are of little use in this regard, being of the quality indicated above.

Today, in Your Majesty's name, I have petitioned the Father Provincial of the Society of Jesus, gathered in congregation with most of his religious here in the city of Córdoba where I am visiting, to send preachers of the gospel into the Chaco to see whether, by preaching the gospel without resort to arms, we can obtain from God our Lord the conversion of the people there who already have an initial knowledge of the faith; and also to send religious missioners to travel throughout the province where there is a total lack of ministers or of competent ones, preaching, reforming morals, administering the sacraments, and curbing the many mestizos, Castilians, and Portuguese who live depraved lives among the Indians (they are more numerous than those living in the cities). He indeed represented to me that in carrying out this commission his men would bring upon themselves the same persecution which they have suffered and still suffer in Paraguay; for they endure both the domestic hatred of the Castilians of the diocese for the protection they give to the Indians of the reductions, defending the natural-born freedom guaranteed them by Your Majesty and instructing them in the gospel, and at the same time the hatred of the inhabitants of São Paulo in Brazil, who with their Tupí auxiliaries inflict havoc, death, and captivity upon the newly converted Indians, and *insults, blasphemies, maltreatment, wounds, and affronts upon the religious themselves, as was the case recently when they invaded the towns that were already Christian, killing many innocent people, taking many away as prisoners to Brazil, profaning the churches, altars, and images of our Lord and his Blessed Mother and the saints, and inflicting equal distress upon the religious, helpless to prevent it, by the pain in their hearts at seeing the travail and misery of those whom they had begotten spiritually in the gospel.*

All this notwithstanding, he has, for the service of Your Majesty and of God our Lord and the good of so many souls, directed all his rectors, where they have insufficient subjects, to take it personally upon themselves to make the circuit of all the valleys, rivers, and settlements of Indians; and I have furnished them with ample faculties for this. I am convinced, however, that they will either be unable to do this or will have to abandon their colleges, since their numbers are so small and particularly since they are an order in which the members neither live in residences nor go on missions and ministries without a companion.

In view of this I humbly implore Your Majesty by the mercy of God to have pity on this poor nation, and, inasmuch as Christ our Lord has confided to Your Majesty the salvation of these Indians who have cost him his blood, to help me with your generous and powerful hand to achieve this by supplying the order with forty men for this diocese of Tucumán, with the exclusive obligation and duty of all performing their ministry in this diocese of Tucumán and no other, since this is the neediest in the whole Church of God. Certainly, Sire, were I not constrained by the expenses of my office (on the small income of four thousand pesos), I would bring them here at my own expense. Your Majesty will order what is his will; for in the discharge of my conscience I appeal to the final instance in sending this report to Your Majesty, the king and natural lord of these lands and the patron of our churches. May our Lord protect your Catholic and royal person, for the safeguarding of Christianity and the increase of many realms.

Córdoba, August 11, 1637.

The same need and zeal are displayed by the other bishops and secular governors of these provinces, who request substantial numbers of Fathers for their dioceses and provinces.

CHAPTER 80

Two portions of a letter to His Majesty from Don Pedro Esteban
Dávila, governor of Buenos Aires

S IRE: I *have received information about the reductions or missions which the*
Fathers of the Society of Jesus had in this jurisdiction in the district of Uruguay
and the province of Tape, and of the harm they have suffered from the townsmen
of São Paulo on the Brazilian coast. When I arrived in Rio de Janeiro, I saw and
learned the truth of the report that had been given to me: in that city they sold
before my very eyes Indians who had been brought there by the townsmen of São
Paulo as though they were slaves and were regarded as such by Your Majesty.
Making inquiries, I ascertained verbally that between 1628 and 1630 the
townsmen of São Paulo had taken more than sixty thousand Indians from the
reductions of the Fathers of the Society, out of this jurisdiction and that of
Paraguay, wherein the said habitants of São Paulo committed incredible deeds of
cruelty and inhumanity, failing even in their Catholic and Christian duties. In
hopes of remedying this, I appealed to the then governor of that province, Martín
de Sa, as Your Majesty may deign to have verified from my note and his reply
which accompany this letter. I await a remedy from His Majesty's clemency, in
view of Your Majesty's Christian piety and the damage produced by the continued
incursions of the raiders from São Paulo into this realm and its provinces—thereby
also facilitating an entrance by which it is but a short distance to Peru, as Father
Antonio Ruiz of the Society of Jesus can inform your Majesty at greater length; he
is traveling from this province because of these matters, since they are for the
service of God and of Your Majesty.
Buenos Aires, October 12, 1637.

DON PEDRO ESTEBAN DÁVILA

In chapter forty-five I mentioned the lack of gold and silver among these
people and the general wish that they did have it. I find there are two
witnesses who allegedly claimed that there were streams and hills of gold, and
that I was the one who enjoyed this magnificence and concealed it (which
shows how far envy can go). We demanded that the witnesses on whose
word this charge was laid against us should make known these streams. In
three tribunals (whose authentic records I possess) they swore that such an
accusation was falsely imputed to them. The Indians will sell a vassal into
slavery for a bit of old tin as a neck ornament—a means by which the
habitants of São Paulo have acquired many Indians. If they had possessed
gold, would they not have brought it out and made use of it? The truth is
what was written by Don Pedro Esteban Dávila, former governor of Buenos

Aires. As His Majesty's conscientious servant he made a diligent investigation, about which he wrote to His Majesty. The pertinent passage in his letter states:

The fertility and abundance offered by these provinces promises so much that it is believed to contain metals and precious substances. I have informed Your Majesty of this in greater detail and forwarded authentic documents on this matter which I understand are in the possession of the Royal Council. Vague rumors of this sort did arise in the time of the governor Ruiz Díaz Melgarejo, founder of Villa Rica; but after a thorough investigation he found they were unreliable. More recently, pursuing the same object, his son-in-law Manuel de Frías, first governor of Paraguay when these two jurisdictions were separated, made an engagement to Your Majesty apparently guaranteeing that these metals would be found. He too, as I am informed by trustworthy persons, made a thorough investigation which turned up nothing. I have sent Your Majesty the reports to which I refer, and understand they are in the possession of the Royal Council. I put little credit in them, for two reasons: first, because of the vigorous investigation made by the persons just mentioned; and secondly, because I consider the witnesses to be prejudiced, little inclined toward the Society, and lacking in the dutifulness imposed by the veracity demanded of reports rendered to Your Majesty. Thus far the letter.

My own truthfulness in this matter is considerably buttressed by the efforts we made to have the province visited. We have begged and petitioned the governors to do this, alleging to them His Majesty's order and will. In proof of this I offer as a highly authorized witness the *licenciado* Don Andrés de León Garabito, who, in his memorial or report to His Majesty regarding his visit under royal mandate to Buenos Aires, states as follows: *During my stay in Buenos Aires, the Fathers urged to me on several occasions that it would be good to have the settlements there visited, and that those past the ten-year period of grace should have their taxes assessed according to the decree, being placed in* encomienda *directly to Your Majesty, in view of the high cost of settling and preserving them. Hearing this proposal, I immediately reported it to the Council, to the viceroy of Peru, and to the Audiencia de la Plata. The Fathers continued to make frequent representations, out of their desire for a visitation by a suitable person having experience of the land. Nothing was ever decided.*

And in paragraph 34 he writes: *The Fathers did not rest content with petitioning the viceroy in Lima, but appealed to the governor; and as there was no discussion of visiting the reductions, etc.* [154]

The gold might easily have been discovered on such a visitation. But how could it be discovered when it did not exist? The truth, at least, would be discovered, despite deceitful jealousy's efforts to mask it.

CHAPTER 81

Appendix: royal letters patent

T O INDICATE how zealously His Majesty, the king our lord, defends the Indians and desires their full liberty, honoring them with the noble title of his own vassals, I will conclude this work by appending the letters patent which His Majesty ordered dispatched to Peru. They run as follows:[155]

The King. — Conde de Chinchón, kinsman, member of my Council of State and War, gentleman of my chamber, my viceroy, governor, and captain general of the provinces of Peru, to the person or persons charged with its administration.

You are well aware that it has been laid down in numerous letters patent and ordinances of myself and my royal forebears that the native Indians of those provinces should have and enjoy complete freedom, serving me just as the other free vassals of these my realms. You likewise know that, since this freedom is incompatible with the personal service in lieu of tribute which in some places has been assessed the Indians and which they pay and are forced to pay to their encomenderos, it has been strictly and repeatedly ordered and commanded that said personal service be ended and altogether abolished, and that the Indians be assessed their tributes, calculated in currency, in the form of wheat, maize, cassava, fowl, fish, cloth, cotton, cochineal, honey, or other fruits, vegetables, and commodities which are available and which can readily be gathered and paid over by said Indians, according to the climate, quality, and nature of the lands and places where they dwell; for no land fails to yield products which are of some value and benefit for human use, commerce, and need.

And whereas, despite this, I have been informed that in those and other provinces the said personal service still continues, and this to the great harm and affliction of the Indians, since the encomenderos use it as pretext to hold and treat them like slaves and worse and do not allow them to enjoy their freedom or go to their own crops, plots, and farms but instead, with inordinate greed, keep them constantly occupied on theirs, with the result that the said Indians flee, sicken, and die, and have decreased greatly in number and will soon cease to exist unless a quick and effective remedy is provided; and inasmuch as in my Royal Council of the Indies numerous letters, reports, and memorials on this subject have been examined which had been written about this matter and presented by persons zealous for God's and my own service and for the good and preservation of said Indians, in addition to what the attorneys of my said Council have petitioned at various times in this regard—I have, after having consulted on what seems the better course, determined to order and command, and by the present document do so order and command, that directly upon receipt of it you take measures to stop and eliminate punctually and absolutely said personal service in whatever place or form it has been or may be found to be established in that province; and that you take steps to convince and make clear to the said Indians and encomenderos that this is what is good and most suitable for them; and that, implementing this as smoothly as possible, you meet with the archbishop, royal officials, superiors of religious orders, and other informed and impartial individuals of that province, to discuss and confer with them about which fruits, articles, and commodities said Indians can be readily assessed as tribute, so that they will correspond and be equivalent to the value which would justly and legitimately accrue to said personal service if there were no excess in its practice, exaction, and payment. Once this commutation is made, you will see to it that to each Indian is assigned what he must give and pay by way of said fruits, money, and other commodities, making a new registration of the Indians and of said assessment in the form herein described; and you will see to it that the encomenderos understand that they may levy and collect from the said Indians only this amount and no more, as is done in Peru and New Spain.

Moreover, you are to carry out this assessment within six months of receiving these letters patent, and put it immediately into execution, unless you happen to encounter particular great and insurmountable obstacles of which we are unaware here and ought to be informed before you proceed with the execution of this provision, this being the only case in which you may suspend and override it, advising me immediately of the fact and of the reasons and motives that have obliged you to do this.

And should any encomienda thus assessed in terms of personal service presently be vacant, you are to delay filling it until after this assessment has been effected; and the new holder should receive it on these terms and with the awareness that he is to be satisfied with its fruits and commodities. And you will advise me at the earliest opportunity that this has been done and carried out, sending me the report and registration of said Indians and of the new assessments, in the knowledge that should there be any delay, omission, or dissimulation in this matter I shall consider myself badly served, and that over and above the serious accounting for this which will be demanded of you in the review of your tenure, you will also have upon your conscience the injuries, damages, and detriments that the Indians will have suffered on this account, compensation for which will be exacted from your own goods and property.

Done in Madrid, April 14, 1633.

I THE KING

By order of the King our Lord,

DON FERNANDO RUIZ DE CONTRERAS

Report made by Father Antonio Ruiz de Montoya
regarding graces received from our Lord[156]

THE FIRST time Your Reverence ordered me to write you the great mercies done to me by the Divine Majesty through the intercession of our Lady, the most glorious Virgin Mary, I decided not to do so (I confess my disobedience and fault in this) since I had already given you an oral account of them. Now, however, that you have a second time ordered and commanded me to do it, I shall comply, to the glory and honor of God our Lord and of the Virgin, his Mother and my Lady, and for the confusion and shame of my wretched self.

From when I was quite small I felt a very great attachment to our Lady; at that age I was constantly experiencing her protection almost miraculously in situations which that age brings with it. When I would finish saying the rosary, I used to hit my chest as hard as I could with a stone and make acts of love (even though at the time I was not familiar with them), producing bruises on my chest. I delighted to shut myself up in my room in the dark late in the evening after taking a discipline (having had no human instructor for this) and spend time thinking of the act with no further reasoning, wherewith I used to find myself very heartened. Within a few days friends inveigled me away and I was turned aside and had no concern any longer except to enjoy myself and run around, going to confession once a year. Eventually I went three entire years without confession.

During the last of these three years I experienced numerous misfortunes and dangers of losing my own life and causing others to lose theirs, so that I was at times a prisoner, a fugitive, or sentenced to banishment. I was afraid that they were out to seize me in a certain house and hurt me badly. One midnight our Lord willed that, as they tried to kill me, I fought them off as best I could for half an hour, until they tired and let me go. I kept on guard against being killed in this house without confession.

Thus, as I was leaving this house with a couple of friends at about eleven or twelve o'clock one very dark night, I was gripped by the thought that God's justice was very angry with me and that he was about to loose his arm against me. I thought I could already feel it bringing a severe punishment. As I walked along absorbed in this thought, one of my companions said to me, "Hey, this man must have died here all of a sudden or else been stabbed to death and thrown here."[157] I got so agitated at this that I spent the rest of

the night sleepless and sweating heavily. This continuing, the thought came
to me as I lay there in bed that what had happened the night before was not
real but a dream. Finally I got dressed just to see if the body was still there.
I found a sign on the ground: it had drizzled and the spot where the body
had lain was not wet. I went into the square but found no corpse there.
However, I asked a friend whether he had heard about anyone being killed.
He answered yes and said they had taken the body to a certain parish. This
left me profoundly frightened, but the devil kept alluring me with pleasures
that sweetened the bitterness in my conscience. One night they caught me
in that same house and gave me three wounds above the heart and came
close to leaving me there dead. I finally escaped; the night was so cold and
I was so oppressed by my conscience that I thought I would lean against a
wall and die.

I finally decided it would be best to go to Chile or leave for a long time,
for I deemed myself already plunged into hell. I spoke to the governor,
Ramón, and together with him to the count of Monterrey, volunteering to
go for two years at my own expense. I had purchased arms and was quite
eager to go when, on the eve of my departure, the Lord willed to deter me
from going by means of a friend of mine, an influential and honorable man,
who supplied me with a good excuse for the viceroy and the governor. I then
got a notion to go to Main[158] to buy myself a half-dozen suits, and later
return to Lima to break them in; I believed that with this absence all would
be forgotten. It occurred to me that I could easily drown and go to hell, and
so I decided to go to confession—consoling myself with the thought that
being a good dresser would be of no consequence for the confession and that,
even if the confessor took other things away from me, he would not take
that.

I went to make my confession to a Father to whom I had gone when I
was little. After hearing me, he said he could not absolve me, that I should
call Father Juan Domínguez, a learned man, and he would hear my
confession. I was so irked by this that I resolved never to go to confession
again: if they were not interested in my confession, neither was I. But of a
sudden I felt a strong interior impulse that I should return to the Society,
that they would hear my confession right away. I went back, and on entering
the vestibule met the Father who would not hear my confession; he was
leaving the house, and at his side was Father Domínguez. The first Father
spoke to him, and he heard my general confession of my entire life and gave
me absolution.

As I was coming in nightly to take a discipline at the Society, I once saw
a Father come after me; the night was so dark I could not tell who it was.
He called to me, but I thought he was calling somebody else, and the Father
immediately halted. However, a few days later he came up behind me and
spoke to me. I then said to myself that the Father had been quite mistaken

the other night, since he was speaking to me without knowing who I was. This was Father Gonzalo Suárez. However, he gave me such clear indications that I had to believe him: for two years, he said, he had felt an inclination to speak to me and implore me at least not to offend our Lord. Our Lord willed that I became so fond of this Father that night that I would not part from him. My converse with him strongly moved me towards a more orderly life, but not to give up the voyage I planned or my intention in making it.

One day during this period I went as usual to hear Mass in the church of St. Francis, at the altar of our Lady's Conception. I heard Mass, and after reciting our Lady's rosary on my fingers because I had lost my rosary, I offered it to our Lady and asked her to accept it and pardon me, telling her I would buy or obtain another rosary. When I finished saying this, it seemed to me that from her statue on the altar I heard our Lady say within me, without my hearing anything outwardly, "I will give you a rosary today." Until that day I had never experienced anything of this sort, and at the time I did not understand how it happened. But I was incapable of doubting it in the slightest. Interiorly abasing myself to the ground, I spoke to her and told her I welcomed it and would keep it in her name. I never gave any thought to how she was going to give it to me.

From this moment on I was so transformed that I did not know myself. Immediately, as I went out into the square to attend to some business I had, men and things seemed different to me; everything seemed a mockery or a game, and nothing was important any longer except to serve God and the Virgin. And so from that day on I always went around with the rosary in my pocket, saying rosaries or performing acts, trying to keep conversing with the Virgin.

On the evening of the day when this happened I went to the Society. I had forgotten what my Lady the Virgin had promised me, but I met Father Suárez, who said he had just been given a rosary and had immediately destined it for me. At that moment what had happened to me at the altar of the Conception came back to me, and I felt an enormous consolation. That very day, as soon as I heard those words, I felt a strong inclination to begin living a chaste life immediately, and so I made a very firm resolution to live chastely and give up my occasions of falling. I have kept this resolution—although shortly afterwards I made a vow to do so.

I spent the remainder of Lent fasting and doing penance; however, I was still set on my voyage. On the second day of Easter I felt myself instantaneously transformed. My desire now was to study, renounce the world altogether, and become a religious in the order of St. Francis. I immediately told my confessor, and he approved my resolution. However, he advised me to make the Exercises before starting, and I did so.

Before beginning them, I was standing next to a column in the square one day at noon. I felt somewhat weak since I was fasting at the time, sometimes eating only every twenty-four hours. As I offered this deprivation to our Lord, with considerable consolation, I turned my face slightly towards the column. Suddenly I seemed to see a devil. He looked not very old, with the appearance of a negro, a long snout, burning eyes, and a devil's feet and hands, though proportioned to his body. But what most fixed my attention was the way he appeared to stare me intently in the face. I took considerable consolation from seeing him distanced from me.

I began the Exercises. The first four days I was extremely upset. I could not stay either standing, kneeling, or sitting. My body weighed me down heavily, and my imagination weighed me down even more with my past follies. What most bothered me was that I kept hearing inside myself, "Are you going to have to give up forever the pleasures you enjoyed yesterday, your friends, your pastimes?" However, I felt more distress over not being able to quell this thought than over actually leaving the friends and pleasures.

But finally on the fourth day, as I was on my knees, I had the impression that the longer I stayed there the less they hurt me. My senses seemed gradually to fall asleep. I found this pleasant, although from time to time I felt a twinge of fear and deliberately woke myself up again. Just as a man in a windowed room who wants to spend time in recollection in the dark will shut the windows one by one and, as he closes them, feel progressively more recollection in his senses until he is in complete darkness and neither sees, hears, nor touches anything—the same thing happened to my soul. My senses gradually went to sleep: I neither saw, heard, nor smelled anything, although my powers were quite alert.

As I abided in the midst of this quietude and let myself go, the first thing I experienced was a great detachment from all created things, good or evil— from being or not being a religious—as if there were no longer any desire or craving in me at all.

In this state, I seemed to be seeing the members of the Society. I did not recognize them by their habit, since I saw them in a white so transparent that the whole interior of their bodies was open to view. I do not know how I recognized them but I know that I did, although I did not hear them saying anything to me. I understood that the transparence I saw in them was their complete candor with their superiors, although at the time I was unaware that the Society had a rule about this.

Then I seemed to behold a large number of unbelievers in a broad field. I felt strongly inclined to help with their salvation, and what spurred me most to this was seeing how the members of the Society were hurrying towards them, aflame with charity to make them Christians and save them. I could see the great hardships they would have to suffer doing this; also the Society's obedience and institute, and their taking no man as their model but our Lord Jesus Christ himself in his desire for the salvation of the pagans.

Suddenly it seemed to me that Christ our Lord was coming towards me, so close that his side, streaming blood, reached my mouth. The consolation I felt is beyond words. This last was the part I felt most sensibly. *Evanuit*—he disappeared, and I was left so consoled and transformed that everything I saw seemed to me a delusion. I had such an eagerness for prayer that I could think of nothing else. From that day on I had great ease in prayer and many spiritual experiences.

I was left so in awe of the members of the Society that I lacked the courage to request admission or tell about this, for I thought they would not accept me. It was the Virgin who obtained all this for me, and who brought it about that within a year and half I managed to learn Latin, which I would need for admission to the Society. I straightway made a vow to her that I would enter the Society to work among unbelievers and that, if they refused to accept me because of my faults, I would go wherever I perceived I was being called by the Lord for the conversion of the pagans, wearing the garb of an honest priest and begging alms for my support as long as my studies lasted.

For several days in the College of San Martín, as I was leaving the refectory for recreation, I seemed to see above myself a Christ crucified and alive on the cross, although this would pass quite quickly like a flash of light. The effect this produced in me was an inability to speak of anything worldly, but only of virtue and perfection; and so I would seek out one of our Fathers or a devout layperson with whom to talk about holy things. The whole time that I studied at San Martín, I had at least an hour and a half of mental prayer, and on Sundays and feast days three or four hours together—usually with strong interior perceptions. There were other times when my knees hurt so badly that I felt as if awls were being thrust into me from the knees all the way up the thigh. From that time I remained with a pain in the right knee which only recently left me. However, it only hurt me when I had spent over an hour in discursive prayer; in the other kind of prayer I feel nothing.

One night I was praying under a tree, weeping and as it were complaining lovingly against our Lord that he had allowed me to be born a natural and not a legitimate child, and that because of this they would not let me into the Society. I heard within myself: "Nothing God does is by chance, and neither was this—nor was your having wasted the estate he left you. Everything is for your good, to keep you from placing your trust in anything in the world. You will enter the Society, and what is lacking to nature God will supply by his grace."

Meanwhile, I heard that Father Diego de Torres was coming from Quito to be provincial of Paraguay and go to the help of the wretched people there. I remembered what had happened to me in my first Spiritual Exercises. Accordingly, I decided to wait for him and follow his orders. My confessor was pressing me to enter the Society, since all the consultors thought the same as he. But since my goal was to get to Paraguay, where I knew the Lord was calling me, I put him off and said I did not know enough Latin and that they should let me study for four more months. This was simply so I could volunteer to Father Diego de Torres; I thought that those in Peru would never let me go to a different province. I was rather in turmoil, until I went to a very spiritual Father with whom I discussed my affairs; I told him my story and asked his opinion. He said, "Do not let this opportunity slip; if the Lord has chosen you for this enterprise, he will send you there even if nobody else wants to." Calmed by this advice, I entered the Society.

One day, when I was weeping over my great sins, like a flash I seemed to see Christ our Lord holding a cross in his hands and giving it to me. This increased my desire for hardships and for the conversion of unbelievers. Three times during these same Exercises it seemed to me that I was on my knees next to an enormous cross, and that I was being lifted up on it with the greatest sweetness. During these Exercises I had very special sentiments of love for the Virgin, and I offered her my life and the hardships I would suffer in Paraguay.

One day I gave to a superior an account of the desire which the Lord was giving me for the conversion of the Paraguay Indians. His reply was that if Father Diego de Torres came and asked who wanted to go with him, claiming that he had permission to take them, I was not to say a word to him.

I followed this order, but remembered to appeal to a higher authority through the intercession of the Virgin. One night when I had decided to ask our Lord for this, while in the chancel of the sacristy at Lima, I began to be deeply recollected within myself; as I earnestly besought the Virgin and Blessed Xavier, I seemed to hear coming from the Virgin the words, "Do not be grieved, son; you will go." The Lord alone knows the joy and assurance that I felt. I wanted to burst into shouting. I said to myself: "No longer do I feel envy for those who are going; we are all companions." And even though superiors said nothing to me for a long time, I did not mind because I was already sure it could not be otherwise; and finally they told me.

During the Exercises I made for going to Paraguay, it occurred to me that I should ask St. Mary for her love, and that this was the best occupation I could have. And so I began them with the resolve to obtain some little love, through the intercession of our Blessed Father Ignatius and Blessed Xavier. As I was praying one day, I began to lose my senses as described above. I seemed to be going out along a rough, rocky, uphill road, which I traveled in a certain distress. At the end of the road stood St. Mary; she was very beautiful, so bright that I could hardly look at her. I came to her with great trust, exhausted. I entered a door where was she standing watch, and she led me through a delightful meadow, so sweet-smelling that its mere odor seemed to put me to sleep and hinder my steps from going on. There is no way to give an idea of this even by comparison with sweet and aromatic things on earth, for the sweet and aromatic things of earth are without exaggeration stinking and bitter.

Then it seemed to me that the Virgin was beckoning me forward with her hand, and there I came upon Christ our Lord, on a cross and alive. He was holding one hand to his side and with two fingers was opening it; he beckoned me with his head to come and drink. I drank and was not slaked. A dense vapor seemed to come forth which penetrated my whole body, giving me such pleasure that I would have wished to remain that way my whole life. *Evanuit*—he disappeared. But even later, when I was fully awake and doing manual work in my cell, I seemed really to smell the flowers. This lasted for two or three days.

In these Exercises I asked our Lord, if it was his will, to take away my consolations in prayer, for I was anxious because I had always heard that the Society's way of prayer consisted in much mortification and that everything else was deceit and delusion. I went through some bitter times because of this. But in prayer I was receiving constant assurance that what was happening to me was genuine. However, as I asked our Lord for this, I suddenly seemed to be placed within Christ our Lord's side, with the most intense joy. Once there, it seemed to me that there was nothing further for me to desire or ask in heaven or on earth. But I saw that I still had a great step to ascend. I saw nothing, but I realized that what I was missing was something great. I saw it as in a little book.[159] I realized that it was contemplation of the divine essence—that what had been shown me so far had been through material things, but that this other was incomparably higher, although not even this can be expressed in this life except by images.

One day I was hauling stones in the novitiate garden. As I made acts of love to the Virgin, I felt myself becoming interiorly inflamed with love for her. Through my guardian angel I offered her my heart. Even though I loaded myself down heavily with stones, it seemed at times that I was not walking on the earth or carrying any load, large or small, and that the brothers walking there looked like angels to me. Then the bell for afternoon prayer rang, and I went to it with this feeling. It suddenly became fixed. I placed myself before our Lady and offered her my heart in all sincerity, and our Lady offered hers to me. This left me the most consoled person in the world. The bell then rang to leave, but I seemed to have just gone in. I was left so weak that I could barely get up. Finally, by leaning against the walls, I got back to my cell, which I had to myself, intending to pray there because the bell for that had rung. I could not open my mouth or kneel: all I could do was to sit propped up on the floor, as if stunned by what had transpired. In this I passed another hour in a breath.

Then, when I went to the refectory, all the food made me want to throw up my bowels when I smelled it. Forcing myself, I finally began to eat; it felt as if I were eating a piece of wool. Going to recreation, I could not bear the voices and the racket, and so asked permission to recollect myself. I regretted giving an account of all this to the superior, since it occurred to me that I was saying it out of vainglory.

In Córdoba I had a number of special interior perceptions. Among those I have noted down is that one day, just after receiving Communion, I offered my heart to our Lord for him to dwell in, and it seemed to me that inside my heart the host had become a beautiful child with whom I was taking delight.

Another time, as I was loving my Lady, I seemed to see her holding her Son in her arms and giving him to me. The chastity which I received then is beyond saying. On the way from Córdoba to Mendoza a wagon fell over. Seven persons could not lift it, one wheel being wedged in the ground and the other up in the air. Commending myself to the Virgin, I got under the wheel and told an Indian to help me. With no special effort on my own part and very little on that of the Indian (as he himself said), the wagon was righted. This was because the Virgin helped us.

On this same trip, some oxen together with an Indian fell behind for a whole night. We could not go on and felt quite uneasy, fearing that they might have gotten in with some wild cows they had seen. Seeing Father Rector's anxiety, I went aside to a little grove and began to pray. After a while I heard the words "Here they come." I opened my eyes and looked, but saw nothing. I returned to prayer and heard, "Here they come." Again I looked and saw nothing. I thought it was a delusion. I fell flat on the ground and heard, "Here they come." I looked, and they could just be seen in the distance, the Indian with them.

Almost every time I prayed—that is, for a short period in Córdoba—I would perceive the devil so vividly that I was driven out of my cell by the terror I felt. I would perceive him in three ways. First, as someone shooting darts of evil thoughts straight into the soul to disturb it. Second, as a great panic and fear felt in the soul, with no accompanying image. Third, in the form of a huge black man holding a thick club in his hand. Sometimes the fear was so great that I could hardly overcome it with good thoughts until the soul had become totally fixed in its prayer; then there was no fear at all.

Once as I was speaking with the Virgin in prayer, my senses were going to sleep as on other occasions. But then I experienced something I never had before. It was this: something, I know not what, was mounting inside me from my feet upwards. I thought at the time that it was the spirit, which was abandoning those limbs and concentrating itself in the breast, where I could feel the activity of willing and loving take place. But it must have been the natural heat abandoning the extremities.

When I gave my account to a superior, he spoke to me of the acts of understanding and willing, and how they were different. I had never thought or worried about this. But then, that day, I went to prayer. Once I knelt down I began to enter recollection as on other occasions and felt my bodily extremities being abandoned by the natural heat and my breast being inflamed with love. Quite soon, I felt all of this natural heat progressively rise like a vapor and gather in my head, which felt extremely hot. Then, at the top, in the highest place inside the head near what is called the crown, rather towards the middle of the head, I myself saw a brightness. I could not see with the eyes but I did see, I do not know how. I realized that this was the understanding, with which we are to see and know the Godhead. I saw nothing with the understanding, but I did see that what is seen with the understanding is not corporeal—I saw with one eye and on the other side saw nothing. This is gibberish; I cannot explain it but I clearly understood it.

Once during the Exercises I was praying and seemed to see our Lord. I did not see him in human form, but I saw that it was he and that he was saying to me, "Study, because I have called you for these"—for the Indians. Grateful for this, my soul vowed to help them, with a humility so deep that would to God it might remain rooted forever in my heart. My spirit longed to undo itself in service to our Lord; however, this brought not sadness but rather profound consolation. Then I suddenly seemed to glimpse one crucified arm, or half an arm, four or more fingers above the elbow. I do not know what it meant; what I felt was a great desire to suffer and to put myself under the earth for love of our Lord.

After receiving Communion, I once seemed to see Christ our Lord at the age of eight to ten years, a lovely lad in a blue robe. With his left hand he held a tablet leaning against his thigh; with his right hand he indicated to me that I should learn there. I did not see anything written on the tablet, but I felt great love for humility and a great detachment from everything on earth.

Another time, after receiving Communion and being given only half a host, I felt bad that the species would not last as long. But suddenly I felt Christ our Lord seated in my heart, fully adult, and letting me understand that he was wholly present in the tiniest particle. This was because I had had a slight doubt whether Christ our Lord was present there or not.

Once on Holy Thursday I felt a desire to go and sleep on the platform of the sacristy where they place the Blessed Sacrament, in order to keep it company throughout the night. I lay on the floor, and as I rested a little, I felt above me that devils were thronging towards me, gesturing and waking me up. But every joint in my body seemed to have seized up; I could not move or say a thing. I remembered the Blessed Sacrament present there, and could not call upon it. I was going to call on the Virgin and could not. And they remained above me, as if mocking, waking me up. I eventually arose, nearly breathless, saying "Jesus," and feeling as exhausted as if I had been through a long battle. I commended myself to the Lord present there, and then lay back down on the ground. Very soon afterwards they returned as before, making gestures at me. I was terrified, unable to ask help from God or from people. I could hear a Father walking in the church above the monument and an Indian snoring in a room attached to the sacristy, but my limbs were all so locked that I could not move, cry out, make the sign of the cross, say inwardly "Jesus," or call upon the Virgin, though I tried all of these. Finally, after a little while, I got up. I was so terrified and panicked that, when I went to the church to visit the Blessed Sacrament enclosed there and then returned to the sacristy, I could not go in. I had such an extraordinary fear that I was shocked to find myself trembling, although I did force myself to go in and walk through the sacristy in order to overcome myself. Thereupon I experienced a very strong temptation to the effect that I was spiritually very advanced and that the devils hated me for it.

Once, as I was praying the little hours in the choir on St. Anthony's day, I began saying within myself to our Lord: "Is it possible, Lord, that the reason I was unable to be a coadjutor rather than a priest was that in this way I would be humble and serve you better?" At this I felt myself entirely filled with an enormous consolation and tenderness coming from the Blessed Sacrament on the high altar and from there pervading my soul. I felt a great desire to make a vow to work forever among the Indians. Having got permission, I made the vow. So vehement was the impression of joy I experienced in my heart at that time—I mean when it came from the Blessed Sacrament and spread throughout my body—that I then felt a sharp pain in my heart which did not leave me until two days ago, when it gradually began disappearing.

Though I have had other interior experiences, these seemed to me the most special and noteworthy. Blessed be the Lord, who has bestowed these experiences upon a person who has deserved hell millions of times over and who fails in gratitude for them. I know they have come to me through the hand and intercession of our Lady, the blessed Virgin Mary.

APPENDIX II

Spiritual Counsels of Father Antonio Ruiz de Montoya[160]

HE MAY be called a spiritual man who feels himself drawn to eternal life and lives with longing for his sovereign fatherland, who sighs from the depth of his heart for the land of the living, who says with the Apostle, "We have here no abiding city, but seek a future one,"[161] and elsewhere, "I desire to be dissolved and to be with Christ."[162] This can hardly be said by anyone who has not embraced mortification and the cross and tribulations of Jesus, in which are a sweet death and a true life.

2. Tranquillity of soul and peace of heart consist in courageously rejecting all sensual pleasures, even that of a jar of cold water, sacrificing it to God as David did the water from the cistern of Bethlehem; and in giving to His Majesty this enjoyment that one renounces for his love, as one compares it with the enjoyment imparted by the Lord to the soul in compensation, which is without doubt far and away superior.

3. Remembrance of God is the wall that protects the heart. To the extent that one forgets God, this wall crumbles, leaving a wide breach for the enemy vices; the soul thus ends up as poor of spiritual goods as the square of a sacked town is of temporal ones.

4. When anyone thinks that he feels himself forgotten and abandoned by God, finding himself in the murk of a dark night, an excellent help is patience and the surrendering of one's own will to God's, saying with the good thief, "We indeed justly, for we are receiving what our deeds deserve."[163] It is better to confess the faults by which one deserved this frown and neglect, to bewail them, to do additional penances and prayers, and steadily to reject all exterior consolations which nature seeks out in order to discharge and relieve its suffering.

5. You should receive the lights of the consolations that follow upon this darkness with the greatest gratitude and the deepest humility, acknowledging yourself unworthy of visitation from God and saying to him with tender affections of the heart, "Where were you, my Lord, eternal Light, that you felt no compassion at seeing me overwhelmed in this painful slavery?"

6. Very pleasing to God is a humility with these four qualities: to have no wish to be honored, to rejoice at seeing oneself put down, to show dislike at being praised, and to aim at being despised by everyone.

7. One rises to love of God by three steps: being carefully careless of temporal things and placing no affection in them, being carelessly careless of

oneself and of bodily comforts, and being carefully careful of God alone and of always pleasing him in everything.

8. If the imagination contains portrayals of the world and of its glories, the spirit does poorly; if there are images of God, of Christ on the cross and in the Sacrament, of the Blessed Virgin, of the angels, and of the courtiers of heaven, then the soul does well.

9. When trials, griefs, and ill treatment are wrongfully inflicted on us by those close to us or by strangers, the remedy is this: if you were at fault, to grieve over that; if not, to offer them to God and forgive your neighbor the wrong he has done you. In this way you will oblige God to forgive you the wrongs you have done him and also to intervene for your innocence and reputation. So long as the pain of these wounds lasts, do not think of curing them through nature, which is very wretched in the medicines it applies, inflaming rather than curing the wound. Embrace Christ crucified, who, having no fault of his own, suffered far more for yours. Have recourse to his most holy wounds and you will find true consolation in all your trials.

10. Once you have made great progress in the desire to suffer for Christ, you will be able without danger to recall to memory the wrongs you have forgotten in order to savor their bitterness and so increase the merit. You must not complain about anyone, no matter how they have hurt you; rather you must desire to do good and have love towards those who loathe you, imitating your divine Lord.

11. It is an intolerable travail for someone to drudge at amassing riches and then, once they have been acquired, never enjoy them. It is an even worse misfortune to devote much time to prayer and get no use from it in situations where it applies. It is pitiful when, after ten or twenty years of mental prayer and of dealing with God and meditating on the life of our Lord Jesus Christ, you complain with impatience and unrestrained criticism about any adversity that befalls you. You may be sure that for the whole time that you spent on prayer you were digging in a barren mine and extracting not silver or gold but sand and gravel.

12. In nothing that you do in this life ought you to look to your own advantage, or think of yourself or of the reward you can garner for yourself through your actions. The only purpose of all your actions must be God's greater pleasure and glory; it is His Majesty's part to take care of you and to ensure your contentment in time and your good end in eternity.

Method for Living the Present Day

1. Fix your mind on God the moment you awake; this will not be hard for you if you lived the previous day with care.

2. If there is a church with the Sacrament where you are, go there right

away. Kneeling, say the divine prayer of the Our Father, with an inward sentiment of what you say; you will have this sentiment if you forget all created things.

3. Thank God for the favors you have received from his most generous hand. Arouse yourself to acts of contrition and sorrow for the offenses you have committed against His Majesty. Offer him all the good works of your entire life, delighting most in those which please him most and wishing to perform them countless times over again with greater perfection—e.g., your entrance into religion, your vows, the sufferings you have endured. Ratify them all and offer them anew united to the blood and passion of the Savior. Offer him likewise all wrongs done you by your neighbors, praying for the latter from the heart and longing for further sufferings provided that God be not offended.

4. Offer the Lord all your powers and senses and whatever acts they may perform.

5. All honors that have been or could be given you, all human praise, all temporal goods and pleasures, you should renounce at the feet of your Lord Jesus Christ in exchange for his love. If you have him, even though you be utterly poor, you have everything; if you lack him, even though you be lord of all creation, you lack everything.

6. Renounce also, in your dear Friend, even the spiritual consolations which he has given or could give to you. Ask for yourself dryness, afflictions, the cross, and confusion; and for God glory—"but for us confusion of face."[164]

7. Ask for the virtue of mortification in all things, so as to live among your neighbors without offending anyone—"giving offense to no one."[165]

8. Ask him to enkindle in your soul more and more the fire of his divine love, towards which you must strive with all the strength of your will.

9. After this say the Litany in the usual way.

10. Then invite the entire heavenly court to the divine praises and recite with deep devotion the invitatory "Come let us exult in the Lord." Upon finishing it, say the hymn "Come, Creator Spirit" with the prayer to the Holy Spirit.

11. Implore the patronage of the Virgin and of St. Magdalene, that they may teach you to love God much. Then continue with your prayer. When it is finished, give thanks and keep a mouthful to ruminate throughout the day.

12. Recite the hours and then, if possible, say Mass before plunging into other concerns and exterior business. You should say Mass and make your thanksgiving very slowly and with all possible devotion.

13. Enter your affairs, and live with care that they do not enter you. If you attend to this you will be their master; otherwise, their slave.

14. If you learn how to keep silence, you can spend the whole day

speaking with God. Even in speaking about God to other people you need to be prudent, for fear of annoying them—except with persons who you can see enjoy it because they themselves have been wounded by divine love. Listen with pleasure to anyone who speaks to you about God.

15. You should exert the most careful watch over your interior recollection when out on the streets, public squares, and roads, where there is more occasion for distraction.

16. Live with the prudent virgins' concern and vigilance to keep your light trimmed, sprightly, and alive; otherwise it may easily dim and go out. If God does leave you in darkness, keep on working, for the merit is greater then and you have plentiful experience that the light quickly shines again at the moment of greatest oppression and darkness. Be convinced that God arranges these fluctuations for your good, so that you will perform your works in humble awareness that what is given to you is not your own.

17. Teach your soul how to talk. If you do this carefully, you will hear it talking to you in the angels' way, and you will silence the unruly clamor of your passions and senses, which, animal-like as they are, constantly whine for what is passing and let themselves be swept away by what is visible.

18. Recall that the world has its own hell of sufferings and heavenly glory of delights, but that its very glory is a hell. You will escape its sufferings if you refuse its glories. Seek no other glory on earth than to be perpetually united with your sweet Redeemer, conforming your every action to his actions, which were all directed towards suffering for the salvation of men and the glory of his eternal Father.

NOTES

1. C. J. McNaspy, S.J., *Conquistador Without Sword: The Life of Roque González, S.J.* (Chicago: Loyola University Press, 1984).

2. Francisco Jarque, *Ruiz Montoya en Indias (1608–1652)*. 4 vols. (Madrid: Victoriano Suárez, 1900), vol. 1. pp. 41–42. Jarque (or Xarque) was a Spaniard and a younger contemporary of Ruiz de Montoya in the Paraguay missions. Leaving the Jesuit order for reasons of health, he eventually returned to Spain, where he published his *The Life—Prodigious in the Variety of Its Events, Exemplary in the Heroism of Religious Virtues, Admirable for the Favors of Heaven, Glorious in the Apostolic Character of Its Occupations—of the Venerable Father Antonio Ruiz de Montoya, Professed Religious, Son of the Illustrious Patriarch St. Ignatius of Loyola, Founder of the Society of Jesus . . .* (Zaragoza, 1662). Despite its pompous style, it is valuable for its numerous quotations from lost notebooks and letters of Ruiz de Montoya—unfortunately with their rough style touched up, as Jarque loyally informs us, to meet the standards of a literary work.

3. See Appendix I, p. 199.

4. For Montoya's own accounts of these events, see his account below in chapter 4, and the earlier description of his spiritual experiences, written around the time of his ordination, in Appendix I.

5. It is interesting to note that the Thirty-first General Congregation of the Society of Jesus, 1965–1966, clarified the requirement for solemn profession, making clear that it included "those who show outstanding apostolic or ministerial capability" (decree 11, n. 4).

6. Op. cit., p. 426.

7. Pierre Delattre, S.J., and Edmond Lamalle, S.J., "Jésuites wallons, flamands, français, missionaires au Paraguay,

1608–1767," *Archivum Historicum Societatis Iesu* 16 (1947), p. 130.

8. Hugo Storni, S.J., "Antonio Ruiz de Montoya," *Archivum Historicum Societatis Iesu* 105 (1984), p. 431.

9. Jarque, vol. 4, pp. 46–47; quoted in Furlong, *Antonio Ruiz de Montoya y su Carta a Comental* (Buenos Aires: Ediciones Theoria, 1964), p 59.

10. Jarque, op. cit., vol. 3, pp. 350–53; cited in Furlong, *Antonio Ruiz de Montoya y su Carta a Comental*, pp. 61–63.

11. In his *Lost Paradise: The Jesuit Republic in South America*, chapter 5.

12. A brief account of the Venerable Francisco may be found in Joseph N. Tylenda's recent volume *Jesuit Saints and Martyrs* (Chicago: Loyola University Press, 1984), pp. 100–101.

13. Antonio Ruiz de Montoya, *Silex del Divino Amor*, Introducción, transcripción y notas de José Luis Rouillon Arróspide (Lima: Pontificia Universidad Católica del Perú, Fondo Editorial, 1991).

14. For a sample of Montoya's spiritual teaching, see Appendix II, which gives two sets of maxims excerpted by Francisco Jarque from Montoya's now lost notebooks.

15. See François Roustang, S.J., ed., *An Autobiography of Martyrdom: Spiritual Writings of the Jesuits in New France*, translated by Sister M. Renelle (St. Louis: Herder, 1964).

16. Bartomeu Melià, S.J., "El 'modo de ser' guaraní en la primera documentación jesuítica," *Archivum Historicum Societatis Iesu* 100 (1981), pp. 212–33.

17. See pp. 53–54.

18. For the arguments of Nezú and Potiravá, see McNaspy, *Conquistador Without Sword*, pp. 183–85.

19. Ps. 80:14.

20. 1 Cor. 15:10.

21. Aphraates, the earliest important

writer of the Syriac church, lived in Persia in the early fourth century.

22. Julian (Flavius Claudius Julianus) was Roman emperor from 361 to 363. A nephew of the first Christian emperor, Constantine I, he reverted to paganism and is accordingly often called "Julian the Apostate."

23. Montoya's marginal note: "V. Histor. de Chiapa, cap. 20. Licendiado Antonio de León, De escudas y armas, fol 17 y Garcilaso, lib. 2 cap. 8." The references are apparently to Antonio de Remesal, *Historia general de las Indias occidentales y particularmente de la gobernación de Chiapa y Guatemala* (Madrid, 1619), and Garcilaso de la Vega, *Comentarios reales que tratan del origen de los Incas* (Lisbon, 1609) or *Historia general del Perú* (second part of the foregoing) [Maeder].

24. See 2 Macc. 4.

25. The word "reduction" is a transliteration of the Spanish *reducción* and has become the standard term for self-contained mission settlements, especially among the Indians of South America.

26. Two thousand leagues, some six thousand miles; the league occasionally varied in length.

27. Montoya's marginal note: "Consta de informaciones auténticas que se presentaron en el Real Consejo de Indias." Montoya here alludes to the threat from southern Brazil against the Spanish viceroyalty of Peru, particularly its southeastern outpost of Potosí (in present-day Bolivia) with its "mountain of silver."

28. The meaning of the word Paraguay is uncertain; some scholars suggest "River of Parrots" and other derivations are offered. The word is also the name of the river and the present republic. In Montoya's time it designated both the civil area and the large Jesuit province which included present-day Paraguay, most of Argentina, Uruguay, parts of Bolivia, and the southern part of Brazil.

29. Manioca or cassava is a tropical plant whose fleshy edible rootstocks yield a nutritious starch from which bread is made.

30. The final clause is perhaps an example of the author's gentle humor.

31. In 1549 the Jesuit founder, St. Ignatius Loyola, sent a team of six Jesuits to Brazil and a few months before he died in 1556 wrote that they had received an urgent petition for help from "a Spanish city called Paraguay [Asunción], since people are needed to teach not only Indians but Spaniards as well." But the beginning of Jesuit apostolic work in the Paraguay area can be fixed at the year 1586, when the bishop of Tucumán, Francisco de Victoria, O.P., requested help from the Jesuit provincials of Peru and Brazil. When, in response, Jesuits from Brazil landed at Buenos Aires they were asked by the bishop of Asunción, Don Alonzo Guerra, then residing there, to go to Paraguay. Three did so. The new mission, part of the Peruvian Jesuit province, barely survived until reinforcements arrived some fifteen years later. In 1607, Paraguay became a separate province with Father Torres Bollo as the first provincial.

32. Thomas Fields was born in Limerick, Ireland, in 1549, and became a Jesuit at Rome in 1574. He arrived in Brazil with Blessed José Anchieta and was for a time his traveling companion. He entered Paraguay in 1587 and died at Asunción in 1625. He was one of the first three Jesuits to reach Paraguay; a second group arrived at Asunción in 1593.

33. Claudio Aquaviva (1542–1615) was the fifth superior general of the Society of Jesus, being elected in 1581 and dying after almost thirty-four years in office, the longest tenure in the order's history. Aquaviva had a great deal to do with the establishment of the Paraguay reductions.

34. Diego de Torres Bollo was born in 1551. He became a Jesuit in Castile and joined the Peruvian Jesuit province. He was named first provincial of Paraguay, serving from 1607 to 1615. He died at Sucre (the former Charcas) in Bolivia in 1638.

35. Montoya himself. For a fuller account by Montoya of his vocation and spiritual experiences, see Appendix I.

36. Tob. 12:7.

37. Marciel de Lorenzana was born at León, Spain, in 1565 and entered the Society of Jesus in Castile in 1583. Ordained in

1591, he came to South America in 1593. In addition to founding the first reduction, San Ignacio Guazú, he served twice as rector of the college in Asunción, where he died in 1632.

38. Diego de Boroa was born in Cáceres, Spain, in 1585 and entered the Toledo province of the Jesuits in 1605. He reached Buenos Aires and was ordained there in 1610. He served as provincial from 1634–1640, and after a long and active life died at the reduction of San Miguel in 1657.

39. Giuseppe Cataldini was born near Ancona, Italy, in 1571 and entered the Society of Jesus at Rome in 1602. He came to South America in 1605 and served as superior of the Guaraní missions from 1644 to 1646. He died at San Ignacio Miní, Argentina, in 1653.

40. Simone Mascetta was born in Castilenti, Italy, in 1577 and entered the Jesuit order at Naples in 1606. He arrived at Buenos Aires in 1608. He died in 1658 at San Ignacio Miní, Argentina, where his name is inscribed in the sanctuary of the church.

41. Villa Rica is a city well known in Paraguayan history and cultural life. Founded in 1570, its site was changed several times, but in Montoya's time was in what is now southern Brazil. Two of the eighty-three Paraguayan-born Jesuits before the expulsion in 1767-68 were born in Villa Rica.

42. Antonio Moranta was born in Palma, Majorca, in 1579 and entered the Aragón province in 1596. He came to Buenos Aires in 1610 and died in Asunción in 1645, after years of service in the reductions.

43. Large grants of land were made to Spanish conquerors and colonists to attract them to settle in South America: the system was known as *encomienda*. The settler, known as an *encomendero*, received payment in tribute and services ("personal service") from Indians, supposedly in return for protecting them and helping in their conversion to Christianity. In fact the Indians were often treated as slaves under the system.

44. The *yerba mate*, now a common beverage in the Southern Cone of South America.

45. Francisco de Alfaro, an important lay figure in reduction history, was appointed by the Audiencia de Charcas to inspect and, if possible, to better the condition of the Indians. His *ordenanza*, referred to by Montoya in chapter 7, against any form of Indian slavery, overt or covert, became a sort of Magna Charta of Indian rights in the reductions and was much controverted by the colonists. He is mentioned again in later chapters. His son Diego became a Jesuit.

46. Montoya's marginal note: "Ordenanzas." The allusion is to Alfaro's decrees.

47. Montoya's marginal note: "Cédula real del año de 1633, que está en el capítulo LXXXI."

48. There are eight reals in a peso (or piece-of-eight).

49. *Hechicero*, Montoya's designation for the shamans who played a leading role in Guaraní societies.

50. *Caa*: Montoya's interest in linguistics makes him notice the similarity of the Guaraní *caa* to the Portuguese *cha* (the original Chinese pronunciation of "tea" retained in Portuguese).

51. Montoya's marginal note: "P. Acosta, *Historia natural* I, c 22." The reference is to José de Acosta, *Historia natural y moral de las Indias* (Seville, 1590) [Maeder].

52. Pedro Romero was born in Seville in 1585 and entered the Paraguay province in 1607. He was ordained together with Montoya in 1611 and took his final vows with Roque González in 1619. He served as superior of the Guaraní missions before Montoya, 1631–1636, and died a martyr at Itatín on March 22, 1645.

53. Manuel Cabral de Alpoim was born in 1591 on the Azores. He arrived in 1599 with his parents at Buenos Aires. After some years in Lisbon he returned to Argentina and held important civil offices in Buenos Aires and Corrientes (where he mainly lived, dying in 1660). With six whites and two hundred Indians of Itatí he went to put down the rising of Caaró and Ijuhí. He was wounded by arrows in the

affray at Candelaria in 1628. He was a good friend to the Jesuit missionaries.

54. Montoya's marginal note: "Escribe a su Magestad el ilustrísimo de Tucumán; puédese ver en capitulo LXXIX. El señor presidente de los Charcas trató que para apaciguar esta gente se volviese a encargar della la Compañía."

55. Audiencia: an administrative unit under several magistrates exercising most functions of government within a large area of the Spanish empire. The Audiencia of Charcas (now Sucre) had jurisdiction over modern Bolivia and parts of present-day Peru, Chile, Argentina, and Paraguay. At this time it was attached to the viceroyalty of Peru.

56. St. Thomas the Apostle was widely believed to have evangelized Latin America. Montoya treats the subject at length in chapters 21 to 26.

57. San Ignacio (Miní): the reduction at Itambzú in Guairá, founded in 1611. Together with the reduction of Loreto it was moved during the transmigration of 1632—described in chapter 38—to the present Argentine province of Misiones. It is called Miní (Guaraní for little) to distinguish it from San Ignacio Guazú (the greater).

58. The original of this obscure passage (omitted in the 1892 Bilbao edition) reads: "del nefando huyen como de la muerte: ayuda a la naturaleza para evacuación por la vía, antes se morirán que admitirla."

59. Tupá is believed by many modern ethnologists to have been the god of thunder; even today the word is used in Guaraní as the equivalent of the Christian God.

60. This custom, called by ethnologists the couvade, has been observed among American Indians as well as in many other parts of the world, such as Africa, India, and parts of China and Japan.

61. Montoya's marginal note: "Fray Alonso Ramos." The reference is to Agustino Alonso Ramos Gavilán, an Augustinian friar and author of *Historia del célebre santuario de nuestra Señora de Copacabana y sus milagros, e invención de la cruz de Carabuco* (1621) [Maeder]; he is cited again in chapter 23. The general deluge is a tradition noted in many cultures.

62. Martín Javier de Urtasun was born in 1590 at Pamplona, Navarre, and was a relative of the great Jesuit missionary to Asia, Francis Xavier. He entered the Society of Jesus in 1604 in Castile, arriving in Buenos Aires on May 1, 1610. His death at Loreto in 1614 is described in chapter 14.

63. Congregation: a chapter meeting of members of a Jesuit province, not to be confused with the pious associations for the laity called congregations or sodalities of the Blessed Virgin Mary.

64. Masses: on a Jesuit's death, each priest in his province offers a number of Masses for his eternal peace.

65. See Acts 5:1–11.

66. *Maloqueros*: raiders who hunted Indians to enslave them.

67. 1 Cor. 14:22.

68. Jean Vaisseau was born in 1583 at Tournai in Belgium, and joined the French-Belgian province in 1606, but withdrew from the novitiate and was ordained a priest in Paris the following year. Reentering the Society of Jesus in 1612, he came to Buenos Aires in 1617. Having been trained as a musician, he is often credited with founding the reductions' strong musical tradition. He died in 1623 while ministering to the Indians during a plague.

69. Agnus Dei: an image of Christ as the Lamb of God, often worn around the neck.

70. Diego de Salazar was born at Jaén, Spain, in 1592 and entered the Andalusian Jesuit province in 1612. He came to Buenos Aires in 1617. He was recognized as a remarkably vigorous missioner up to his death in 1659 at San Ignacio Miní, Argentina.

71. Cristóbal de Mendoza was born in Santa Cruz de la Sierra, Bolivia, in 1598 and entered the Society's Paraguay province in 1616. He was ordained in São Paulo, April 19, 1629. After participating in the foundation of several reductions, he was martyred in Rio Grande do Sul, Brazil, in 1635.

72. Francisco Díaz Taño was born in Las Palmas, Canary Islands, in 1593 and entered the Andalusian Jesuit province in

1614. He came to Buenos Aires in 1622. He was twice sent to Europe as mission procurator to recruit new missionaries (1627–1640 and 1658–1663). He was also superior of the Guaraní missions for two terms, 1646–1649 and 1657–1658. He died at Córdoba, Argentina, in 1677.

73. *Tierra Firme*, the Spanish Main, i.e., the Spanish South American coastal lands stretching from Panama eastward.

74. Portuguese: at that time all the white and mixed-blood inhabitants of Brazil were loosely referred to as Portuguese.

75. Spiritual conquest: here for the first time Montoya uses the term which is also the title of the work; it is intended obviously to refer to the peaceful evangelization of the Indian inhabitants in contradistinction to the armed conquest of the conquistadors.

76. Lorenzo de Mendoza was the "prelate" of Rio de Janeiro from 1633–1637; the prelacy lasted just one hundred years, from 1576 until creation of the bishopric in 1676. Dr. Mendoza wrote the approbation which precedes the *Spiritual Conquest*.

77. Montoya's marginal note "Fray Alonso Ramos, *Historia de Nuestra Señora de Copacabana*, c. 7, 8, 9 10, y 11."

78. Diego Alvarez de Paz (1560–1620) was born in Toledo, Spain, and went as a missioner to Peru. One of the eminent spiritual writers of the Society of Jesus, he died in Lima.

79. Toribio Alfonso de Mongrovejo (1538–1606) was born in Spain and served as archbishop of Lima from 1581 until his death there. He is an important figure in the story of the evangelization in South America and was later canonized.

80. Guarcar Inga: the Inca ruler Huáscar (1495?–1533).

81. Lorenzo Pérez de Grado was named bishop of Paraguay (i.e, Asunción) in 1615 but did not take possession of his see till 1618; the following year he departed to become bishop of Cuzco. Copacabana is a peninsula on Lake Titicaca, bordering Bolivia and Peru, the site of one of the great shrines of the Blessed Virgin Mary (since 1583).

82. Matt. 28:19.

83. Montoya's marginal note: "Origen, In Genesim., lib. 3; Eusebius, lib. 3, c. 1; Martyrol. 21 diciembre."

84. Montoya's marginal note: "San Juan Chrys. *Oratio duo apos.*" Ethiopians: in Montoya's time, this word was used as a general term for all black Africans.

85. See note 45.

86. Montoya's marginal note: "P. Pedro de Ribadeneira 2, folio 715." Pedro Ribadeneira (1526–1611), one of the most prominent early Jesuits and first biographer of St. Ignatius, composed an encyclopedic Lives of the Saints (*Flos Sanctorum*), to which Montoya apparently refers here.

87. Manuel da Nóbrega (1517–1570), a Portuguese, led the first Jesuit mission to Brazil in 1549. He and Blessed José de Anchieta (1534–1597) founded the mission of São Paulo and are recognized as the "Apostles of Brazil."

88. Montoya's marginal note: "P. Acosta, *Hist. mor.* ca. 27, folio 377."

89. Montoya's marginal note: "Ribadeneira, *vid. sup.*"

90. Montoya's marginal note: "Dr. D. Francisco de Alfaro."

91. "Holy wood," i.e., lignum vitae.

92. Montoya's marginal note: "Ribadeneira."

93. Montoya's marginal note: "Fray Alonso Ramos, *Historia de Copacabana.*"

94. José Doménech was born April 28, 1602, in Alicante, Spain, and entered the Aragón province 1617. He arrived in Buenos Aires in 1622, and died at the reduction of Candelaria (Argentina) in 1642.

95. See note 73.

96. São Paulo: the city originated from the Jesuit college of São Paulo de Piratininga, founded in 1554 by Father Manuel da Nóbrega. Portuguese, Indian and mixed-race settlements developed around it.

97. Montoya's marginal note: "Consta y mucho más de informaciones auténticas que se han presentado."

98. Montoya's marginal note: "En Oriente lo hicieron así, como lo dice Pinto en su historia." The allusion may be to Fernao Mendes Pinto (1510–1583), *Historia oriental de sus peregrinaciones* (1614) [Maeder].

99. Josse Van Suerck (hispanicized to Justo Mansilla or Banciur) was born in Antwerp in 1600. In 1616 he entered the Flemish-Belgian province, where he was a fellow novice of St. John Berchmans. He arrived in Buenos Aires in 1628 and died in Paraguay in 1666.

100. Cristóbal de Aresti, O.S.B., was Paraguay's only Benedictine bishop, serving from 1628 to 1631, when he was appointed to Buenos Aires. He is known in Paraguayan history principally for holding the second diocesan synod at Asunción.

101. Francisco Vázquez Trujillo was born in Cáceres, Spain, in 1571. He entered the novitiate in Peru in 1588 and joined the Paraguay province in 1607. He held several important posts, including those of mission procurator to Europe (1620–1622) and provincial (1629–1633). He died at Córdoba, Argentina, in 1652. (The famous migration, or "exodus," which Montoya begins to describe in this chapter, took place in 1631.)

102. Pedro de Espinosa was born in Baeza, Spain, in 1596 and entered the Andalusian Jesuit province in 1614. Coming to Buenos Aires in 1622, he made his solemn profession at Loreto, Argentina, in 1632 (shortly after the "Exodus"), and died a martyr between Santa Fe and Yapeyú, Argentina, July 3, 1634, as recounted in chapter 44.

103. Jacques Ransonnier was born in Burgundy in 1600 and entered the Flemish-Belgian Jesuit province in 1619. He arrived at Buenos Aires in 1628 together with Josse Van Suerck and died in 1636 after a short but energetic missionary life. He was among some forty-six Belgian Jesuits who worked in the reductions.

104. Nicholas Hénard (1596–1638) was born in Toul, France, in 1596 and entered the Champagne Jesuit province in 1617. He arrived at Buenos Aires together with Ransonnier and Van Suerck in 1628. After being solemnly professed (probably in 1636) he died in 1638 while working among the Itatí Indians. He and Ransonnier founded the reduction of San Carlos.

105. Diego de Alfaro, son of the Francisco de Alfaro mentioned in chapter 7 and elsewhere, was born in Panama in 1596 and entered the Society of Jesus in Castile in 1614. He reached Buenos Aires in 1617. He became superior of the Guaraní missions in 1637 and was killed in 1639 while defending his Indians against the bandeirantes in Rio Grande do Sul, Brazil.

106. This is the Southern Hemisphere.

107. The sodality, or "congregation," of the Blessed Virgin Mary was a pious association for laypeople, sponsored and guided by Jesuits.

108. Juan Augustín de Contreras was born in Pastrana, Spain, in 1601 and entered the Toledo Jesuit province in 1621. He came to Buenos Aires in 1628. After long service in the missions, he died at the reduction of Santa María de Fe, Paraguay, in 1668.

109. Prov. 3:32.

110. 1 Cor. 14:11.

111. Montoya eulogizes the skill of the Guaraní in music and various crafts. His enthusiasm is shared by other missioners in the reductions, notably by Anton Sepp and later writers. This is perhaps the earliest documentary reference to these artistic skills.

112. Banciur (Van Suerck): see note 99.

113. An oblique reference to the Spanish monarchy's obligations, from agreements with the Holy See, to supply and support missionaries in newly conquered non-Christian territory.

114. The reductions discussed in this part of the Spiritual Conquest are situated mainly in present-day Paraguay and the northeastern province of Argentina aptly called Misiones. Their remains are handsomely photographed by José Maria Blanch and treated in some detail in Lost Cities of Paraguay: Art and Architecture of the Jesuit Reductions 1607–1767, by C. J. McNaspy and J. M. Blanch (Chicago: Loyola University Press, 1982). Many of these reductions were either founded or developed by Roque González.

115. Roque González de Santa Cruz was born in Asunción in 1576 and ordained as a priest of the diocese in 1598. He entered the Society of Jesus in 1609 and became one of the outstanding missionaries among

the Guaraní Indians and founder of a number of reductions; martyred in 1628, he was canonized a saint in 1988.

116. Wis. 1:14.

117. Juan de Porras was born in 1596 at Ciudad Real, Spain, and entered the Society in 1619. He arrived at Buenos Aires in 1622 and the last record of his life indicates that he was at the reduction of Encarnación in 1681.

118. Alexis and John Calybites were two fifth-century saints who are said to have fled their families (Alexis on his wedding day) and later returned in disguise to live out their lives as hermits in their own households.

119. Alfonso D'Aragona was born in Naples in 1585 and entered the Society there in 1602. He taught Hebrew and other humanities for some years, and finally was admitted as a missioner to Paraguay. He reached Buenos Aires in 1617 and after a short but energetic apostolate died at Asunción in 1629.

120. The reduction of Nuestra Señora de los Reyes was founded in 1628 by Pedro Romero, in the spot known as Yapeyú, where Roque González had done preliminary planning with local Indians. Yapeyú, as the reduction is often called, later became famous as the musical center of the reductions, especially under the leadership of the great Tyrolese Jesuit, Anton Sepp (1655–1733).

121. Claude Royer (or Ruyer) was born in Champlois, France, in 1582 and entered the Society at Naples in 1612. He arrived at Buenos Aires in 1617 with the same missionary expedition as Jean Vaisseau, Diego de Alfaro, Alfonso D'Aragona and other outstanding reduction Jesuits. He served as superior of the Guaraní missions from 1639 to 1644. He died in 1648.

122. Francesco Broglia (hispanicized to Francisco de Céspedes) was born in Turin in 1599 and entered the Society in 1615. He arrived at Buenos Aires in 1628, and died at Encarnación in 1647.

123. The reduction of la Asunción is not to be confused with the capital city of Asunción; both were founded, in different years, on August 15, the feast of the As-

sumption of the Blessed Virgin Mary—the city in 1537, the reduction in 1629.

124. Cristóbal de Altamirano (1602–1698) was born in Santa Fe, Argentina, in 1602 and entered the Society in 1617. He was twice superior of the Guaraní missions (1660–1665 and 1678–1680) and was chosen as procurator to Europe, serving from 1670 to 1674. He died at a very advanced age, at the Apóstoles reduction, Argentina, in 1698.

125. This and the following two chapters deal with the martyrdom of the three Jesuit martyrs: Fathers Roque González de Santa Cruz, Alonso Rodríguez, and Juan del Castillo, who were canonized together by Pope John Paul II on his visit to Paraguay in 1988. See C. J. McNaspy, S.J., *Conquistador Without Sword: The Life of Roque González, S.J.* (Chicago: Loyola University Press, 1984). Twenty-three other Jesuits—priests and brothers—also gave their lives as martyrs in witness of the faith during the period of the River Plate reductions.

126. The then bishop of Asunción, Fray Reginaldo de Lizárraga, living abroad and without personally knowing González, named him vicar general; Roque declined and very shortly afterwards became a Jesuit.

127. Juan del Castillo was born near Cuenca, Spain, in 1596, entered the Society in 1614 and arrived at Buenos Aires in 1617. He was martyred at the reduction of Ijuhí (Rio Grande do Sul, Brazil) on November 17, 1628.

128. Alonso Rodríguez was born in Zamora, Spain, in 1599, entered the Society in 1614, and arrived at Buenos Aires in 1617. He was martyred, with Roque González, at the reduction of Caaró on November 15, 1628.

129. The reduction of Caaró, known afterwards as "of the Martyrs," was refounded in 1638 from various groups who had fled from the *bandeirantes* and is situated in the Argentinean province of Misiones.

130. The heart of Roque González was taken to Rome in 1634; in 1928 it was returned to South America and is at present preserved, together with the hatchet and

the arrow, in the chapel of the Martyrs at the Jesuit high school of Cristo Rey in Asunción.

131. Mark 9:47.

132. Pablo Antonio Palerm was born in Palma, Majorca, in 1602. He entered the Aragón Jesuit province in 1624, and came to Buenos Aires in 1628. After working in several missions, he died at Encarnación in 1665.

133. Louis Ernot was born in Marienbourg, Belgium, in 1597, the son of an officer in the Spanish army. He became a Jesuit in 1622 and arrived at Buenos Aires in 1628. He was in charge of the San Javier reduction when the *bandeirantes* attacked; he escaped alive only because one of their arquebuses misfired. He disagreed with Montoya on his handling of the "Exodus," on grounds which he later wrote to the superior general. In 1638, together with Noël Berthot, he founded the reduction of Santo Tomás, which soon had to be moved to escape another *bandeirante* invasion. He instructed the Christian Guaranís in defense tactics. He died at San Ignacio Miní, Argentina, in 1667.

134. Noël Berthot born in Marboz, France, in 1601, entered the Lyons Jesuit province in 1621. He reached Buenos Aires in 1628 in the same expedition that brought Louis Ernot. He was sent to work in reductions beyond the Uruguay River, in what is now the state of Rio Grande do Sul, Brazil. He and Ernot founded the Santo Tomás reduction in 1638. Berthot later worked in several other reductions and, unlike his companions Pedro Romero and Cristóbal de Mendoza, who died martyrs, had to witness the destruction of much of his life's work by the *bandeirantes*. Applying in vain for the French Canadian mission, he was reduced to teaching in Paraguayan schools instead of working in the reductions. At the age of seventy, however, he was able to resume work there, in Santo Tomás and later in Candelaria. After sixty years of service in Paraguay, Berthot died at Santa María Mayor, Argentina, in 1687.

135. St. Alphonsus Rodríguez (1533–1617) was a Spanish Jesuit lay brother. He

was not beatified until 1825.

136. Miguel Gómez was born in Buenos Aires in 1606 and entered the Society in 1623. After completion of the usual studies at Córdoba, he worked as associate pastor at Ignacio Miní, and later as curate at Santo Tomás, where he died in 1673.

137. Francisco Jiménez was born near Albacete, Spain, in 1602 and entered the Society in 1619. He reached Buenos Aires in 1622 and, after working in the reductions, died in that city in 1668.

138. Tupís: an Indian people living on the Brazilian coastland; their involvement with the *bandeirantes* in the slave trade is described by Montoya in several chapters.

139. Giuseppe Oreggi was born in 1588, entered the Society of Jesus at Rome in 1606 and reached Buenos Aires in 1617. He died at the San Javier reduction, Argentina, in 1664.

140. Pedro de Mola was born near Huesca, Spain, in 1602. He became a Jesuit in 1619, came to Buenos Aires in 1622, and died at the Apóstoles reduction in 1660.

141. The original mistakenly has 1626.

142. See Luke 6:5–6.

143. Given the perils of travel at this time, two or more copies of important correspondence would be sent by different carriers.

144. Montoya's marginal note: "Paulo III, año 1537." The reference is to the brief *Sublimis Deus* of June 9, 1337, in defense of the Indians [Maeder].

145. The sanctuary of St. James of Compostela, in northwest Spain, is one of Europe's oldest and most popular pilgrimage sites.

146. The original mistakenly has 1637.

147. "Castilians": in the context of the period this could just mean "men-at-arms" or white men, though there would undoubtedly have been Spaniards among them.

148. Brother: apart from priests, and seminarians (scholastics) who are studying for the priesthood, the Society of Jesus includes those who enter without the intention of being ordained, namely, Jesuit Brothers.

149. Montoya's marginal note: "Consta de informaciones jurídicas que se presentaron al Consejo."
150. Isaiah 1:3.
151. John 1:11.
152. Montoya's marginal note: "Congregación a 20 de julio de 1637."
153. *Doctrinas.*
154. Montoya's marginal note: "Licenciado Andrés de León, en el memor[ial] discurso No. 33." And further below: "Cédula Real en Madrid, 30 de enero de 1607, Ordenanza del doctor don Francisco de Alfaro visitador, confirmade. Ubi supra No. 34."
155. Montoya's marginal note: "En Madrid, 14 de abril 1633 años."
156. This document probably dates from about the time of Ruiz de Montoya's ordination to the priesthood. It was published by Guillermo Furlong, S.J., in his *Antonio Ruiz de Montoya y su Carta a Comental* (Escritores Coloniales Rioplatenses XVII, Buenos Aires: Ediciones Theoria, 1964), pp. 159-70.
157. Francisco Jarque (vol. 1, p. 105)

tells us that the dead man was a close friend of Antonio's.
158. The Spanish Main, i.e., the Caribbean coast of Panama and South America.
159. This translation is conjectural. Furlong's transcription reads *Vilo como en liobrico. Liobrico* does not occur in any of the dictionaries, and the diminutive *librico* (assuming an error in transcription) is unusual, besides rendering uncertain sense in the context.
160. These maxims, drawn from Montoya's spiritual notebooks (now lost), were published by his seventeenth-century biographer, Francisco Jarque. They are also reprinted in José Luis Rouillon Arróspide's edition of Montoya's *Silex del Divino Amor* (Lima: Pontificia Universidad Católica del Perú, 1991), pp. 271-82.
161. Heb. 13:14.
162. Phil. 1:23.
163. Luke 23:41.
164. Bar. 1:15; 2:6.
165. 2 Cor. 6:3.

SELECT BIBLIOGRAPHY

Caraman, Philip. *The Lost Paradise: The Jesuit Republic in South America*. New York: Seabury, 1976.

Delattre, Pierre, S.J., and Edmond Lamalle, S.J. "Jésuites wallons, flamands, français, missionaires au Paraguay, 1608–1767." *Archivum Historicum Societatis Iesu* 16 (1947), pp. 98–176.

Furlong, Guillermo, S.J. *Antonio Ruiz de Montoya y su Carta a Comental*. Escritores Coloniales Rioplatenses XVII. Buenos Aires: Ediciones Theoria, 1964.

Groh, John E. "Antonio Ruiz de Montoya and the Early Reductions in the Jesuit Province of Paraguay." *Catholic Historical Review* 56 (1971), pp. 501-33.

Huonder, Anthony, S.J. Art. "Ruiz de Montoya, Antonio." *The Catholic Encyclopedia* 13, 223-24.

Jarque [Xarque], Francisco, *Ruiz Montoya en Indias (1608–1652)*. 4 vols. Madrid: Victoriano Suárez, 1900.

McNaspy, C. J., S.J. *Conquistador Without Sword: The Life of Roque González, S.J.* Chicago: Loyola University Press, 1984.

——. *Lost Cities of Paraguay: Art and Architecture of the Jesuit Reductions, 1607–1767*. Photographs by J. M. Blanch, S.J. Chicago: Loyola University Press, 1982.

Ruiz de Montoya, Antonio, S.J. *Conquista espiritual hecha por los religiosos de la Compañía de Jesús en las provincias de Paraguay, Paraná, Uruguay y Tape*. Bibao: Imprenta del Corazón de Jesús, 1892.

——. *Conquista espiritual hecha por los religiosos de la Compañía de Jesús en las provincias de Paraguay, Paraná, Uruguay y Tape*. Estudio preliminar y notas: Dr. Ernesto J. A. Maeder. Rosario, Argentina: Equipo Difusor de Estudios de Historia Iberoamericana, 1989.

——. *Silex del Divino Amor*. Introducción, transcripción y notas de José Luis Rouillon Arróspide. Lima: Pontificia Universidad Católica del Perú, Fondo Editorial, 1991.

Storni, Hugo, S.J. "Antonio Ruiz de Montoya." *Archivum Historicum Societatis Iesu* 105 (1984), pp. 425-42. (Gives complete bibliography of Montoya's writings and of writings about him.)

——. Art. "Ruiz de Montoya, Antonio" *New Catholic Encyclopedia*, vol. 12, 706.

INDEX